Sanity, Insanity and Common Sense
The Missing Link in Understanding Mental Health

SANITY, INSANITY AND COMMON SENSE

The Missing Link in Understanding Mental Health

by
E. M. Suarez, Ph.D.
and
Roger C. Mills, Ph.D.

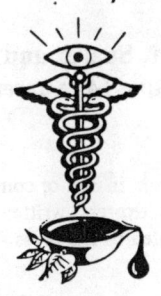

Published by
Med-Psych Publications

Pine Mountain Press, Inc., Publishing Group
P.O. Box 19746
West Allis, WI 53219

Editor: *Timothy E. Knier*
Typeography: *Quality Plus Phototypesetting*

First printing, March 1982
Second printing, Sept. 1982
Third printing, July 1983

Copyright 1980 by E. M. Suarez and Roger C. Mills
Copyright 1982 by Enrique M. Suarez and Roger C. Mills

All rights are reserved. This book, in part or complete, may not be reproduced in any manner without the express written consent of the publisher. Customary privileges are granted to the press and other reviewing agencies.

Manufactured in U.S.A.

ISBN 0-89769-049-4 Hard Cover
ISBN 0-89769-024-9 Soft Cover

DEDICATION

We would like to dedicate this book to the many people who have assisted us in our professional work, and who trusted our "hunches" about the direction that led to the discoveries presented in this book.

We want to thank all of the people who stayed with us as we began to shift our direction away from the traditional formulations within psychology to tread on new ground. While many of our former colleagues dropped away, those who did follow provided support and encouragement that helped us far beyond what they probably realize.

We also want to especially thank our "natural" teachers; the people we learned from who exhibit this common sense and live it to a degree far beyond what we ever learned from any text on psychology. It was their wisdom, natural enjoyment of life and beauty as people that initially triggered our inquiries.

TABLE OF CONTENTS

INTRODUCTION

SECTION I: *The Nature of This Book in Relation to the Need for a More "Scientific" Psychology.*

CHAPTER 1: The Nature of a "Science" and the Need for Unifying Principles Within Psychology 23
CHAPTER 2: The Basis of a Scientific Psychology of Human Behavior 31

SECTION II: *The Principles of the Evident Psychology: The Route to Sanity.*

CHAPTER 3: The Need for an Advanced Psychology: Toward a Deeper Understanding of the Mind 57
CHAPTER 4: The Simplicity of Sanity: The Common Sense Beneath Our Concepts of Mental Health. 67
CHAPTER 5: Understanding Thought: What Mental Health and Sanity Are In Relation to Our Conditioned Realities. 75
CHAPTER 6: Individual Thought Systems: A World of Separate Realities. 81
CHAPTER 7: Thought and Our Image of Self-Importance: How We Learn Insecurity. 89
CHAPTER 8: Levels of Consciousness: The Knowledge of What Our Thought Systems Are. 97

SECTION III: *Thought Systems and Insecurity: A New Light on Mental Health versus Mental Illness.*

    CHAPTER 9: A New Framework for Psychology: A Context for a Deeper Understanding of Human Behavior. 107

    CHAPTER 10: The Mental Health Field versus the Route to Mental Health. 121

    CHAPTER 11: Insight in Relation to Mental Health. 135

    CHAPTER 12: The Many Faces of Insecurity: Looking Past the Disguises. 141

SECTION IV: *The Relationship of Present Day Psychology to Our Evolving Understanding of the Mind.*

    CHAPTER 13: Today's Psychology in Theory: A System of Thought. 157

    CHAPTER 14: Today's Psychology in Practice: The Search for More Problems. 167

    CHAPTER 15: Today's Psychology in Effect: The Price for Treating an Illusion. 179

    CHAPTER 16: Today's Psychology in Essence: The Self-Fulfilling Nature of Its Orientation. 191

SECTION V: *A New Direction for the Fields of Psychology and Mental Health.*

    CHAPTER 17: The Evolution of the Helping Professions: The New Direction of Therapy. 205

    CHAPTER 18: Therapy Beyond Techniques: The Principle of Listening. 213

    CHAPTER 19: Recognizing the Placebo Effect in Mental Health and Mental Illness. . 223

CHAPTER 20: The Direction and True Role of the Therapist: Beyond Our Theories, Beyond Burnout. 231

CHAPTER 21: The Process of Therapy: Guiding Clients to Their Own Mental Health. 241

SECTION VI: *These Breakthroughs in Practice: The Results in Major Health Care Settings.*

CHAPTER 22: Applications of This Breakthrough to the Functioning of Health Care Organizations. 253

CHAPTER 23: Applications of This Breakthrough to the Effectiveness and Quality of Work Life of Health Care Professionals. 263

SECTION VII: *Implications of These Discoveries for the Future Evolution of the Fields of Psychological Research and Mental Health Practice.*

CHAPTER 24: The Future Evolution of Psychological Research: Building on the Clues Already Recognized......... 285

CHAPTER 25: The Direction Provided by an Understanding of These Principles: The Emergence of a New Understanding of the Mind. 293

INDEX.. 301

INTRODUCTION

During the course of our professional work, research and teaching over the past several years, we have recognized and uncovered a deeper set of principles about the mind that determines our experiences and behaviors as human beings. These principles give us a more profound understanding of what mental health is and a deeper cognizance into the sources of our behaviors as human beings than has up to now been understood or recognized by the fields of psychology, human relations and other disciplines involved in the study of human behavior.

These principles provide simpler, more profound and yet more "common sense" answers to problems we now call *"mental illness," "emotional disturbance," "stress,"* and *"addictive"* or *"compulsive"* behaviors. These principles also shed a new light on the true nature of psychosomatic or psychophysiological illnesses and on the power of thought in relation to the general state of physical and mental health.

The dissemination of these principles and insights will answer questions to which the fields of psychology and mental health are still seeking solutions. These principles will, in fact, alter our entire frame of reference in terms of how we now think about all categories of mental illness or emotional reactivity.

The magnitude and the scope of this breakthrough is such that it will bring into new perspective and significantly change the underlying assumptions and framework within which we presently study human behavior. Furthermore, this breakthrough will dramatically alter the approach to treating all forms of abnormal behavior, emotional breakdowns, stress and interpersonal problems.

This book is written for people who are honestly interested in achieving better states of mental health and well-being for themselves; or in helping others live lives with emotional maturity, well-being and success in their families and professional lives. We are not interested in adding another theory, model or method to a field already inundated with techniques, methods, approaches and conflicting theories. To do so would be to introduce another potential psychological dependency and to foster further in people the illusion that their mental health is dependent on something other than themselves.

Since we are presenting something new, a breakthrough, a new direction and a new framework for psychology and mental health, we would like to make a request of the reader. If at all possible, read this book with no preconceptions, *apriori* ideas of what we are talking about, or prejudgments. Once you have read the book, of course, you will do whatever you want with what you feel it has to offer.

What we are hoping to contribute through this book is a deeper common sense understanding of how emotional and behavioral patterns are generated now, every day on a moment-to-moment basis, so that each individual can change them by going directly to the source. The source is not any particular event, trauma, past relationship, or any other cause outside the person. The source is the overall "thought system." This notion is something that psychology has looked at out of the corner of its eye, but has never faced directly. If psychology faced this fact directly, it would get a surprise, an answer that would shake the field of psychology to its very core in the same way that the principles of relativity shook the foundations of Newtonian physics.

This book is designed as a comprehensive text of human behavior. However, its starting point is discontinuous with what is known today as the science of human behavior. We mention this because the present book is neither based on the contents of any psychological theories or models, nor on the literature which these concepts have produced. Consequently, few references are provided for the simple fact that few exist. Furthermore, we are not directing or referring the reader to anyone else's realities but his own. What we are presenting is not a theoretical construct psychology but an Evident Psychology. The evidence for such a psychology is to be found in everyday moment-to-moment experience of life and nowhere else.

The implications from what is presented in this book will point the field of psychology in a new direction, one that cannot be seen at all from the field's present base of assumptions and theories. Therefore, this work must be discontinuous with the collection of theories, ideas and concepts now included in the discipline we call psychology. The direction in which we are attempting to point the field with this book involves a clearer, deeper understanding of the state or the condition of mind that we would call mental health or emotional maturity in all human beings.

What we have discovered and will further develop in this text is that mental health in all individuals is the most natural, ordinary and accessible condition in life. At the same time we acknowledge that very few people have actually realized this fact in their own lives. The reason for that is that present-day psychology is oriented toward attempting causally to define and to explain mental illness in terms of specific neuroses, specific learned negative behavior patterns, specific traumatic events in the past, specific life histories, and so on. Most of psychology is preoccupied with figuring out mental illness or abnormal behavior. Consequently, the field of psychology has very few studies and little research aimed at telling us what mental health is and how to achieve it. Yet in order to remove mental illness all we really need to do is to go directly to the state of mental health. From that state we ourselves understand what mental illness is and, therefore, how to avoid it.

We also wish to dispel the widely held beliefs that the details of a person's previously acquired personality traits or conditioned reactive behavior patterns, attitudes and habits are important to understand what mental health is and to achieve the state we are calling mental health. Rather, what we emphasize is that the person understand how all of these experiences have developed into a systemic network or framework of beliefs and underlying assumptions; that is, how they create the person's personal thought system. The way that this unique, individualized and subjective thought system operates now to create what is seen and to interpret what is seen is what must be understood to be at a deeper level of clarity than has up to now been obtained by modern psychology.

Over the last five years of our teaching and research, we have seen literally thousands of individuals from all walks of life develop this common sense understanding of the workings of their own thought systems to attain levels of mental health, maturity and enjoyment of life that they never previously had thought possible. We have not observed any similar or comparable results from any form of therapy or mental health intervention program. The reason for this significant difference is that all therapy programs we know of actually work to keep people immersed in, focused on, and encapsulated within a reality of their problems and negative behaviors. This effect of today's therapies cannot be avoided because of the theoretical foundations and techniques upon which these therapies are based. No practitioner can help but do this, although this is not his or her avowed intent. From our observations of these results, we know that the breakthrough presented in this book will eventually turn psychology around to a new direction.

One of the purposes of this book, then, is to assist the field of psychology in taking a look at itself from the perspective of this breakthrough. We do not mean looking at the present collection of theories to see what more is needed. Rather, we mean looking honestly, even ingenuously, at the underlying assumptions and beliefs on which present theories and models, techniques and methods are based. If psychology, as a field, takes a deeper look at these underlying assumptions, we would realize the extent to which we are limiting our knowledge and understanding of mental health and the inherent capabilities of our minds. In fact, one of the implications of what we are learning is that the framework of present psychological theories and approaches and the proliferation of techniques is now itself a frame of reference or a thought system that is keeping people from seeing something new, just as the framework of Newtonian physics kept physicists from grasping relativity for many years following Einstein's initial discoveries. We are addressing, among other things, the misconceptions of the frame of reference of psychology.

In order to break through this frame of reference and go beyond its present limitations, the field must take a simpler, more truthful and common sense perspective on itself. Gaining this perspective involves stepping outside the boundaries of what the field now knows and into unknown waters. Yet all this step really takes is a willingness to realize that this kind of letting go is what is needed, along with the courage to not attempt evaluation in the context of what we think we already know. In the case of this book, attachment to the present frame of reference of the field will hinder anyone from appreciating the implications of this work for adding new dimensions to our understanding of the mind and of human behavior and mental health.

The present book is founded on our realization that there is much more knowledge, understanding and wisdom available directly to people than what psychology presently thinks. While we are making some strong — and what will sometimes sound like critical — statements about the field, we must truthfully state that we would rather not talk about the field at all. We are forced to do so only to illustrate why the field, limited by its present frame of reference, has not yet discovered that the state of mental health is a natural condition, a real condition, one available to every human being and one that has nothing to do with any particular method, technique or therapy existing now within the collection of modern-day psychological concepts and theories.

Because the field of mental health has been functioning within the boundaries of a framework of psychological theories it has not realized the primary role that thought plays in the reality we see, including our desires and attempts to explain it. Accordingly, previous psychological works have attempted to understand human behavior from a definite set of relative human behaviors that collectively we call psychology. Our intent is to provide the reader with a bigger picture with which to realize what human behavior is, including the behavior we call psychology. This is *per se* a discontinuous departure for the present work. In fact, when one of the authors and a colleague published the first article reporting some of our initial findings, they immediately received a letter from a national psychological accrediting body requesting that they cease and desist because they were saying something that did not fit within the existing framework of accepted psychological theories and methods. Yet, this is the most valuable contribution these insights give: a new, fresh look beyond the context of the present set of assumptions, beliefs and accepted theories in the field of psychology.

Another possible misperception is that we in some way are attacking, maligning or putting down the mental health professions. It is of the utmost importance for the reader to realize that this is not in any way our intent. We simply are sharing a breakthrough about the present frame of reference of psychology in much the same manner that allowed the medical sciences to go beyond a given frame of reference to realize that such practices as bleeding people in shock — although at one time widely used, accepted and supported — was not in the best interests of the patient. Such a suggestion was at the time considered to be an attack on the medical profession by many physicians who truly believed bloodletting to be therapeutic. Yet it was such changes that accounted for the very development of that profession.

Finally, the knowledge which we have realized and are introducing is not new in the sense that we (the authors) are the first to think of or to discover it; we have, however, uncovered something which is relatively unknown. In fact, what we are directing the reader towards is the realization that this knowledge is the basis for the existing ability of individual human beings to create any thoughts about themselves they wish. Such knowledge is new only in the sense that we as human beings all somehow forgot our innate responsibility and power in life. Thus, this common sense knowledge does not belong to any science, group, theory or model; neither does it belong to anyone, including ourselves. It simply exists within all of us. To read this book from the perspective of anyone's theory, model, belief or way of thinking will keep the reader from experiencing his or her own understanding of this book. It is, therefore, important to read this work as free as possible from what anyone presently thinks the psychology of life or human behavior is or includes.

The two chapters which follow (Section I) have been written to create a scientific context for the remainder of the book. In these chapters, we make a series of analogies to Einstein's breakthroughs in the field of physics. If the reader finds these passages difficult, please bear with us. The point here is not to explain any of Einstein's theories, but to make relevant analogies to the implications of a breakthrough of the same magnitude in terms of scope and direction for the field of psychology. The rest of the book (starting with Section II) has been written in as common sense a way as possible, so the average person may benefit from the text as much as a mental health professional.

In Section II of this book, we will present the basic principles of this new psychology in as common sense a way as possible. In Section III, we will discuss more fully how insecurity acts as the source of all mental health problems and how mental health is related to our thought systems and the ego. In Sections IV and V, we will discuss the implications of what we are learning in terms of the present *status quo* of the field of psychology and our present knowledge of human behavior. In Section VI, we will talk about how this common sense has been applied in hospital settings and other areas of mental health consultation. In Section VII, we will broaden this discussion to include the implications of what we are learning for mental health practice and psychological consultation and therapy in general. In Section VII, we will talk to the implications of what we are learning for the evolution of the fields of psychology and human behavior in the future. Section V includes material which may be of interest to people involved in therapy and counseling, offering some more practical, directional guidelines or pointers that may be of help to people in these professions in their work with clients. In these chapters, we will also discuss how this understanding is related to stress and burnout and the ability to live and work without stress.

SECTION I

THE NATURE OF THIS BOOK IN RELATION TO THE NEED FOR A MORE "SCIENTIFIC" PSYCHOLOGY

CHAPTER 1

The Nature of a "Science" and the Need for Unifying Principles within Psychology

There has been continual debate throughout all areas of the field of psychology over the last 100 years, as to whether the field of psychology is really a science yet, or still an art form. There are a wealth of psychological treatment techniques and methods around; each based on different and often conflicting theoretical schools of thought. We really have not yet achieved the consistency or uniformity of results within psychology that has been achieved by other "sciences," such as math, physics, chemistry or engineering. Physics is assured the status of a science by virtue of the fact that the phenomena studied are "observable" and measurable. Yet math is also accepted although the phenomena studied are highly abstract (non-tangible) as is the case in psychology.

THE NATURE OF A "SCIENCE"

What is it that makes a discipline a "science" or not yet a science? The commonality among the hard sciences, from math through physics, is that there is a consistent, uniform set of underlying principles that are generally accepted, and which apply across the board, to all phenomena included within that discipline. This level of agreement has not been reached yet within psychology.

Math has been accepted as a science because the principles upon which mathematical relationships are based are logically consistent and precise. Certain transformations and relationships are defined in terms of principles that, if properly used, always give the right answer. These relationships are defined by principles that are "universal" (i.e., they apply equally to all problems that fall in that area of mathematics). In some areas of physical phenomena (physics and chemistry) the phenomena are not directly observable to the senses. (For example, atomic level, molecular level transformations, the actions of electromagnetic and gravitational fields). Yet, the "scientific" principles used to describe these phenomena are generally accepted as scientific. The reason they are accepted is again that they apply universally to provide the most consistent, predictable and "generalizable" answers that can be found.

THE STATUS OF PSYCHOLOGY

These conditions are not met yet in the field of psychology. We have not yet achieved uniformity, precision or consistency between our theories and the results of our mental health treatment and education programs. Nor is the logic consistent and uniform. There are a myriad of theories and models around, many of which operate from a base of assumptions or principles that are mutually inconsistent, or even contradictory to other theories. Yet each of these schools of psychology gets support from its adherants within accepted academic and professional ranks.

This lack of agreement is evidenced by the fact that patients going to these different therapists will often receive three completely different diagnoses, and three different treatments. Rescidivism rates to state hospitals of 85% national averages indicate that we have not yet achieved "solid" cures.

Psychology, as a field has not yet achieved the unambiguous status of a science, not because of our object of study, but rather because our formulations, and thus our results, have been neither consistent nor as precise as those of mathematics, physics, or chemistry. The perspective or framework which has been adopted in our thinking, as a field regarding human behavior, has resulted in obvious inconsistencies in our results and acknowledged gaps in the knowledge of the realities we live in. There are, in fact, quite a few conflicting formulations within psychology each of which has been based on different underlying assumptions about the source of human behavior, that are considered factual. The variance within the field of psychology, as a science, is equal to the variance outside of psychology (the world) pointing to the conclusion that we have not made "significant" advancements in our understanding of human behavior, relative to the whole of society. We have not accounted for the observed variance.

Psychological research and mental health practice have been earnestly searching for solid answers to problems of stress, emotional distress and mental illness in our society; to date no real answers have been found. Our inconclusive and uncertain results are evidenced by the national high rescidivism rates in state hospitals pointing to lack of sustained results in our mental health programs, in therapy, and also by the current proliferation of theories, methods and techniques, that are offered to the public today.

After one century of development, perhaps the best characterization of our present state of the art in our psychology of human behavior and therapy is the trend toward further diversification and specialization Some psychologists, in fact, go so far as to suggest that we need to develop specific procedures and techniques to accomplish specific kinds of behavior change with specific kinds of clients, applied by specific types of therapists. The field of psychology as a whole appears to be convinced that this direction will eventually yield results. The results, however, from this direction documented to date are not significant with regard to this state of affairs, it has been suggested that what would be needed to accomplish such a feat would be: (1) a classification system for clients; (2) a classification system for problems; (3) a classification system of therapeutic approaches; and

(4) a classification system for therapists.

We are even questioning ourselves, as a profession, regarding whether or not we may be causing more harm than good by not being able to recognize mental health when we see it. As the science of human behavior, we are still in the same boat as described by Jerome Frank of John Hopkins University:

> "At this point it must be emphasized that the failure to find differences in improvement rate from different forms or amounts of psychotherapy is a sign of ignorance, not knowledge . . . In short, the inability to prove that a phenomenon exists is quite different from proving that it does *not* exist. The difficulty in demonstrating by statistical or experimental methods that therapy works or that one form is superior to another may lie in our inability to define adequately any of the variables involved."*

One predictable outgrowth of our inability to provide direct answers to the psychologically troubled is that it has led to the overgrowth of "pop psychology" or "personal growth" gimmicks which offer "awareness," "enlightenment," or "consciousness raising" gimmicks. Many of these offerings end up as not much more than a form of a conversion process (conditioning) aimed at recruiting people into an organization which then becomes an integral part of their lifestyle.

The necessary clues, nonetheless, pointing to psychology's next evolutionary step are all around us in our journals and in our jobs. What has been missing in psychology has been the unifying principles or perspective which would bring what we already know alive and into clear focus for us to understand and utilize.

THE MECHANICS OF PRESENT PSYCHOLOGICAL THINKING

In discussing the scientific level of our present framework

---

* *Persuasion and Healing: A Comparative Study of Psychotherapy.* Jerome D. Frank. Baltimore: Johns Hopkins Press, 1961, p. 15, 16.

of psychological approaches, Ivan London and Warren Thorngate have noted:

> "But for the social sciences, where are the promised successes? Despite all his [social scientist's] efforts and firm faith in an ultimate payoff, these successes are still to be exhibited. The radical reorientations that initiated the great advances of physics (relativity and quantum theory) have no counterpart in the social sciences. Instead, the social sciences continue to be bound futally to the orientations of classical physics, from which they have elaborated naive conceptions of force, energy, least action, equilibrium, etc., seeming to promise much but accomplishing little...
>
> The fault may be in what we are trying to do. The model for progress we have been emulating may have misdirected us and dissipated our energies not because it was wrong, but precisely because it has been wedded to classical orientations . . . yet even in physics classical orientations have been replaced, while in the social sciences they tenaciously persist in spite of their record of failure and skepticism of the few mavericks in the field." (London and Thorngate, 1981, p. 203-204).

The primary reason we have not experienced success in advancing our working knowledge of human behavior and mental health is that we have not taken into account the role of our own frame of reference, as behavioral scientists in what we observe to be psychologically happening to create the reality we live in (the fact that we are part of the field we are studying). Throughout the history of modern day psychology, we have focused on specific classes of behaviors, "problems," and/or undesired behaviors (variables) as absolutes. We have constructed theories which relate our behaviors, problems and perceptions to one another within a mechanical cause and effect framework.

BECOMING A SCIENCE

Each evolutionary step within a branch of "Science" demands looking in the direction of "simpler," more profound and more universal principles. Such principles connect in a more logically consistent and satisfying way the variety of

---

London, I. and Thorngate, W. Divergent amplification and social behavior: Some methodological considerations. *Psychological Reports*, 1981, *48*, 203-228.

manifestations of human behavior. Einstein and Infeld (1938) in their book, *The Evolution of Physics* stated that the purpose of scientific research and discoveries is to: "reduce the apparent complexity of natural phenomena to some simple, fundamental ideas and relations . . . to discover some essential common features, hidden beneath the surface of some external differences, to form, on this basis, a new successful theory is important, creative work" (p. 287). Yet, in psychology today, we have gone almost totally in the opposite direction. We have specialized, segmented and divided up our study of human behavior into hundreds of competing schools, disciplines and personal growth "gimmicks." The lack of consistency, in terms of achieving a deeper overall understanding of the psychology of human behavior, is evidenced in the variety of techniques that are presently "marketed" for personal growth, therapy and happiness. Almost everything is now tried, from behavior modification to diet, astrology and re-birthing. At the same time the "track record" of our mental health treatment programs has hovered between 15-20% nonremission (people who actually experience a lasting reduction in their symptoms or problem behaviors).

THE LIMITATIONS OF OUR PRESENT MODELS

It does not appear that psychology will derive a more universal, more accurate description of the relationship of our mind to our behavior from the currently accepted theories or assumptions. We must begin to look at our observations, our data and our experience from a new perspective, one that is outside of and free from, the biases or limitations of currently accepted models. In the same vein, Einstein noted:

> "Successful revolt against the accepted view results in unexpected and completely different developments, becoming a source of new philosophical aspects." (Einstein and Infeld, 1938, p. 259).

THE NEW "SCIENCE" OF PSYCHOLOGY

From our own research and from looking at the results of a broad range of research and treatment pilot programs over

---

Einstein, A. and Infeld, L. *The evolution of physics.* New York: Simon and Schuster, 1938.

the last ten years, we have seen a pattern, or a trend, that reveals a direction toward a more universal set of principles of human behavior. These principles do, in fact, make the field more consistent and precise. These principles reveal a deeper connection of "logical consistency" in terms of causality relationships among all the data; whether the research was done from a base of "Freudian," "Gestalt," "Social Learning" theories, or other models of personality dynamics. These principles connect in a very precise way, the more central "systemic" source of our behavior to our actual emotions, behaviors and fears; to our everyday moods and perceptions; and to our reactions to events and to other people.

THE NATURE OF PSYCHOLOGICAL PRINCIPLES

True psychological principles are not amenable to personal "use," in the sense that they could be used *on* people, or by people in a manipulative way on one another. They are "impersonal" in the sense that they are like the principles of mathematics, they impersonally describe the results of certain key relationships between our thoughts, our experiences, and our behavior, that are precise (constant and accurate), irrespective of the details of our personalities, life situation, or past history.

When some degree of true knowledge about any phenomenon is uncovered, a "principle" emerges that acts as a directional guide to the next degree of understanding. That is, a principle *points* toward another, still deeper level of understanding of a phenomenon; it points to the unknown. A totally valid principle does not point toward contradiction as an answer. It points in the direction of a, as yet unknown answer, which when recognized results in an unambiguous correct answer. Such is the case in mathematics whereby the principles which guide the mathematicians toward the solution to any mathematical expression either totally resolves the problem or produces a recognizable contradictory answer which leaves no doubt regarding its falsity as an answer.

Present day concepts in the field of psychology do not qualify as "scientific principles" for they result in more questions and lengthen the list of probable answers about human behavior. The concepts and theories we in psychology refer to as principles usually point in the direction of complexity rather than simplicity, and fragmentation rather than unification.

The principles we will introduce in this book represent a totally new direction for the field of psychology in which to look for answers to mental health problems. We will develop a set of principles which are related to four psychological common denominators or constants shared by each and every human being that has ever lived: To these ends we will discuss the total psychological experience of what we call life from the perspective of:

a) Thinking and the workings of the "thought system" each of us as human beings have acquired.

b) The separate reality of individual differences which every unique thought system creates.

c) The capability of human beings to increase their conscious understanding or knowledge regarding the nature of their own psychological functioning.

d) The capacity to experience feelings and emotions which vary from negative to positive.

These principles are very practical in the sense that when anyone recognizes these principles, in relation to how they themselves are operating emotionally or psychologically (in relation to their own behavior) everyday, they can see for themselves what causes their ups and downs, their "reactions, irrational fears compulsive," or destructive behaviors and various emotional states, from feeling good to feeling "down" or upset.

CHAPTER 2

The Basis of a Scientific Psychology of Human Behavior

We originally "stumbled onto" these principles in the course of a series of research-demonstration programs carried out in conjunction with the State of Oregon Mental Health Division, The National Institute of Mental Health and the Veterans' Administration. The nature of the positive psychological changes that we observed in professionals themselves, and subsequently in their patients, were such that it left no doubt that a breakthrough in our understanding of mental health was eminent. The changes were not only significantly different from control group improvement, but far and away more powerful than changes reported from any other training or educational experience (i.e., a recognition or grasp of these principles led to a better view of what is happening psychologically on a moment to moment basis in people, which in turn led to further positive changes in their own mental health, i.e., feelings of well-being and emotional stability). This process is similar to learning a principle of mathematics, then practicing the application of that principle and how it works in practice. When we make a mistake in mathematics, it is because we have misunderstood the principle, or made an error in addition, subtraction, etc. The principle itself is still accurate.

The breakthrough revealed by the identification of these more accurate psychological principles will change psychology to become a more exact science. We realize that no science is ever totally exact. Even physics, math and chemistry keep discovering new levels of understanding that bring more precision and consistency. We can see the results of these continued breakthroughs in our rapidly evolving technology, yet we have not seen these types of breakthroughs and the accompanying results yet in our mental health treatment programs.

Initially a field normally resists the re-conceptualizations that any true breakthrough signifies, because these insights are outside of the bounderies of the accepted "legitimized" frame of reference. Yet the proof comes as people begin to see the deeper logic in the relationships revealed by such a breakthrough.

What these principles contribute to psychology is a beginning in a new direction. The direction is one of a better integration of our knowledge; a unification in terms of more logically consistent, universal and more fundamental principles of human behavior that cut across modalities, and theoretical boundaries.

THE BASIS OF THIS BREAKTHROUGH: THE BARRIER OF THOUGHT

Each of us, as people, has developed, as we have moved through all of our experiences in life, what we would call a "thought system." This system has all of the characteristics or attributes of all other "systems." It tends to be internally consistent as an interlocking network of ideas, beliefs and biases (in other words there is a unique form of interdependence of the units, beliefs, within this system). There is adaptation, as say in a natural ecological system, in that any modification or adaptation, to new ideas is limited and affected by what is there already, and therefore whatever comes in from the outside is filtered and colored by the existing network of beliefs. In other words, the content of each person's thought system is their beliefs, arranged in a logically consistent way.

Given these "system" attributes, we could accurately state

that each of us is immersed in, (i.e., lives life viewing things through) *the perceptual filters* of our own subjective frame of reference (thought system). In other words, we make an interpretation or judgment, based on the *content* of our particular thought system, and the reaction we have is then based on this interpretation.

The analogy to the psychological phenomenon of a "thought system" in mathematics is called a "set." What a set means in math is a framework within which we define a certain *set of rules* or *laws of transformation*. Once we have defined these rules, when we plug numbers into that set, they change, by following the rules we have defined for that set. For instance, the rules set for division are different from those set for multiplication. In the same way, psychologically, we each collect and combine learned attitudes, ideas and values into an accumulation of beliefs, combined in a way that is unique to us. Any external event or situation then follows the "rules" of our interpretations and biases, becoming transformed into what we think these things mean.

RELATIVITY IN PSYCHOLOGY:

One of the reasons that this fact, or principle has been "hidden" to a large degree is the fact itself; that each of us lives within our own view, (or perceptual field) which therefore seems real to us. Einstein, in order to gain acceptance for a more unified "field" theory of the physical universe had to first show people that they were a part of that field, and therefore that every measurement and observation was affected by their relative mass, position, and velocity with regard to what was being observed (the fact of relativity itself). In order to start to see beyond our acquired "thought system," we must begin to look at this system impersonally and objectively, from outside of its limitations, in terms of the principles of how all such systems work. We can then go back and apply these more general principles to our own thought system. We will then see that even our academic training as psychologists has in itself become part of a self-limiting thought system.

THE SCIENTIFIC APPLICATION OF A SYSTEMS' PERSPECTIVE

When scientists began looking at the world through "systems" lenses, (i.e., when we began to see cultures or ecosystems or our bodies and so on, as *systems* with all the characteristics of systems) we first studied principles that determined the behavior of the entire set of phenomena in terms of system dynamics. We then went back and plugged in the content (for example, what type of physical attributes I personally exhibit) and found what we observed to be consistent with those systems' principles.

The same shift in our thinking about human behavior in terms of individual personalities and behavior patterns is needed today. Once we began to realize that each of us possessed a *thought system,* we began to look at and become aware of the underlying principles of how these thought systems operate as systems. We wanted particularly to understand the relationship of these thought systems to our mental health, to stress, to psychosomatic illness, to all forms of what we now label "mental illness" or compulsive behavior patterns.

A "SYSTEMS" PERSPECTIVE: A STEP TOWARD A FIELD UNDERSTANDING

Many authors and researchers in psychology have begun to write about the need for a broader "systems" approach in psychology. In the field of physics, prior to Einstein's introduction of a general field theory, Maxwell, Faraday and others had begun to write about specific kinds of fields they had observed, or discovered in the course of their work. These included electric, magnetic and gravitational fields. Einstein showed the commonalities of all of these and created a more general field theory, which encompassed the others as well. Any new development of a field of study that is "scientific" in this sense does integrate and make sense out of a wide array of apparently conflicting, inconsistent, partially understood data. A "field," as used in physics, means a configuration of forces acting in a particular area of space (for example the space around a magnet, or between two electrically charged plates). Our "thought system" acts in a manner analogous to these fields in the sense that any stimulus that comes in from the outside is distorted, affected or interpreted by the nature of our beliefs (our particular field of forces). We can visualize this process as in Figure 1 (see pages 36 and 37).

When first introduced the principle of the "field" represented another scientific evolutionary step. We began to glimpse an entirely new dimension (the field) which, on the basis of a single continuum, reveals how seemingly qualitatively dissimilar systems are interrelated. For example, prior to Einstein's breakthrough, physicists saw space and matter as being separate qualities which comprise the physical world. Consequently, the different phenomena associated with the mechanical behavior of separate material bodies (i.e., heat, light, gravitation, electricity) were also seen as being separate. Systems were proposed to explain each class of phenomena, yet the connection between these phenomena, or the systems to explain them, was missing. Each system could only account for itself. Einstein, however, realized the context within which all of these phenomena were, in principle, the same. He realized that the missing link did not lie in any aspect of the specific phenomena. With the specifics out of the way, "only field energy would be left, and the particle would be merely an area of special density of field energy. In that way one could hope to deduce the ... field equations — the disturbing dualism would have been removed" (Einstein, 1949, p. 37).

In a manner analogous to magnetic and other physical fields, if we turn off the current or otherwise remove the field, the distortion of forces acting on these external stimuli no longer exists. It does not then matter what the nature of the particular or detailed configuration of forces were, because when they are taken away, they are no longer a factor. Thus the key to the solution lies in finding out the process by which

---

Einstein, A. Autobiographical notes. In P. A. Schilpp (Ed.), *Albert Einstein: Philosopher-Scientist* (Vol. 1). New York: Harper and Brothers, 1949.

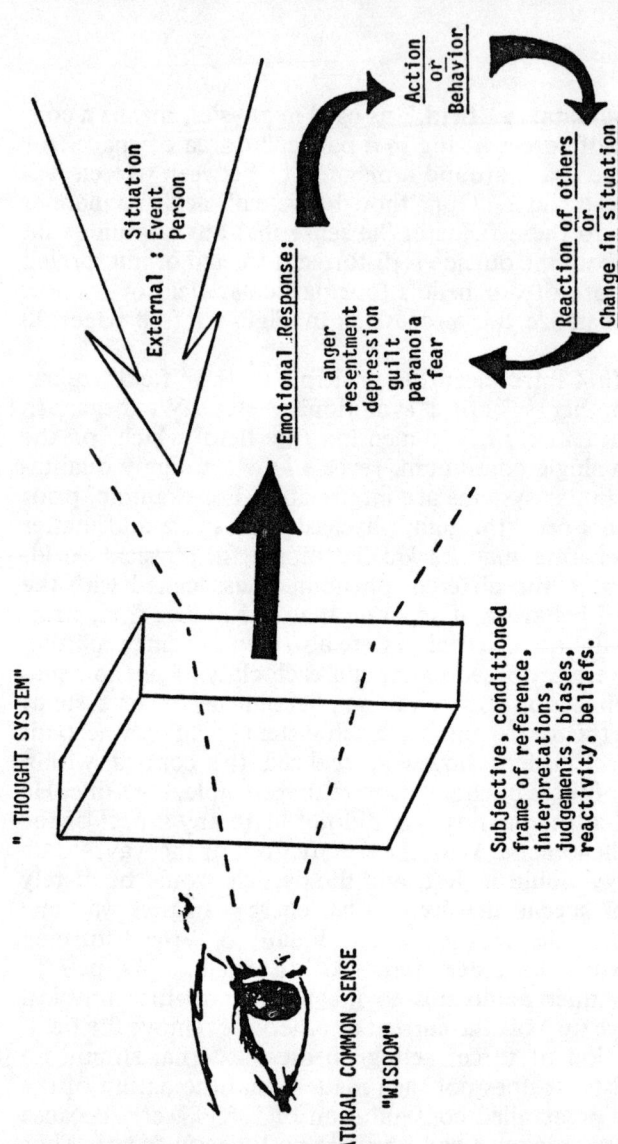

FIGURE ONE:

these systems or fields are activated and maintained in ourselves psychologically, at a level of understanding that applies irrespective of the details or particular beliefs of each unique thought system.

THE RIDDLE OF INDIVIDUAL DIFFERENCES AND OUR PSYCHOLOGICAL REALITY

The content of each persons' subjective frame of reference or thought system is unique. We cannot find the commonalities in analyzing this varied content, except perhaps for broad cultural similarities. In other words, everyone sees things differently than anyone else.

A much simpler, more elegant and profound answer exists when we look deeper to grasp the underlying principles of how all thought systems work as systems, at a level of generalization outside of the unique content of each particular system. The beauty of this systems' view in one sense, is that we then do see our own biases more "impersonally," and objectively to a much greater degree than when we are taking the content of our own thought system seriously. We are then in a condition or state of mind where we are using our own "common-sense" to look at the way all people function psychologically.

THE ANALOGY TO NATURAL SYSTEMS

ALL NATURAL ECOLOGICAL SYSTEMS OPERATE ACCORDING TO THE SAME PRINCIPLES, WHETHER THE "CONTENT" IS A RAIN FOREST OR A DRY SEA COAST TERRAIN. THIS NEW FORMULATION OF THESE PSYCHOLOGICAL PRINCIPLES APPLIES EQUALLY TO ANY INDIVIDUAL REGARDLESS OF THE DETAILED NATURE OF HIS PAST, OR THE QUALITY OF PAST EXPERIENCES.

The psychological principles describing how "thought systems" work are not complicated, and in fact are quite "common-sensical" in terms of their logic. They have not yet been realized by the field of psychology because we have not looked at the matter yet from this new vantage point, *or* in this comprehensive a manner. These systems' principles determine how our thoughts, perceptions and feelings are generated now, in the present moment, to create whatever reality we personally experience. Perhaps we can more graphically visualize that our subjective frame of reference (made up of all our habit patterns, attitudes, opinions, beliefs, expectations, and so on) exists in the present as memory stored in a computer-like fashion in the form of a thought system. In terms of the principles that describe how this system actually works, the detailed content of this frame of reference, where and how it was acquired, who was involved, or what experiences contributed to it, has nothing to do with what is now called "mental health" or maturity. Operationally, what this means is that the solution to eliminating any problem (being generated from any given acquired frame of reference) cannot be realized by analyzing our specific habit patterns, our personal interactions, or by behavioral manipulation of our environment or symptom patterns.

We can see this point perhaps more easily with regard to physical fields, say a magnetic field. It is the entire field that must be understood to change it. We cannot try to move or manipulate one line of magnetic force within this field. When we try to change specific symptoms or specific problems we have, it is like trying to change each line of force in a magnetic field one by one.

Psychologically, as well, if we are attempting to work with the results of the effects of our thought system, we are taking this system as a given, thereby giving it the continuing power to affect our behavior, our reactions and our mental health in the future.

THE CONDITIONAL RELATIONSHIP OF OUR
THOUGHT SYSTEM TO OUR BRAINS

The thought system, as a bundle of memories, is stored in our brains. The input-output characteristics of our brains have been more than adequately delineated operationally and phenomenologically, as a result of the work of the Russian physiologist Ivan Pavlov, Harvard's B. F. Skinner and Canada's renowned neurosurgeon, Wilder Penfield, respectively. We are now factually justified in saying that there is no longer any doubt that our brains are biological computers capable of projecting a sensory-motor and cognitive experience. As human beings we are capable of attaching or associating any event (experience) with any other experience in terms of an associative experience of cause and effect. Learning and conditioning are undeniable potential sources of bias to human experience due to the fact that we are capable of storing and recalling any experience we have had. The brain, then, can be viewed as the "hardware" of the computer, while the thought system is the program or "software."

INDIVIDUAL DIFFERENCES AND THE PRINCIPLE OF SEPARATE REALITIES

Because our thought system is built up from whatever unique associations we have stored up in our memory regarding the experiences we have had, the resulting psychological frame of reference is unique for each one of us. This bundle of memories then becomes a potential source of bias, when activated. This occurs because these "memories" are locked, so to speak, to the relative reality of what we thought occurred in the past, a past which is no longer real in the sense that it is *present* as a function of our memory. As such, this past exists in our present reality only via the activation of our thinking. The more our thinking is based on our stored memories, the more circular the thinking process becomes. Thus, to the degree the reference function is activated in the process of thought, there ensues an accompanying inability to recognize or understand (by degrees) anything not already included within the conceptual boundaries of our referenced thinking. The end result is a pattern of thinking which is separate, by virtue of its uniqueness from anyone else's thinking. All psychological problems result from the dilemma that no human being is capable of understanding any other reality from within the confines of their own acquired pattern of thinking.

THE SOLUTION LIES IN THE PERSON ACTUALLY UNDERSTANDING FOR HIM OR HERSELF *UNDER WHAT PSYCHOLOGICAL CONDITIONS* WE TEND TO ACTIVATE AND UTILIZE THIS BUNDLE OF STORED THOUGHT PATTERNS AND REACTIONS TO LOCK OURSELVES IN A SEPARATE REALITY.

We can think of this solution again in terms of these "systems' principles," particularly the notion of "succession" or the evolution of a system to higher levels of adaptation. We, as human beings are much more "adaptive" when we can view every situation from an objective, mature perspective, applying "common-sense" to see clearly and make sound judgments not based on insecurity or filtered by emotional "reaction" personal "vested" interest, emotional upset or stress. We are then more able to understand and help ourselves, our friends and people in our work.

IT IS, IN FACT ACTIVATING OUR OWN INNATE COMMON-SENSE THAT ENABLES US TO SOMETIMES STEP BACK AND ADMIT THAT WE ARE "CAUGHT UP" IN SOMETHING, OVER-REACTING, FEELING IRRATIONALLY (I.E., OUT OF PROPORTION TO THE SITUATION) INSECURE, ANGRY OR UPSET IN SOME OTHER WAY.

IRRESPECTIVE OF THE PRESENTING PROBLEMS:

This new psychological formulation which we are presenting has allowed us to bypass having to delve into the details of peoples' lives, their past and their problems to go directly to the source of their difficulty in their own thoughts. In this respect it is the details of peoples' past, their present lives, and their habit patterns which they activate and then they cannot see through when they become insecure. Every time we talk about them we are in essence activating what we would call a patient mentality or a therapeutic life-style in which they do not eliminate their problems but simply recontaminate their own reactive tendencies by talking about their problems and analyzing their marital interactions, their impact on others, and so on, when they are in these "reactive" states. In this sense, there is no one in the world who is not schizophrenic, yet we often promote the schizophrenia.

THE DEVELOPMENT OF SPECIALIZATION:

Psychology as a yet fairly young field, has become highly specialized. Experimental and clinical psychology have little in common. Alcoholism specialists would not treat marital problems, experts in weight loss would not attempt to treat depression or schizophrenia and so on. Drug abuse specialists, different age group specialists (old age, youth, middle age, college age, etc.) sex specialists and people who study stress all seem to have a corner on their type of problems, in spite of the fact that people who are, for example, heavy drug users also typically have a terrible family life, bad work habits, poor relationships, and could be any age or occupation, while many claim their dependency developed due to stress.

SPECIALIZATION IN THE PHYSICAL SCIENCES

As physics evolved as a science initially, people also studied manifestated phenomena separately. Some scientists were specialists in heat, some electricity, some in gravity, some in optics, others in mechanics and so on. However, at a certain stage, we began to realize that heat could be turned into electricity, which would be turned into light and mechanical energy, or generate magnetic forces, and that we could even reverse these processes. Once scientists began to see these similarities and to then recognize the universal wave-like nature of energy, the similarities in the ways that gravitational, magnetic, electric and electromagnetic fields worked, became clearer. These different specialities and categories then broke down even further and became less important. Maxwell's equations, the principles of the Lorentz transformations, and the fundamental formulas of Einstein's principles of general relativity showed clearly and convincingly that all energy and substance could be broken down to the same basic phenomena which undergo transformations from one form to another in very predictable and understandable ways.

LINKING OUR THEORIES, A PRINCIPLE OF CONSCIOUSNESS

These new principles of the mind reveal and clarify the same types of connections and relationships for the field of psychology. Any individual with a given "thought system," having gained a certain level of understanding of the nature of that thought system, when entering into any environment will have predictable feelings, reactions, stresses, thoughts and behavior patterns. All of our psychological tests and experiments to date have ultimately, but in a piecemeal fashion, been aimed at documenting these relationships.

The variable that can change is the individual's level of consciousness, or understanding of what is really happening. At higher levels of consciousness our acquired or conditioned "thought system" is of less consequence, (i.e., it is not used to interpret, judge and produce defensiveness, stress or other negative feelings). This is a key dimension linking all human beings regardless of their culture, personality, education, age, life style or personal history.

THE PSYCHOLOGICAL ENERGY OF THOUGHT SYSTEMS

The concept in physics of electromagnetic and gravitational "fields" showed that movements in physical space are created and altered by certain types of configurations of energy that cover an area of space, creating force in a particular direction. The psychological interactions of different peoples' "thought systems" in any setting will create a network or a field of feelings, positions and behaviors. Anything then that a group of individuals wants to accomplish will be affected by the nature of the total field. For example, we found that, as consultants in hospital settings, if the staff on a ward sent us a "problem" patient, even if that patient changed, when they went back on the ward, they were still treated as a "problem patient" and their behaviors responded to on this basis.

While these more complex systems act to reinforce a particular set of assumptions, judgments and responses in a social or work setting, it is only necessary for an individual to see how their own "thought system" works, to then easily see the nature of the interactions in any setting with others as the predictable result of the interactions of these individual systems.

THE RELATIVITY OF THOUGHT SYSTEMS

One of the arguments that Einstein had to put forth and defend in the evolution of the general theory of relativity was the erroneous assumption of the absolute "inertial" system or frame of reference, from which we can measure all phenomena (for example, standing at rest on the earth won't work because the earth is not only spinning but also rotating around the sun). Since, psychologically our own thoughts create our reality, there is also no absolute psychological frame of reference to be found within the context of any particular thought system. There are on the other hand some more "absolute" psychological facts, just as Einstein demonstrated that electromagnetic fields operate across different coordinate systems or physical frames of reference and that the speed of light is a limiting velocity for anything with mass. Because of these facts certain laws of transformation across different physical frames of reference are true as well irrespective of the nature of each individual frame of reference.

In a similar manner these deeper psychological facts have to do with realizing the power of thought itself and the nature of how we all go in and out of the "thought systems" we have learned in our lifetime. These principles hold up *regardless of the nature of* our subjective, psychological frame of reference.

THE RESULTS OF THE CURRENT MODALITIES AND APPROACHES IN PSYCHOLOGY

The fields of psychology and human behavior have to date

missed uncovering these principles because they have based current theories and models almost exclusively on empirical and epidemiological data which itself has been based on peoples' subjective perceptions or misperceptions, reactions, feelings and so forth (what people see when they are in "reactive" states). That is, these theories are in essence based on a misperception of people in terms of how we operate now psychologically. The resulting models and theories are conceptualized versions of these misperceptions and thus exhibit the same limitation experienced by the data points themselves, that is the people in the samples. In this sense, even though the fields of psychology, human behavior and mental health are honestly attempting to help people, the process by which theories and models have been developed with their associated therapies, is analogous to developing surgical techniques in the absence of any knowledge concerning microbiological contamination or sterilization procedures. In that situation we have a problem that, regardless of the approach, the result of applying the technique produces contamination which overshadows any possible positive result. In this same sense, a therapeutic approach which directs a person to dwell into the details of his or her life, past or present to search out habit patterns and negative emotions is contaminating the result. This is unavoidable when the frame of reference of psychology assumes that our behavior now is caused by our past or learned reactions to external stimuli, the quality and quantity of which is determined by the particulars of our past associations.

To date we have seen consistently positive results in mental health patients suffering from a variety of problems including affective, addictive, compulsive, or adjustment disorders as well as psychophysiological disturbance. In addition, we have found that these same principles have also reversed the trend of negative perceptions in feelings that people are experiencing today in their jobs and professional lives. That is the problems that are being labeled "job stress" or "burnout." We have seen these positive results not only in physicians but in nurses and other allied health care professions in a variety of settings, which include: spinal cord injury, intensive care, rehabilitation, dialysis, laboratory, and surgical units.

INTEGRATING THE CLUES IN PRESENT DAY PSYCHOLOGY: A COMMON DENOMINATOR

Perhaps the single most important and more accurate fact or principle that we must take a look at is the power (or role) of our own thoughts in relation to our emotional state and our mental health, in relation to stress and to other psychological problems. *"We are what we think"* at first seems like a tired truism we all have heard before. Yet, when looked at from a deeper psychological perspective, there is a much more profound fact in that statement about our experience as human beings than we realize.

Most schools of therapy would admit the truth of that principle to some extent. Freudian psychologists would say that much of our personality and "habitual" behavior patterns and beliefs came from our early relationship with our parents. Social learning theorists would say that, through repeated exposure, we "learned" certain "conditioned" ways of behaving and thinking. Environmental or cultural psychologists would say that certain stimuli in our environment, or values in our culture have contributed to our present personality, our self-image and how we view the world. From looking at all of these hypotheses and experimental correlations of their studies from a broader, cumulative perspective, all the data point to the facts that:

1) Our mind, acting in a manner analogous to a computer, stores (as programs) every learned response and experience from our past.

2) These experiences are then connected to values and attitudes, due to our ability to think creatively. We then combine these beliefs into an interlocking, internally consistent frame of reference; a "thought system" that acts as a set of perceptual filters through which we view life.

3) The end result of this process is that each of us lives (and therefore acts and reacts) within the framework (a cacoon or our "fishbowl") of a unique set of beliefs, interpretations and biases, all of which are related to our self-image (our picture of who we are, what is important to our well-being and happiness, etc.).

4) The evidence of this "thought system" (as a system that is internally consistent, and self-validating) explains why people tend to see things quite differently because of their parenting, culture, peer influences, unique experiences, socio-economic conditions, education, and other "factors" from their past or "lifestyle."

5) While this "thought system" is a conditioned, or learned view of reality, it is our reality, we see and experience our version of reality as real, no matter how bizarre or out of the ordinary (try to talk to a "schizophrenic" patient out of thinking they are from outer space when they are in that particular delusionary state).

6) This "thought system" is the source of our interpretations, and therefore our emotions, and reactions to events. Therefore, this "thought system" is also the source of our stress, our emotional upsets and compulsive behaviors.

THERAPY FROM AN UNDERSTANDING OF THOUGHT SYSTEMS

In relation to these logical correlations to the first principle, we have discovered, primarily from our own research over the last five years, that once people begin to discover for themselves what their thought system is, not in terms of its detailed content, but rather the principles of how these subjective frames of reference actually act to form our "illusionary" view of the world, they can begin to drop these filters to see more clearly and objectively what is really going on, from what we would call a more "mature," "rational" or "common-sense" vantage point.

1) We can see the evidence for this shift in perspective in a variety of "common-sense" ways. For example, we

all go in and out of different moods, emotional states and ways of viewing our lives everyday. When we are in what we call "good" mood, we are usually enjoying ourselves, appreciating our work, family and friends and often have insights about things. We feel alive and energized. Our problems don't seem like such a big deal. When we drop into a lower mood, our self-confidence wavers, we become anxious, worried and upset. It is at these times when we feel "caught up in" or overwhelmed by things. We cannot catch up on our work, we feel tired, get sick easier, and everything unexpected is either a petty annoyance, or a sign of impending doom. Our mood has changed, and our version of reality has also changed.

2) We all know, or have heard about people who are respected for their wisdom, good judgment, their perspective on problems. We have a respect for people with a lot of "common-sense." We often go to these kinds of people for help when we are in trouble, (caught up in, or overwhelmed by our problems to the point of confusion and an anxiety that does not allow us to think "straight"). We go to these people because we feel they will have a clearer perspective. Yet, when we are in these lower "reactive" states, we will still argue with them, defending our negatively distorted views.

3) We can see in athletics, games and other activities, the adverse effects of "pressing" or thinking too much about what we are doing. If we are self-conscious and thinking of how well we are doing, we usually tense up and blow the shot or drop the pass or lose the ball. It is this shift to a sudden thought of insecurity that actually triggers our lower, more reactive and emotionally distraught, distorted views of reality. (Our subjective "thought system.")

The final conclusion, emerging from these propositions is that (a) everyone lives in their own world (their subjective frame of reference), (b) at a given level of understanding or insight about the illusionary quality of that reality at any given time. In lower "moods" or states of insecurity, we habitually activate our "conditioned" thought system to more rigorously defend and become more affected ourselves by those thoughts.

THE NATURE OF MENTAL HEALTH:

As we understand these dynamics better, we begin to drop our insecurity (self-consciousness about the image of self-importance we would call our "ego" or self-image; i.e., the sum total of our personality traits and learned attitudes), our conditioned thought system is then referenced less, and we have access to deeper states of "common-sense" or sanity. These more positive states we could call deeper and deeper levels of "mental health." These states are characterized by a natural high self-esteem, emotional stability, compassion or understanding, good judgment and the ability to effectively communicate our ideas and hear what others are saying. We could call these states conditions of more psychological clarity or objectivity.

In these higher states of objectivity, we understand the nature of "thought" systems and how they work to the point where we are no longer caught up in our own. We can see the relationship between everyone's subjective thought system and the results in the emotional conditions, relationships and life situations of the people around them.

THE INTERNAL CONSISTENCY OF THOUGHT SYSTEMS

When we look at these "thought systems" we see that for most of us, they comprise a total reality; a view of reality that creates predictable correlations, (or certain precise kinds of relationships) between our self-image, our values, our life style, how we view and react to others, our clothes, our diet, recreational and social habits and the kinds of people we want to impress or to be accepted by in relation to our self-image. Thus we do find experimental correlations between certain groups of symptoms (i.e., heavy drinking, chronic anxiety, drug use, spouse beating, irresponsibility, different categories of psychosis and nonproductive behaviors) and cultural or social backgrounds; in relation to experiences in our past, and to our other personality traits.

All of these relationships may be, and often are correlated; however, none of them has a causative relationship to the cure. What these data achieve is to validate the internal consistency of a given thought-system, at a given thought level of insecurity or level of understanding of what that "thought system" really is, and how it works.

The book "The Evolution of Physics" describes the change from a mechanical description of the physical universe to a "Field Theory" description in the following way:

> In the beginning, the field concept was no more than a means of facilitating the understanding of phenomena from the mechanical point of view . . . The recognition of the new concepts grew steadily, until substance was overshadowed by the field. It was realized that something of great importance had happened in physics. A new reality was created, a new concept for which there was no place in the mechanical description. Slowly, and by a struggle, the field concept established for itself a leading place in physics and has remained one of the basic physical concepts. The electromagnetic field is, for the modern physicist, as real as the chair on which he sits (Einstein and Infeld, 1938, pp. 157-158).

Today, as far as classical psychology is concerned the principles of "Thought Systems" are not yet real. Particularly, recently we have been moving perhaps more in a mechanistic direction by studying specific behaviors (social learning theories), measuring and locating discrete patterns of electrical brain wave activity and so on.

Until physics evolved to understand field theory, the phenomena of light for example was confusing because it exhibited wave-like characteristics, yet the mechanical theories allowed only for waves that moved through a medium (water, gas, etc.). Therefore classical physics had to invent or hypothesize an "ether" in the vacuum of space which was jelly-like, in order to accept the wave properties of light.

The existence of fields revealed that light was an electromagnetic wave that indeed moved through a vacuum influenced only by the properties of the "field" as a whole. yet these fields cannot be seen, touched, weighed or measured, they are intangible. We discovered their existence by noticing the resultant physical phenomena (the pull of gravity, electric currents, magnetic forces, the diffraction of light), and the *connections between* these phenomena.

The existence of thought systems is similarly revealed by the resulting feelings and behaviors, although a "thought system" itself is intangible. The existence of levels of consciousness is also evidenced in the way we are sometimes more easily upset, "reactive" or insecure, while at other times we are less attached to our personal ways of seeing things.

THE PRINCIPLES OF OUR (A) LEVEL OF INSECURITY AND (B) THE ACTIVATION OF OUR ACQUIRED "THOUGHT SYSTEM" DETERMINE EXACTLY WHAT IS HAPPENING IN OUR LIVES PSYCHOLOGICALLY AT ANY GIVEN POINT IN TIME.

In order to fully comprehend what is actually occurring, we must look at the whole thing from this new perspective with a more comprehensive frame of reference, a perspective that includes all the different versions of reality and types of psychological reactions we all experience, all the time.

One thing that we start to see when we adopt this broader perspective, is that we have gotten the relationship of our "mental health" to our feelings confused, and in most cases backwards.

We can look back at Figure 1 to illustrate this point (see pages 36 and 37).

Everything we observe when filtered through this conditioned thought system is given an interpretation. After we apply this interpretation, we become "locked in" to seeing that situation with certain feelings, expectations, judgments and reactions. If we analyze or talk about these feelings and reactions, we are in a situation analogous to looking at the picture on the screen at a movie theater to find the projector.

Figure 2 will illustrate a more accurate perspective on this process (see pages 52 and 53).

As we can see from this diagram, looking at and analyzing specific symptoms is three steps removed from the actual source of these symptoms. Working on, or talking about feelings is a step closer, but is still not the source, nor is it productive in therapy to work at this level.

For example, many therapists tell us to "get out" or "express" our pent-up emotions and to be "out-front" or honest about how we "really" feel about others. Yet since *I* originally created the interpretation, *I* can work myself into any feeling I want to whenever I want, via the power of my own thinking ability. If we encourage clients to talk about or otherwise take seriously negative feelings, we are unknowingly encouraging and reinforcing that view of reality, and the level of insecurity and stress involved with that perspective.

We can also observe, from Figure 2, that this process works in the same way irrespective of the content of our thought system, our specific personality traits, or the kinds of symptoms we experience. These details are analogous to the numbers we plug into a mathematical equation, they are subject to certain rules or principles of transformation, but in themselves have no power to change the nature of the relationships described by these principles.

We can actually look at, and understand the relationships among various types of "mental illnesses," and "addictive behaviors" and other symptoms of stress using these principles. The correlation between the details of our "thought system" and the way we live our lives is as precise as a computer-drawn map, in which the computer accurately portrays the information stored in its memory circuits in drawing the map itself. George Kelley studies correlations between "bundles" or groups of values and personality traits, and talked in terms of what he called "personal construct" theory. His work was focused on step one, in which he asked people about their "interpretations" of things, and then clustered these in groups to show people what kind of person

FIGURE TWO:

NATURAL COMMON
SENSE WISDOM

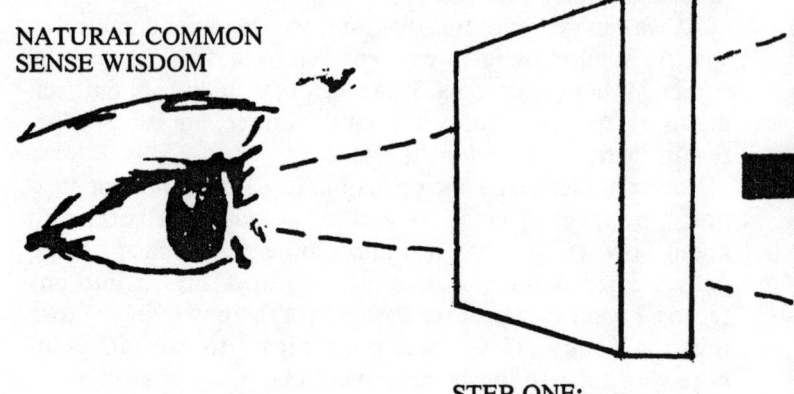

STEP ONE:
Interpretation based
on content of subjective
"thought system"

they are.

In order to really get to the source however, we must begin to look at this entire process objectively from beginning to end, *from outside* that framework altogether. We are only prisoners of our personality, habits, learned behaviors and insecure states when we do not realize what they are, or the power of our own thoughts. We develop this realization when we start to use our "common-sense," our innate wisdom, (i.e., our own states of mental health) to view ourselves and others in terms of how we work psychologically.

POSITIVE FEELINGS; THE PRINCIPLE
DIRECTION TO MENTAL HEALTH

When we follow the direction of all of the data and propositions put forth above, we also come to the unmistakable conclusion that we cannot find the route to our own deeper levels of mental health or well-being through negative feelings, by working with our symptoms, or by intellectually analyzing and "figuring out" how we work psychological. Since we all live within the boundaries of our own subjective

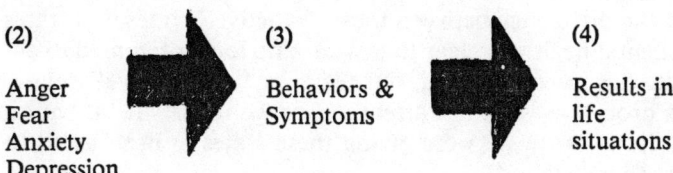

(2)	(3)	(4)
Anger Fear Anxiety Depression	Behaviors & Symptoms	Results in life situations

STEP TWO: STEP THREE:
Actual feelings, Behaviors and
reactions, symptoms emerging
emotional state from feelings

frame of reference, (a perspective that is unique, but seems real to us) we must analyze any input using that frame of reference.

Since we, intellectually, process new information through, and with, our existing "thought system," intellectual comprehension is not the solution. The solution involves, rather, quieting down our mind altogether, to listen and to "experience" as insights the realization of a broader frame of reference altogether.

Our own deeper levels of common-sense actually are reached via positive feelings, not intellectual comprehension. Once we start to realize what we are looking for, what we should then do is to start to enjoy life as we did when we were young and less ridden with anxiety, worry and responsibilities. Enjoying whatever we are doing and appreciating what we have now brings a state of more happiness; in these states our "chronic" negative thoughts and concerns are not being activated. Therefore we use our "common-sense"; a state of mind that is naturally and effortlessly there when we let go of the filters of our insecure thought system. The longer we stay in positive feeling states, the more our common sense is used and the more the results of this frame of mind starts to show up in our lives. At some point, from our observations of clients, ourselves and friends, things become so much nicer, and the difference between these "reactive" states and states of mental health so clear that we are no longer tempted to activate our insecure world, our fears, or "compulsive" behaviors drop away without attention, as we realize the attention and importance we were giving these states in itself acted to keep them around.

THE IMPLICATIONS OF THESE DISCOVERIES

When these results begin to happen, we are in effect, operating ourselves at a more accurate, more profound and deeper level of understanding about the nature of the relationship of our thoughts to our "psychological" functioning. This wisdom is true mental health. With this accurate an understanding, we cannot possibly become "mentally ill" or suffer from nervous breakdowns, "burnout" or emotional instability, because we know how those problems came about. We are then ourselves the best psychologist we can ever get. Just as math students can learn the principles of math, sometimes even better than the teacher, all human beings have the capacity to recognize these principles and apply them to our own experience. If we apply them correctly, we will always get an accurate answer.

In the following chapters, we will develop the principles introduced here in a more in-depth fashion, with concrete examples, case histories and applications that the reader can identify with, in terms of both our professional work and our personal lives. We know that an exposure to these principles, presented in the context of problems and experiences we have all had, allows the implications of these discoveries to sink in, and become more and more obvious. We will also present these principles in the light of current psychological theories and methods, and discuss the future direction of psychological research, teaching and treatment implied by the discovery of these new principles.

SECTION II

THE PRINCIPLES OF THE EVIDENT PSYCHOLOGY: THE ROUTE TO SANITY

CHAPTER 3

The Need for An Advanced Psychology: Toward A Deeper Understanding of the Mind

Never in the history of the study of human behavior has the need been so obvious for a time out, an honest look at what we as thinking human beings are doing. It is truly time to look at the results of our present state of understanding of human behavior and to decide whether or not we wish to continue the search for knowledge about ourselves in the traditional theorizing manner and direction handed down nearly a century ago.

Because the human mind is capable of attaching or of associating any event to any other event in terms of an experience of cause and effect, human beings are capable of making up an infinite number of theories about human behavior. By reason of this attribute, we are also capable of experiencing these theories in our lives because of our expectations, reactions and/or beliefs. It is precisely this fact about how each person's thought system works in the present to generate his or her experience, perception and interpretation of life that we are attempting to assist psychology to understand at a deeper level.

It follows then that since all psychological theories are in themselves thought systems (as theories of cause and effect), there is no answer existent looking within the content boundaries of these theories. Rather we must look at these theories as examples of what we are pointing toward in this book. The process of looking beyond theories, techniques, methods and conceptual models is a tricky one because everyone's experience is itself a product of an individual thought system, including the training, the theories, concepts and techniques that each has learned in a lifetime — in other words, what each of us considers to be the significant content of our lives. It is precisely for this reason that it is important to understand the underlying principles of thought systems at an impersonal level or in a way that applies to all people, regardless of the content of their individual thought systems. As these underlying principles are gradually realized we can begin to experience without fear our own thought systems for what they are, our illusionary versions of reality.

IN SEARCH OF OURSELVES:
THE EVOLVING FIELD OF PSYCHOLOGY

The focused study of ourselves as human beings did not begin with the notion of studying problems. It began as an honest yearning for the knowledge of how our psychic apparatus, the so-called mind, operates to create and/or produce the reality of the experience we call life.

Thus, many of those individuals acknowledged with being the precursors of what would later be known as Psychology approached the inquiry using a much different perspective than that from which our study of the mind is being approached today. Those originally interested in this inquiry sought to understand the very source of human behavior. They attempted to study the existing relationships of *"thoughts," "feelings," "sensations," "images," "perceptions,"* and so forth, to the *"experiences"* called life. These early innovators did not look to find the sources of human experiences and behaviors in the experienced perceptions of the past. Neither were they solely interested in the study of people's problems as a separate class of human experiences or behaviors. They simply suspected that all experience and behavior emitted by a human being originated within the confines of his own mind.

This initial direction was replaced by the increasing tendency to study the parameters and the details of people's mental output in order to begin building a foundation of data. These data would then serve as standards of reference from which to further study other human behaviors. Thus, the study of thought became the study of the varied contents we think about. The study of feelings became the study of what were thought to be the causes of this or that feeling, so on and so forth. Not surprisingly, it was not long before different schools of thought began to appear. Such so-called schools generated their own frameworks of ideas, concepts, theories and data concerning what, how and who should be studied and for what purposes.

It wasn't until the late 1800's, however, when Sigmund Freud would share his thoughts (later called theories) about what he hypothesized to be the source of all human behavior; that the study of man's mind would be formally replaced by the study of people's behaviors, especially the negative ones. This problem-oriented psychology, in time, was to be adopted in direction and methodology and would become the standard framework for the entire field of mental health. To date, the field of psychology has continued in its problem-oriented theoretical approach to the study of human behavior.

As the field turned its analytical attention to the varying aspects of life, it did so using its problem-oriented framework. Utilizing an already ever-accumulating warehouse of theories, models and constructs, it proceeded to attempt to define and to analyze problems as a means of helping people. In a relatively short span of time thousands of theories were thought up to explain the problems of human beings. Each theory in turn generated a specific therapeutic ritual with which to deal with the rapidly increasing list of problems and disorders being defined and described. What the field at that time did not realize was that this process is analogous to adding water to a swamp to get rid of the swamp, when in actuality it was merely creating more swamp, and then trying to show people new ways to try to stay afloat in an ever-increasing circle of problems, traumas, sources of stress, disorders and reasons from the past.

STATE OF THE ART OF MENTAL HEALTH PRACTICE

The present-day state of mental health is reflected by the ever-increasing demand for more mental health professionals and programs to solve people's problems. To a greater extent than ever before people are now focused on and preoccupied with being normal, adjusted and aware. Psychology presently endorses and promotes an unbelievable arsenal of specific theories, models, methods and techniques to assess, evaluate and treat any abnormality in every conceivable area of life.

As a direct result, the present-day cost of mental health services in this society is astronomical. The cost associated with the general decline in the state of mental health is immeasurable to its citizens since it affects all aspects of society. What this society is presently receiving for all this cost is still a matter of debate on the part of the field of psychology.

We were astounded when an article appeared in *Science* in January, 1973, written by a psychologist who had placed eight normal people — a student, a painter, three psychologists, a psychiatrist, a pediatrician, and a housewife — secretly in mental institutions, most of which were well known and respected. There the subjects acted totally normal and sane, and not one of them was discovered. We were even more astounded when this psychologist described what happened to these people and how every behavior, which would be seen as normal out in the community, was interpreted as more evidence of their pathology. Most interesting of all was the fact that nothing happened as a result of the publication of that article. The only response from the mental health fields was in terms of theoretical and methodological critique.

As employees of the mental health system ourselves, we have seen how mental hospitals and most therapies often serve to make patients more convinced they are crazy and make it harder for them to realize normal, sane lives. Many of the employees of this system know that as well, but none have

---

Rosenhan, D. L. On being sane in insane places. *Science,* 1973, *179,* 250-258.

raised a hue or cry. In fact, the first year that one of the authors was director of a community mental health center, he went to a regional meeting of center directors to listen to people complain that their census had dropped and they needed to do better marketing of their programs. The notion that their services may not have been needed, or seen as helpful, was not considered, as a matter for investigation.

A FIELD IN A NUTSHELL

We have personally seen such crazy things happen in mental health centers and hospitals among the staff that even fans of *One Flew Over the Cuckoo's Nest* would find hard to believe. We have seen people intimidated, embarrassed and humiliated in so-called *personal growth* groups. We are not putting these sorts of details in this book because we are not interested in muckraking. Furthermore, we realize that these happenings occur as a result of our present-day levels of understanding, and as such represent only detailed symptoms. We are much more interested in providing something positive, something of value to people who themselves want some understanding, some peace and the ability to live their lives the way they want to live them and be happy.

In spite of the present arsenal of therapeutic defenses against psychological problems, relief has yet to be experienced. This dissatisfaction has led to the overgrowth in this society of *"self help," "personal growth," "awareness,"* and *"consciousness raising"* gimmicks and techniques. It is possible today to go to almost any city in the United States and undergo all combinations and varieties of individual and/or group psychotherapies involving every imaginable gimmick one could think of. The bizarre nature of some of these therapies is something most ordinary people would disbelieve unless witnessed. The relationship of these rituals to enjoying life is questionable.

MISSING THE FOREST FOR THE TREES

Within the ranks of academic psychology, the dissatisfaction with traditional formulation has been manifested by the appearance and/or reappearance of a large variety of literature pertaining to such topics as *"consciousness," "mind," "creativity," "thought," "intuition,"* and so forth. All inquiry in this direction, however, has been conceptualized and approached using the same basic framework which presently dominates the field of psychology. As a result, no true breakthrough of useful practical value has yet been realized by the psychological field.

Along the same vein, there has also been more of an interest recently in the power of thought. There has been a resurgence in psychology of people interested in psychosomatic illness. We know more than ever that many physical probems, like ulcers, heart attacks and other nervous system ailments are generated by stress. Some people are even beginning to see the relationship of cancer to stress. With the recent advance in technology to measure the relationship between our thought patterns, feelings and physical reactions (polygraph and biofeedback machines), these relationships are becoming more and more obvious. However, the field as a whole has taken these phenomena merely as interesting sidelights to integrate into the mainstream of psychological theories, methods and research. In a rush to create a psychological technology, no one as yet has taken a serious and thorough look at the implications of these findings.

SOURCES OF CONTROVERSY

We know that this book will create both positive and negative controversy. We did not write it intending to create a negative controversy; however, we know it cannot be avoided. Because we are sharing principles which are beyond the present frame of reference of the field of psychology, people who have been trained to do therapy, teach, research and develop theories within that frame of reference will find themselves reacting to some extent to what we are learning and sharing. We have already been accused of being *"too simplistic," "too grandiose," "too naive," "too pie-in-the-sky"* and other more unmentionable epithets.

A DOSE OF OUR OWN MEDICINE

When we first began to realize the insights which make up the material in this book, we did not really believe it ourselves. We thought it was interesting and intriguing more as a hobby than anything else. But, we stuck our noses in too far, and our lives and those of our colleagues and friends started to honestly change in positive directions. Our clients got better faster, our friends became happier and more self-assured, and therapists we knew started getting excited about their work. The results of our then microscopically deeper understanding of human behavior had tremendous results we had not nearly anticipated. In fact, even now although we see people becoming happier, having more common sense and enjoying every moment of their lives more fully, without analysis, diets, gurus, bio-feedback, rebirthing, rolfing, massage, encounter, gestalt, T.A., primal scream, or anything, we still feel as though we do not really understand or appreciate what is going on.

So, although we are still relatively somewhat in the dark ourselves, the more we learn the more we know we are on the right track and in the right direction. Therefore, we welcome all skeptics. What we are pointing to is controversial only due to its obvious absence in what today is known as human behavior. The implications of what we are learning cover the entire field of psychology, from family and relationship counseling, and working with the severely emotionally disturbed and physically handicapped, to all us normal folks.

As stated above, what is reported in this book gives us a deeper understanding of behavior across cultures, of our behavior as societies and as interest groups or factions within societies. This understanding clarifies why people join groups or movements, and how our self-esteem is attached to whatever conditions we feel are important for our own personal happiness.

It may sound grandiose to say that this understanding has

application to all of these areas. Yet if the reader can see the relationship of this understanding to any one of them, he or she will then see its relevance to all of the others, and most importantly, to the individual. By talking to people in all different areas of life and all disciplines, we have learned a tremendous amount ourselves. This type of learning has already contributed to this book, to the quality of our personal lives, and to our professional work.

We are especially grateful to those who have already accused us of heresy since this reaction has helped us to gain a deeper understanding of dogma, rituals, and the power of orthodoxy in relation to what we are learning about the power of thought. We are even, sometimes, grateful for the people who have caught on that there is something different here, and yet have held back because of their reputations or the lack of agreement that existed around them. These reactions have given us a deeper understanding of the power of agreement and authority in relation to introducing something new to an existing frame of reference, and to assisting people to see something beyond what they know now.

We are interested in reaching people who will get excited about the relationship of these deeper patterns to their field or profession, so they can gain a deeper wisdom about what they are studying and teaching. We, therefore, would welcome all inquiries, questions, and/or open discussions from those who are interested, regardless of how much or how little they understand of what we are saying. For those who would mostly like to argue, we must say that we have never known people to enter an argument with the purpose of learning something new about themselves or anyone else.

Although we have learned tremendously, observing people caught up in arguments over issues, ideologies and theories, there is absolutely nothing of value for those caught up in the argument itself. When we are caught up in argument, we are merely arguing from our present thought systems. This will guarantee that we can learn nothing new until we begin to see the effects of those thought systems on our perceptions and reactions. Thus, we would like to ingenuously request that readers having any negative reaction to the notions and the principles presented in this book first take a look with as little judgment as possible at what personal beliefs may have been triggered to generate that negative reaction.

In the following chapters we will try to explain in as concrete, practical and common-sense terms as we possibly can what a thought system is and how it works in each of us as an individual human being. We have intentionally attempted to talk about this in very ordinary, straightforward language that both psychologists and lay people can understand. We have found that lay people, who have no professional or career investment in a particular model or theory of human behavior, often pick up this common-sense understanding of their own thought systems faster than professionals in the field of psychology. Yet understandably lay people are also often put off by the excessive use of jargon and professional terminology. Therefore, our intent is not to be insulting to the field of psychology, but rather to talk about what we are learning in as ordinary terms as possible, when we can, so that these insights will benefit as many as we possibly can reach with this book. Although the book was initially written for psychologists, we know that many people who have no education whatsoever in the field of psychology will be able to read it and achieve more sanity and peace of mind as a result.

CHAPTER 4

The Simplicity of Sanity:
The Common Sense Beneath Our Concepts of Mental Health

True mental health has nothing at all to do with concepts or theories. The condition of sanity is a natural condition in which the principles of how we go in and out of different moods, feeling states and ways of looking at situations that trigger our fears and reactions are so obvious and simple that they hardly seem worth talking about or explaining. The people we know who have realized what sanity is are often surprised by the lack of understanding of people around them, and the complications people create when they analyze their pasts, their patterns, their relationships and their personality styles, in relation to the events of their lives.

Every negative feeling that we experience as human beings comes about as a direct result of our own thought systems. That is, our acquired negative thinking patterns become activated by something that happens or that we think has happened to us, which we interpret as being harmful to our self-images. Once we begin to actually observe this process in operation without interpretation, the route to mental health becomes obvious. The way that this process actually works is quite simple, in fact, much simpler than any currently accepted theory or model of human behavior in the literature today.

MAKING THE COMPLICATED SIMPLE

One set of assumptions that will absolutely stop anyone from understanding the deeper principles of psychology is that this answer is too simple. Do not be fooled by this reaction. Again, because of our present-day conceptualization of intelligence and the theoretical role of intellect in problem-solving, the field of psychology is losing itself in the tendency to make things complicated, to break things down into categories, to find out more about the details of one category than anyone else.

The answer is simple and has nothing to do with intellectual or conceptual understanding. We are talking about a totally different dimension, a new dimension we will be referring to as wisdom, common sense or maturity. The wiser we become, the more simple life gets. The deeper we as individuals go into our understandings and the realizations of the power of thought, the more obvious becomes the connection between our individual thought systems and mental health, happy marriages, raising our children, having successful businesses, our social, political and even economic problems.

THE RELATIVE NATURE OF PSYCHOLOGICAL THEORIES, METHODS AND INFORMATION

While the fields that study human behavior come up with more and more causes, types of traumas, neuroses, syndromes and special categories of disturbances, the more problems continue to worsen. The answers seem further and further away, although we continue to document more symptomatic details and characteristics of the variety of emotional problems we experience as human beings. The solution does not lie in all of these details, but rather in the opposite direction toward a more simple but more profound understanding of our minds and the power of thought.

The reason underlying this state of affairs is that the answers that we as behavioral scientists seek will not be found in the results of statistical manipulation of the psychology data that we are creating. The long sought-after answers will be realized when we are willing to take perhaps a deeper, more objective look at the logic of how we create these data. We must take a more objective perspective and then look at the basic fundamental assumptions underlying what we presently call psychological measurement. It is at this new level of inquiry that the field of psychology will find the gateway to a deeper understanding of what the source of human behavior is.

The first thing we as a field will find is that our scientific methodology can only insure relative objectivity in our data. The scientific method can guarantee that our measurements are consistent, but only within the relative limits of the framework of assumptions which we are using as the measuring stick for those measurements.

The predicament of early astronomy illustrates this point beautifully. When astronomers were first charting the movement of the planets and stars, they did so under the assumption that the earth was a stationary center from which these measurements were being made. Astronomers objectively described what they saw. Without knowing it, however, they were objectively describing an illusion created because they lacked the knowledge that they, too, were moving. Their measurements, therefore, were relative measures; that is, relative measurements that were true only if one assumed that the earth was stationary. When all of these data were pooled, the resultant formulations were accordingly relatively true, yet far from being factual. All of the problems and the inconsistencies within the field of astronomy at that time were in fact self-generated. The solution to many of these problems was only realized when the field began to see the relativity of its measurements.

The fields of psychology, mental health and human behavior as they stand today are in the same predicament as these early astronomers. Although sincerely attempting to find solutions for the psychological problems that we experience, we have been unable to provide anything that truly works. Rigorous research methodology continues to be utilized in the behavioral sciences, and yet no breakthroughs have occurred.

Such a breakthrough has not come because the answers to the riddles which we are seeking have nothing to do with the objectivity of our research methodology, but rather with the underlying assumptions to our questions. We are measuring ourselves with our own theories, models and concepts, which are already biased measurements. As far as true objectivity goes, we are always too late, the moment we study our behaviors as human beings using arbitrary and relative sets of beliefs. When we begin to more fully understand the principles of relativity, we will once again be brought back to a fact: it is all our own thinking that we are measuring a reality we are simultaneously creating, perceiving and measuring via our own thoughts.

SEEING BEYOND INFORMATION

No amount of research alone can produce the answers we in the behavioral sciences are searching for. There is already an immense multitude of studies that have been carried out of our behaviors as individuals within and across cultures; of the rituals and belief systems of different cultures; of the behavior of people in groups, in societies, in political parties and factions, in relationship to authority and all other relative forces affecting behavior in groups and in organizations. There are refinements of studies that are themselves refinements of other studies. Epidemiological studies of psychological cause and effect carried out from the perspective of present-day assumptions, whether conceptual or empirical, will only serve to further obscure the true dynamics of what we are doing each moment to ourselves that creates our emotional states.

There are thousands of libraries, microfilm files and computers already storing a multitude of descriptive data on human behavior in every kind of situation, condition and organized group. We honestly do not need any more information on our emotional or social problems. The information is already there on television, in the news, in computers, in dissertations and journals, and in people. Common sense or wisdom gives us a truer understanding of the meaning behind the results of all these studies. Wisdom and the absence of insecurity give us the courage to use that information to the best of our abilities in a way that will help people and ourselves.

A consultant with wisdom can talk to people as individuals in organizations or social groups, get information from them about their situations and problems, and show them exactly how to solve their problems. This wisdom, however, is only useful to the clients, if they themselves can see beyond their own biases and theories to see the common sense to which the consultant is pointing. It is only then that they will be able to carry out any solutions that do not in themselves create more problems.

We cannot help anyone with information alone. Only the wisdom that puts this information in perspective is helpful. In the same way, the contents of this book are irrelevant as information to any insights or wisdom people get out of reading it. We talk about psychology and mental health neither from a descriptive viewpoint nor through details about what is happening, but through the perspective of why the results we get now are occurring. The readers who find their own common sense somehow triggered through reading this book can forget that they read the book, take their own common sense and see what the problems are in their own lives.

What is important are the insights and the sense of direction that actually occur in the readers from anything in the book. As we begin to see how to develop our wisdom, then we ourselves become the source of understanding rather than someone else's theories, ideas, insights, or books. If we have honestly learned something about insecurity and common sense, we are on the way to saner lives.

BRIDGING THE GAP BETWEEN DISCIPLINES

The exciting thing about this wisdom we are talking about is that, as we learn more about how it works, we see the connections to anthropology (how people behave as cultures), to our behaviors in terms of political beliefs, to our behaviors in social groups and in businesses and other organizations. The variety of the settings and situations in life to which this knowledge applies is endless. Therefore, there is no end to learning how the principles laid out in this book apply across the wide variations and arenas of human behavior. With a grasp of these principles, we can go anywhere in the world, enter any culture, group or situation and soon see clearly what is happening, what people are doing and for what evidently simple reasons. The results of this clarity in return show us more about how these principles operate.

Einstein saw things in simplicity. His original principles were simple but profound. As people began to grasp the meaning of these principles, they saw how they were connected to every form of physical phenomenon. Once we begin to get a grasp of the simple principles of the mind and our thought systems, we begin to actually see the relationship of these same principles to all our problems, to social problems and even to international relations. These discoveries make the simplicity exciting as we discover an underlying principle of human life at a deeper level of understanding, and then begin to see how it is connected to an endless variety of phenomena in all aspects of human behavior!

The evolution of the field of psychological thought is on the verge today of turning in this direction. As we have previously noted, more and more of the field is exploring such areas as altered states of consciousness and mind-body connections, particularly in the areas of psychosomatic medicine. Yet we have merely scratched the surface in terms of our understanding of the power of our own thoughts. The main reason we have not gone deeper in this direction is the tenacity of our accepted theoretical frameworks.

It is the objectivity of an unobstructed panorama that will assist the field of psychology to understand more clearly and in practical terms the power of thought and how it works every day in all individuals to generate their relative versions of reality. Once this connection is understood, we will understand truly what mental health is. Until that time we will merely continue to surface more and more theoretical problems, forms of emotional disturbances, and specialties for solving each particular type or category of trauma or problem.

THE NEED FOR BETTER UNDERSTANDING: RESULTS

We have found recently that the common-sense nature of what we are seeing is relatively more obvious to people in other professions than to people in the field of human behavior. These people have less attachment to present-day theories of human behavior. They can see the results in their work from seeing past their fears and insecurities, to develop not only expanded visions of their professions or businesses, but also deeper understandings of the perceptions and frustrations of their colleagues and employees in a way that helps them to maximize the potential productivity of their workers. These people are interested more in results than in protecting or preserving their theories about human behavior. In order to begin to grasp the implications of what is being pointed out through this book, psychology as a field must shift its priorities in the same direction.

CHAPTER 5

Understanding Thought: What Mental Health and Sanity Are in Relation to Our Conditioned Realities

It takes some degree of courage to stop and look at the way we are thinking now in a more relative way. That is, we must consider and recognize the possibility that our theories, beliefs and ideas comprise an illusionary thought system. But we must be willing to do this stepping back and looking at our views of reality in this way in order to begin to realize the role and the power of our own thoughts. This is the route — the only route — to sanity.

A WORLD OF THOUGHT

If we go one step deeper than the field of psychology has up to now and look at what is really happening, we realize something that has profound and far-reaching implications for our understanding of all human behavior. We see that our experiences as human beings are products of our own thought systems. The way we see life, perceive and give meaning and significance to events, how we react, solve our problems and feel about other people are all products of our own thought systems.

The only significant change in our experiences comes when we see this fact at a deeper level of common sense, and begin to drop our own beliefs and conditioned responses. In Sections 4 through 6 of this book, we will describe in more detail how this process works. What we are starting to realize, in terms of the notion of psychological theories, is that all theories and concepts are themselves illusionary thought systems. Every theory of personality comes from the imagination of the founder of that theory!

Freud is a prime example of the type of theorizing that has been characteristic of the field since his time. In order to explain people's behaviors, he invented something called the *"id,"* the *"ego,"* and the *"superego."* Anytime somebody did something wrong, he claimed that the *"id"* made him do it and the *"superego"* was too weak to stop it. Freud felt these entities or units such as the *"id"* were the mind, and thus controlled and determined the behaviors of the person. All he was really doing was inventing a new way to blame people's behaviors on some kind of internal battle of evil and good which was beyond the person's control. He might as well have been saying that "the devil made me do it," and the conscience was too weak to stop it.

THE SUGGESTIBILITY OF THOSE IN NEED

Freud missed the fact that no matter what name or explanation he gave to his thoughts, it was all his thinking, his suggestion. More recently, it has been suggested to those seeking mental health to think in terms of people all having three other entities of some sort inside them — a parent, an adult and a child — who are fighting for control. Others blame all of their problems on the stars, their *kharma* from past lives, their early life decisions, their parents, their cultural factors, their genetic make-up, their diets and on and on.

Each time we test people or categorize them or in other ways tell them about their habitual conditioned patterns, where they came from and how they work, we are driving more nails into the coffin of their own negative expectations. We make them even more prisoners of those realities than they were before. Most of what is now called therapy is in essence countertherapeutic, unless in some way it leads the patients to realizations of their own that they do not have to live at the mercy of these conditioned patterns or with the accumulated thought systems that they possess.

What the field of psychology has not yet realized is that every time we label people, especially those experiencing difficulties in life; or tell them that they have certain problems because of certain experiences or reasons from their pasts, we are automatically and absolutely adding fuel to their fires. This is true because of the way the human thought system works in terms of its suggestibility or implanting, coding and programming characteristics. The human mind has the capacity to take any stimulus response causal connection and turn it into the reality that that mind sees. This is precisely why people have emotional problems in the first place, because they think and subsequently feel that they are the kinds of persons who would have those kinds of problems.

THE CONDITIONAL NATURE OF OUR EXPERIENCES

The actual fact of the matter is that our brains are like computers, they can be programmed with anything, and will then respond based on that program. One need only experience the innumerable and varied cultures and customs on earth today or read any history book to realize this. Pavlov found that he could program a dog to connect the sound of a bell with food to the point where the animal would salivate at the sound of the bell with no food around! In essence, he had accidentally discovered how the condition of illusion could be programmed into the experience of any one of us. In its own conditioned haste to achieve acceptance and recognition as a science, however, the field of psychology has missed the profound significance of this seemingly simple discovery about learning. Instead, it has directed its efforts to explaining, in rare detail, every aspect of conditioned human behavior in terms of some theory, and toward developing a behavioral technology with which to alter people's experiences. Behavior modification approaches today still boil down to the same basic formula of connecting patterns of thought and behavior to one another in the form of stimuli and reinforcement schedules.

Unfortunately, however, because the field of psychology from the very start became so conditioned and accustomed to theorizing, it quickly lost sight of what it was theorizing about in the first place, not to mention what it was using to theorize. Thus, rather than pointing to the relative and the illusory quality of all conditioned behavior — and thus freeing people from even thinking their beliefs and reactions are fixed and absolute — the field of psychology itself literally got caught in the illusion. This is why the field of psychology itself believes in theories of its own making without knowing why. To this day people are reprogrammed from one set of conditioned responses to another — one illusion to the next — all on the basis of a set of theoretical associations acquired nearly one century ago.

What is needed today in the fields of mental health and psychology is to go a step deeper and to give people a clearer picture of the relationship of thought to behavior. Thus they can free themselves from all of their own conditioned reactions with no need to go back into the past to see where these patterns started; no need to re-experience them, act them out or do anything with them.

THE ILLUSIONS OF OUR CONDITIONED FEELINGS

When one of the authors of this book led encounter groups, he encouraged people to release their negative feelings. This was supposed to help angry people to get out their anger. The psychologist could himself get worked into a rage at his father and how he did it to him. All the analyst had to do was to create or to think up an interpretation he had learned of why he was unhappy. That interpretation created a feeling of anger, pain, loneliness, fear, guilt or resentment. Once the analyst began to realize how this worked, he saw the total craziness in encounter groups and in techniques in general. All any technique can do is to create a thought or a belief in the brain that some reaction or feeling is connected to that stimulus (that technique or method). Thus the subjects are no better off than Pavlov's dog.

This fact is the reason people feel temporarily high or good after a weekend encounter group or a therapy session and soon after fall back into old behavior patterns, requiring them to go back for another hit or dose of this medication. Participants think they have just gone through what they consider significant experiences of emotional catharsis or analysis, and literally give themselves permission via those particular thoughts to feel better. However, without an understanding of what is happening, they eventually get caught back up in habitual ways of doing things that bring back their normal feeling states, which leads to the same problems as before. Most doctors, by the way, know the power of suggestion and recommend or prescribe placebos a lot more often than they acknowledge to their patients or to each other. Yet, they see results in their own patients: if the patients think they will get better, they start to get better.

CHAPTER 6

Individual Thought Systems: A World of Separate Realities

In the next three chapters we will spell out, as clearly as we possibly can, the dynamics of how our individual thought systems operate. We will illustrate in ordinary terms how our own thought systems influence our emotions and behaviors, and how these conditioned processes are kept in place psychologically. While we will be utilizing terminology and definitions and talking about connections between thought and experience, we would ask the reader to not read for intellectual understanding. Any way we use to talk about what we are learning can be heard as a concept. If this result occurs, the person has then missed that point as a realization or an experience. If, on the other hand, the reader reads for understanding or insight, then he or she will begin to identify with what is shared in the individual experience. An insight comes with a realization of the nature "You know, that really makes sense," or "Gee, I can see that in myself and other people." Once the connection is made to the person's own experience, then he or she has that wisdom; it is theirs to use every day.

It is this experience of insights that we are calling the common sense of sanity. When we as individuals have insights about the workings of our own thought systems, we immediately have more common sense. What this common sense is is the ability to see how each person's reality is a product of the individual unique illusionary thought system. As our common sense increases it becomes more evident why people get upset at different things, how people get trapped in their own emotional reactivity and paranoia or insecure thoughts. We will see in the following chapters of this text how deepening our own innate wisdom or common sense is the route to true, lasting mental health and emotional maturity. In fact, as we show in Chapters 5, 6, and 7, we are beginning to see that this is the only route to a true, lasting solidly mentally healthy, emotionally mature experience of life.

What we want the reader to begin to realize is that our minds are analogous to, and really nothing more than, power sources, like generators. These power sources have the capacity to take our thoughts and thought systems and project them outward into forms that we call our lives. Wisdom, then, is the actual knowledge of this fact, not in terms of the external mechanics or details, which cannot be figured out, but in terms of the actual experience of using this power source.

Since the whole process is one of thought prior to the formulation of the actual content of the situation; intellectual understanding, intellectual support or intellectual argument are of no value. Most people, when they read a fiction book, do not attempt to remember details or to link that person's theories or story to anything else; they read for enjoyment and satisfaction. If the reader reads this book for that kind of enjoyment and does pick up a good feeling, that good feeling is the route to any value that can be derived from this book. Keep the feeling and forget the content. If we forget the content and then read the book again, we always find that the content seems different the next time. This occurs because our levels of consciousness have changed and we are looking at things from different vantage points than before.

We do not need to go to therapy for years, to study some *ology* or any other structured method or technique to realize the power of your own thoughts. The results of this power are occurring all the time. All we have to do is wake up and look around, see the connection, and we are on our way. We know many students who have gone way beyond their teachers in wisdom, merely from dropping the illusionary forms and methods of those teachers. These things may be a *Linus-blanket,* but they are a *"Linus-blanket"* that holds us down because we are still attached to a pre-conceived form, when what we are looking for does not have and is found only before the development of the external form.

It is for this reason that the words or terms we use to talk about this experience become irrelevant once the principle becomes obvious common sense to an individual. This deeper common sense will then free that person from negative behavior patterns; from personal conditioning; from reacting to others with anger, guilt, insecurity or judgment; in fact, from all insecurity and stress which ties people to details by thinking them crucial.

A WORLD OF SEPARATE REALITIES

The most natural place to begin is honestly realizing the implications of the fact that every person lives in a separate reality from everyone else. This separate reality we have called our frame of reference. These frames of reference are made up of all the conditioning from the past, culture, family experience, education, upbringing, peer influence, social environment and all other possible sources of programming including media, friends and important teachers and mentors.

Within the context of our present discussion, our aim is not necessarily to convince or to get anyone to recognize that separate realities exist. For in fact, most of us would say, "Of course people see things differently." Rather, what we hope to help the reader uncover is the depth and the all-encompassing implications of this fact for our study of human behavior. If we actually begin to understand the psychological principles of separate realities, we will understand everything we are doing ourselves in all areas of our lives. We will realize the source of all of our attitudes, habitual reactions and accepted ways of looking at things, and how these are related to our mental health. We will begin to recognize the nature of our thought systems as separate, unique and subjective frames of reference.

The details of where this thought system or subjective frame of reference comes from is irrelevant. The result is our reality, the world we live in; a unique combination of beliefs, interpretations, biases, attitudes and theories. These thoughts create perceptual filters through which we analyze, interpret, judge and react to life. The sum total of this bundle of thoughts comprises each individual's thought system. In most people this thought system is internally consistent and externally self-validating. If I have the belief, for example, that people do not like me this interpretation results in my feeling bad about myself, which in turn affects the way I behave. I may then act withdrawn, not take care of my appearance and appear somewhat unapproachable to others. Their reactions to my behavior will in turn reinforce the belief system that I am unlikable.

Every pattern of emotional disturbance follows a similar process, which is schematically illustrated in the diagram below:

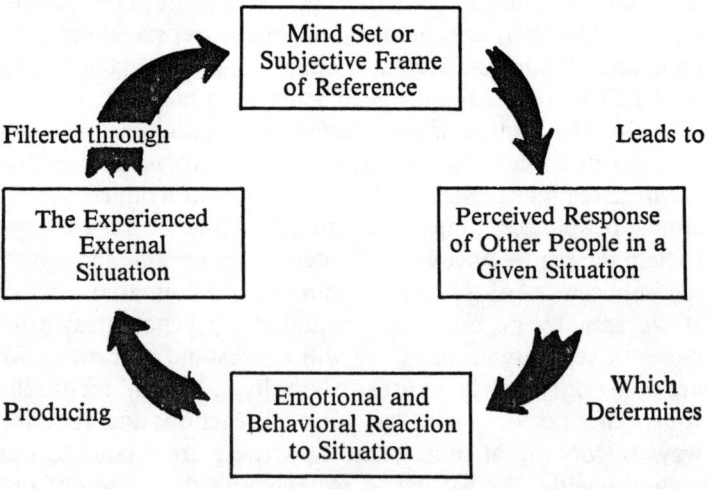

As we can see from the cyclical and self-determining nature of this system, while we think that we are responding to situations, events and causes outside of ourselves, the entire process is in reality determined by our own thought systems! A person who thinks other people are untrustworthy, for example, will never meet a person he can trust. The belief will create that interpretation of others which creates feelings and reactions to others. He will in turn be seen by others as suspicious and defensive, a posture that does not lend itself to other people being open with him.

The same thing is true about people's prejudices against others of a different race, culture or nationality. Their prejudices will lead them to find evidence to support their beliefs, and will also create reactions from the people they are biased about which again reinforces their beliefs.

All media studies have clearly shown that people listen to political or social statements with which they already agree; and don't listen to, or even hear, those that conflict with their belief systems. Most of us, most of the time, are in a condition where we hear and see what we already think we know, and do not hear; or do react negatively to things with which we do not already agree; or have opened up to accepting ideas because they do not conflict with more dearly held beliefs. Most of our deeply held beliefs are not even recognized as such, but are seen as the way that things really are.

In Chapter 7 we will discuss how it is the workings of our own thought systems which create this condition in our reality. We will further show how this is related to our levels of consciousness or common sense and not to our lack of information as it is presently thought.

SEPARATE REALITIES AND INTERPERSONAL COMMUNICATION

The only rationale for interpersonal skills training is that people do not hear what others are really saying, but do listen and react from the interpretations and meanings of their own thought systems. This inability to realize where the other person *is coming from* (that is, what they see and how they are interpreting the situation differently) really is the only source of conflict between couples, friends and people in general. Yet, we find that conflict and misunderstanding in relationships is more pervasive than cooperation and understanding. In fact, it is very seldom that we really know what is going on in somebody else's thought system as opposed to interpreting that person's response or actions within the context of our own thought systems which tell us that what we see is the only reality.

This tendency to misinterpret and not realize the difference between our own and the other person's frames of reference is so pervasive, it is seen as natural or normal. In fact, it is the most unnatural thing in the world! Every person naturally has the ability or the wisdom to see and to understand where others are coming from. Yet this clarity and objectivity is covered up and distorted by the filters of our own illusionary thought systems.

THE NATURE OF A REALITY

In order to more easily grasp the principles we are pointing to, it would be helpful to the reader to begin to have a simpler understanding of what we mean when we talk about a *reality* of *realities*. A reality is an apparency, how something actually appears to us, or how we see things. The principal reason why someone or something appears to us in a certain way and not another way cannot be found among the details of how we see it.

For example, when we go to the movie theatre, we go not only expecting to see a film, but also a story about someone else's life and reality. Once in the theatre we sit back and look at a screen where we begin to see people speaking, moving, interacting and living. As the story develops, we often become so identified with the plot in our own thoughts that we may begin to feel and exhibit different emotions that fit with the story. When the movie is over, the lights go on, and we are back in the reality which includes the theatre, who we are with and the like.

If we go one step deeper with this example, we could say that the total movie is only real by appearance. What we have experienced exists because a movie projector projected a rapid series of still pictures on the screen. Since our eyes and our brains could not keep up with how quickly each picture was flashed on and off the screen, it appeared to us to be one continuous set of scenes which changed with respect to the movement of the characters and scenery over time.

Whatever we as people see, whether in a movie or a day in our jobs, is also only real because it appears so, by virtue of our perspectives at that moment in time and the degree to which we understand the principles of how we as human beings create our own realities. If, for some reason, our perspectives happen to change to higher levels, we would immediately begin to see the principles underlying the perceptions of what we just experienced or saw. In our example of the movie theatre, we may be totally absorbed in the reality being depicted in a movie; yet if, for some reason, the film becomes jammed in the projector, we would for a few seconds before the film melts see a still life scene being projected onto the screen. What the audience has the opportunity to see is that, regardless of the details of the movie being shown, a deeper level of reality has been uncovered about what was a moment ago seen as real.

This is similar to when we are caught up in a bad dream. While these so-called nightmares are being experienced, we are in these realities. The happenings are real at those times and we experience the thoughts that go along with the fear, anxiety or despair. When we finally wake up, we are relieved because we realize a deeper principle about the reality we have just left. We instantly realize that the happenings were real because the mind was making them so in a way we call dreaming. Once awakened, we also can easily see that the principal reason we could not help ourselves or escape from what was scaring us in the nightmare was that it was the thought system creating the whole experience. We were both Jekyll and Hyde at the same time!

In the very same way, when we can begin to look toward the more simple side of life rather than the complexity of details about how real and fixed our perceptions are, we are well on our way to realizing deeper principles about our life experiences. The only reason people do not see the deeper and more simple principles of life is simply that they get caught up at a level of thinking that what they see is absolutely and unchangingly real, and that is as deep as their lives go.

CHAPTER 7

Thought and Our Image of Self-Importance: How We Learn Insecurity

The key principles that we must begin to grasp in order to actually realize and observe how we create our own realities involve a practical understanding of the role of the ego and of insecurity. We do not want to present the notion of ego as a concept or an actual entity, but merely as a word used here to mean the individual's sense of self-importance; a self-image along with standards of behavior and performance to which we attach our own self-esteem or sense of well-being.

Insecurity is merely any form of the thought that "I will not be all right, happy or accepted unless I do something the right way, the way that is correct." There may be insecurity whether we are concerned about our lifestyles, how we dress, how we raise our children, our professions and how we do our jobs, how we treat our spouses, and on and on through every aspect of our behaviors. Both the thought of insecurity and the ego or image of self-importance are themselves illusionary; like everything else they are merely products of our own minds.

Understanding the notion of insecurity is the key that helps us understand the dynamics of how our thought systems are activated and what keeps them in place. To truly understand the dynamics of how insecurity works we must look at it before it manifests itself into any particular form of neurosis, phobia, fear, anxiety, or self-consciousness. Understanding how insecurity works at a practical level is perhaps the most important factor on the route to mental health. This may sound simplistic, but it is true. Insecurity works the same way in every human being and is the only thing keeping a person from a deeper and deeper experience of emotional well-being, maturity and positive state of mental health. The more insecure any person becomes, the more tenaciously he or she will defend the individual version of reality and attempt to impose it upon the world. However, insecurity itself is merely an illusionary made-up thought created from our own minds.

For example, as a teenager, when one of the authors first became interested in the opposite sex, he immediately became insecure around girls to which he was attracted. He could be natural and even witty and entertaining both around his friends and around girls to whom he was not attracted. However, as soon as he met someone he liked, he became insecure, afraid of not saying or doing the right thing. As soon as this insecurity entered his mind, he immediately lost his poise and made a fool out of himself. He once saw a girl he had liked for months sitting alone out by the pool at a party he was attending. He rehearsed his lines for ten minutes, composed himself, caught her attention, and fiercely trying to remember his opening line started over to engage her. He was so distracted that he walked face first into the sliding glass door between him and the pool area! That encounter immediately ended their budding relationship.

The source of every chronic problem in life is insecurity. Insecurity causes us to lose our natural good feelings, clarity and self-esteem. The insecurity itself causes us to not see the situation with self-confidence and good judgment. This thought of insecurity creates a feeling which affects our ability to act wisely and decisively. The same fact is true in sports, in business and in politics.

Books such as *The Inner Game of Tennis* were greeted by the sports world with some controversy. However, what the author of this book was really pointing to is absolutely true. If we have no insecurity, no conscious thoughts about how well we are doing, how well we should be doing, how we should hit the ball and so-on, with practice our body will naturally learn to respond and hit the ball the best way for us. As soon as we become insecure or self-conscious, we lose our natural knowing and learning ability; we lose our intuitive feel for how to do something. One of the authors played high school basketball, but not well enough to play in college. At one point, when he was in graduate school he was asked to play a pick-up game with some friends, all of whom had played college basketball. He immediately became self-conscious about his ability to do well. His ego (image of self-importance) came in, and he thought about what he was doing. He was *trying* to look good. Exactly the opposite result occurred. His passes went out of bounds, he lost the ball dribbling and worst of all, his shots went nowhere near the rim. He finally became so disgusted he gave up, stopped pressing and just decided to enjoy the exercise and his teammates. All of a sudden, when he was not thinking about his game, his passes were accurate, he was dribbling well, and his next four shots went through the basket. However, as soon as he noticed how well he was doing and wanted to be able to keep it up to impress his friends, he lost it again, and started pressing, making bad shots and missing passes.

HOW WE LEARN INSECURITY

We have found this same principle to apply not only in all forms of athletics, but also in all arenas of life. In fact, our thought systems are products of our insecurities. We are taught to be insecure and then taught that in order to survive and feel successful (that is, to have self-esteem), we must believe in this certain way, achieve these certain standards, react to others in certain ways, respond this way in this kind of situation. Our images of self-importance, the other side of the same coin as our insecurity, become attached to these results, beliefs, behaviors and judgments. We start to go through life proving ourselves. We go to college to prove ourselves; if we don't, we feel low self-esteem. We strive to keep ahead of our neighbors and co-workers to prove ourselves, to make more money, to have more sex-appeal, to have well-behaved children, to prove we are our own bosses, and on and on. The driving force behind all of this behavior is insecurity. Insecurity runs people literally into the ground since there is no end to proving. Insecurity — again only an illusionary, made up thought — causes all forms of mental illness.

DROPPING INSECURITY: THE ROUTE TO MENTAL HEALTH

To most psychologists and to people in the mental health field this is a very strong statement. In making this assertion to the field of mental health, we have been called simplistic and naive. However, this is merely because the listener is not hearing what we are saying to him at a deep enough level of understanding. What we are really saying is that insecurity comes first as a thought of being incorrect or imperfect, and is then attached to a specific form. As the reader relates to the examples and principles presented in this text and compares these to the present state of the art of psychological understanding, he or she will begin to realize more and more clearly how it is insecurity, created by each at the moment, that triggers incidents, fears, or memories from the past. These memories have no more power than the power that we ourselves give them in the present. Whatever power we give these fears and memories in the present is determined solely by our levels of insecurity at the time.

The irony of all this is that as soon as we really learn how insecurity works and that insecurity is merely a thought, an illusion of our own minds, then we start to lose our insecurities and our need to prove ourselves. We start to live with a high natural sense of self-esteem, and a clarity and wisdom that makes everything easier. We start to more effortlessly accomplish everything we wanted so badly before. Yet these accomplishments do not have the same seriousness, importance or significance as they did before. The stress, anxiety and effort disappear. We enjoy more the doing of something in itself and migrate toward doing those things that we truly enjoy in life. We then begin to find intrinsic satisfaction in our accomplishments not caring so much what others think, how they would react or compare themselves to us.

THE RESULTS OF OUR IMAGE OF SELF-IMPORTANCE

The freedom obtained from dropping insecurity is tremendous. Since there is no end to the ego proving itself, carrying around an image of self-importance is like going through life with a load of bricks on one's back; constantly worrying about whether one is a good enough parent, worker, lover, friend and on and on. Our lives are then ridden with stress, negativity and doubt. Yet once we drop insecurity, we have the natural wisdom and compassion to become good friends, spouses, parents or whatever we want.

A woman we know recently returned to graduate school at the age of fifty-six, and began working at a family counseling center. She felt naive and insecure around all the other professionals who had years of experience. Every day she worried about how she dressed, what other people (therapists) thought about her ideas, her hobbies, her opinions and what she did with her clients. There were two warring factions in the center between two very different approaches to therapy. One group sided with the director, the other was aligned against the director and wanted her fired. Our friend was again insecure about who was right, whose side she should be on and what other therapists thought about her position.

She came home from work every day totally exhausted. She usually fell asleep over dinner because she was so worn out by the stress. Then she would wake up in the middle of the night to worry about the next day. She was becoming an emotional wreck. Then one afternoon she suddenly realized that she could just be ordinary, be herself, dress the way she liked, talk about what she liked to do, and do the best she could for her clients. She decided she was perfectly fine the way she was. She saw the load of bricks she was carrying for what it really was. She stopped worrying about which side was right and totally dropped out of the cliques and the in-fighting. Once she dropped her insecurity, she started to realize it was only egos fighting over the various theories and techniques, and realized what was really happening. She felt a tremendous relief from stress.

Once she dropped her insecurity, started to mind her own business and become ordinary, she found that she was more effective with her clients since she could see their frames of reference more clearly. She began to be perceived by the other staff as different: she had self-confidence and presence that they did not see in other people. The other therapists began to come to her with their problems. When the director finally quit because her ulcer kept getting worse and worse, the staff met with the Board of Directors and decided to ask this woman to be the director. This family counseling center is now a much nicer place to work, with little conflict and good feelings of mutual support among the staff.

In the example above, we can see how this woman's insecurity affected both her relationships with people at work. We can also see how the other professional staff allowed their insecurities and images of self-importance to affect their working relationships. Over the past several years, we have observed these same phenomena occur in most professional groups, even in psychology departments and mental health agencies. We professionals are as insecure as our clients because we do not really understand the relationship of our levels of insecurity to our own mental health, stress levels and anxieties which we pass along to our clients, irrespective of our own theories or techniques. Our levels of insecurity are what determine our own mental health and the quality of our relationships to other people. All we need to do is drop insecurity or self-consciousness and to recognize this fact, to change our realities to more mentally healthy, stress free and enjoyable experiences.

Over and over again we have seen how the insecurities of people in an organization filter and distort their approaches to problems, their relationships with others, their abilities to listen and to hear good ideas from others, and their levels of cooperation and conflict in any organization. All of these elements have a tremendous impact on overall productivity and organizational performance. Yet in most organizations, this is the last place that people want to look for solutions. Often, because of insecurity itself, we do not want to take responsibility for the ways we are perceiving things and the impact these have on the overall picture. Therefore, it is more comfortable in most organizations for their administrators to look at technical factors or practice interpersonal, social, communication or other so-called psychological skills rather than to take responsibility for their own versions of organizational reality.

In every organization, conflicts between management and workers, or conflicts between departments, between managers and within work groups all can be traced back to insecurity. If managers in a business operate with insecurity, they will focus on protecting themselves; they will talk down to employees; they will be reluctant to acknowledge mistakes; they will defend their position in meetings rather than acknowledging that someone else might have a better solution to that problem; and they will put a lot of effort, time and energy into the politics of the organization at the expense of doing their jobs.

Managers who operate without insecurity treat their employees with respect and consideration, seek their ideas and input, naturally look for ways to recognize and to reinforce positive results and good performance. They have employees who are loyal, who enjoy working for them, and who find ways to make their jobs more productive. These managers are more effective and better problem solvers and make clear, sound decisions because their visions are not clouded by their own self-interests or by insecurity. They are grateful for the opportunity to use the skills and resources of other people, and appreciate the abilities of their peers. When they are free from insecurity, they can see the motivations and the frames of reference of the people around them. They know how to get the most out of people because they understand and have compassion for their insecurities.

We have consulted with major corporations, state agencies, local government and other human service organizations including hospitals and mental health centers. We have consistently found that a deeper understanding of how insecurity is being manifested in that setting leads to levels of productivity, cooperation, and enjoyment of work that those people had previously not imagined would be possible in their professional lives.

The route to mental health, self-esteem and effectiveness is that simple. However, it is not that easy because we have all grown up convinced that it must be more complicated, and thus, our own egos will fight this simplicity. Given this condition of ego, we all want to think we are important, different and have special problems. People who blame their problems on the past and who complain how hard things are because of their difficulties from the past are talking from their images of self-importance. They want to be seen as special or different and to obtain sympathy for their positions. They do not see the harm they are doing to themselves through their images of self-importance.

We all have egos and are all insecure to some extent. The result is that the ego itself hides the fact of its own existence, because it needs to prove itself. If we saw the ego's needs for what they really are — illusionary images of self-importance — the game would be up, and the illusionary nature of the ego would be obvious to us. Since we do not always see the illusionary nature of our worlds of reactions, judgments and interpretations, the ability to notice our states of mind in terms of the principles of levels of consciousness is the key to gaining more wisdom and sanity, beyond the ego and insecurity.

CHAPTER 8

Levels of Consciousness: The Knowledge of What Our Thought Systems Are

Since it is the case that our own thought systems fool us into thinking that the world really is the way we see it through our perceptual filters, we must look for another way to start to recognize the difference between when we are caught up in illusionary realities and when we are seeing things with more perspective, wisdom, good judgment, objectivity and clarity. The first clue in the field of psychology that helped us with this recognition was the notion of altered states of consciousness. What we are talking about are states of consciousness or levels of consciousness, if you will, that are not triggered by external agents or experiences, but merely by the levels of insecurity at the time. The levels of insecurity determine the intensity with which the concerns, worries, anxieties, and beliefs programmed into our thought systems are triggered into conscious concerns and the extent to which they are perceived as real. If we had no insecurity, we would have no self-consciousness and our own thought systems would be less important and, therefore, not activated as much as our common sense or inherent wisdom.

In order to gain more perspective on the workings of our own thought systems in our day-to-day lives, we must begin to understand how insecurity is connected to what we will be calling in this book *levels of consciousness*. Often when people hear that phrase, they associate its meaning with some esoteric study of Eastern mysticism or with the notion of altered states of consciousness induced through some external psychotropic medication or with other unusual or out of the ordinary experience. In this book, we are hoping that people will begin to understand levels of consciousness in relationship to their daily moods, ups and downs, and fears. It is only through this common sense understanding of the true meaning of levels of consciousness that we can begin to unlock our own natural states of high self-esteem, wisdom and understanding of how to live our lives the way we want and be happy.

THE INNOCENCE OF OUR OWN THOUGHT SYSTEMS

When we talk about the ego as an image of self-importance, we know that it is extremely important to clearly state that there is no blame, judgment or wrong-doing implied at all by these statements. Every human being on earth is the same in this respect. We all to different degrees operate from insecurity, at times, and we all have this illusionary ego or image of self-importance. When a person is caught up in a thought system and is seeing life through the perceptual filters of that thought system, it seems that this is the way it really is. It is, in fact, such thoughts and concepts as blame, judgment and wrong-doing that actually keep the person from seeing and realizing his or her own responsibility and innocence and that of others.

LEVELS OF CONSCIOUSNESS: THE LADDER OF LIFE

We all have moods. We all go up and down. We know that when we are in a low mood everything seems harder, less enjoyable, kind of gray and hopeless. We wonder why we even married the old battle-ax, why our children are turning into juvenile delinquents, why we cannot get a more interesting job. Every aspect of our lives is colored by our low mood. If something nice happens and we feel good, all of a sudden everything changes and looks better. The world has not changed, but only our mood, our internal state of mind.

We are all so-called schizophrenic in this respect; we move in and out of separate realities many times even in one day.

People who are labeled schizophrenic are only more extreme versions of ourselves. The trick is to begin to see how this process actually works and how these changes are connected to the ego and to insecurity. If something triggers individual insecurity, there is a drop to a lower mood or frame of mind, and life is seen through the filters of the insecurity of the thought system.

To date the field of psychology has not realized that levels of consciousness exist, much less how they actually work. Each level of consciousness, as it goes higher, is a level of understanding or knowing what mind and thought are, and how our thought systems are related to the realities we see as life. These levels of conscious state account for the truly separate realities in which each and every one of us lives. The particulars or details of what is seen in the reality we call life is a function of a person's thought system. How this reality is seen and understood is a function of the level of consciousness. In other words, the knowledge and the understanding that any given reality is a reality of our thoughts coming from our thought systems is dependent on and subject to the levels of consciousness at which we are living.

Lower levels of consciousness are states of mind characterized by a lack of understanding (ignorance) of our own lives or realities. At these levels, we urgently rely upon our thought systems to figure out the causes of the reality we are creating and seeing as life, using the same units of the reality we see. Said differently, if some aspect of life is thought of, felt and seen as negative, we mobilize the very same thought system which created the situation to explain the negativity within the very same framework. Experientially, the negative feelings are accordingly perceived as coming from an external negative reality and not from our thoughts. Consequently, the ultimate illusion of non-responsibility is created by thinking that the causes (and thus, the justification) of our feelings (hate, resentment, sorrow) lie in some aspect of an external world, a world which is external to us and is independent of our thoughts about it. The aspect will be seen as anything but what it is — Archie Bunker come to life.

In contrast, higher levels of consciousness are states of mind in which our realities, what we call our lives, our thought systems in action, are more clearly seen for what they are: programmed bundles of accumulated and stored information from the past brought to life, so to speak, via thought. Thus, we as individuals become free from the particulars of our pasts regardless of how negative, ignorant, or misdirected we may have been. With these bundles of information out of the way and no longer utilized as the thought bases for life, the negative aspects of life begin to evaporate and, literally, disappear. In the process, we truly begin to experience what is called responsibility. It is in these higher states of consciousness where success is encountered, creativity expressed, and the power of the mind realized. This is true growth, insight, wisdom or common sense awakening in a human being. The awakening of this wisdom is the true source of mental health. In fact, the only way that any person's reality actually ever changes for the better is through allowing this wisdom or common sense to emerge.

Experientially, as our wisdom or common sense is realized, our lives begin to appear more effortless and simple because the stored bundles of information, most of them based on relative misperceptions, are removed from thought. The stored information becomes secondary and the appearance of a new reality becomes primary. This is the tranquility of humility which calms and clears a thought system, allowing a human being to be open to a higher understanding and positive reality that was previously unknown.

THOUGHT SYSTEMS, INSECURITY AND LEVELS OF CONSCIOUSNESS

When we actually begin to experience how our thinking and feelings of insecurity relate to our levels of consciousness, we at once begin to live our lives with more understanding and, therefore, with more mental and emotional stability. We devote less and less time and effort to using our stored memories to try and figure out why we sometimes alternate between thinking of ourselves or others as attractive and ugly, strong and weak, confident and insecure, loving and hateful, innocent and guilty, interesting and boring, intelligent and stupid, and so forth.

We begin to more clearly relate our thoughts, perceptions and feelings to our levels of consciousness, rather than to what we see as external causes. As this growth progresses, we can look at our worlds with less of a tendency to judge and to fix matters to fit our biases. Interestingly enough, we become better helpers because we see more objectively that the realization of the knowledge of these higher states of consciousness or their existence does not exist within the boundaries of anyone's frame of reference composed of intellectual information. The clearer we can see for ourselves that everyone's bundle of information is in and of itself neutral, the more our help also becomes neutral or objective and thus becomes more helpful and its use as a benefit or barrier is dependent on their levels of consciousness.

The lower our levels of consciousness, the greater will be the tendency to use our stored information in a rigid and irresponsible manner. Accordingly, we will ignore that we are the causes of the negative results we will experience. This is because the information is not experienced as information but as reality. In contrast, at higher levels this very same bundle, if used at all, will be put to use in a positive and creative way which brings greater ease and comfort to life. It is the level of consciousness and not the information which determines whether or not it will be evident to an individual that such an illusion of the thought system is, in fact, occurring. This is why no one at a given level of consciousness can possibly use the intellect to understand, to comprehend, or to experience a higher level. Information in and of itself is of absolutely no use in helping to raise one's level of consciousness. It is, in fact, an innocent reliance on the frame of reference created from the information stored in the thought system which is used as the barrier to experiencing higher states of consciousness!

The reason we get caught in this self-limiting predicament is that most of us have not realized we really cannot think of something truly new within the boundaries of our given information storage. Until experienced, the new is simply non-existent, or will be seen as something already known. As with any truly new discovery, the realization of a new fact has without exception shed light on how little was previously known which *per se* was the resistance to the new (for example, Einstein).

A SPADE BY ANY OTHER NAME

For each individual, the thought system is different. Therefore each person's insecurity will emerge in a different form. For one person insecurity will appear as non-specific in all aspects of life. For another it may be the relationship to spouse or children which leads to arguments and child-beating. For others it may emerge as anger toward a boss or even toward society. Some people attempt to numb this feeling of insecurity through alcohol or drugs, others through aggressive behavior, others through withdrawal into depression.

In actuality the form in which insecurity comes out is irrelevant. We know personally hundreds of ex-alcoholics who have started to realize how insecurity works. As a result they have begun to drop their own thoughts of insecurity. Their drinking behaviors have begun to disappear on their own. We have had many phone calls from people saying that they had stopped drinking for over a month before they even noticed they had stopped. Alcoholics Anonymous and most professionals who specialize in addictive behaviors would never believe this result could possibly happen.

Since all destructive or self-destructive behavior, whatever its form, is the result of insecurity, there is no value in focusing on the behavior. Even if we manipulate or if we force an individual to alter that behavior, insecurity will emerge in another form, and in most instances the person reverts to the original form once away from the treatment program.

We have observed tremendous success with all kinds of emotional and mental illnesses on the part of therapists who have themselves realized the role and the power of insecurity and its relationship to individual thought systems and levels of consciousness. Again, they have gained this understanding not as an intellectual or theoretical conceptualization of the relationship of these factors, but rather as real insights into how their own thought systems have functioned to generate their experiences of life.

In the following section, we first want to lay out some definitions in order to give the reader a more concrete grasp of what we are talking about when we refer to *"frames of reference,"* the *"ego," "insecurity"* and *"wisdom."* Since these terms are now used quite differently or not at all by psychology today, we want to make sure the reader is able to relate to and to identify with what we are pointing to in their own experiences.

SECTION III

THOUGHT SYSTEMS AND
INSECURITY: A NEW LIGHT ON
MENTAL HEALTH VERSUS
MENTAL ILLNESS

CHAPTER 9

A New Framework for Psychology: A Context for a Deeper Understanding of Human Behavior

The principles we will lay out in this chapter are impersonal in themselves. They make no statement about any person, situation or actual condition now existing in the world today. They are principles, rather, that discuss the source in people's thoughts of all these phenomena.

The purpose of this chapter is to lay out the framework for a deeper understanding not only for mental health, or what commonly is included in psychology as a field, but also for the entire arena of human behavior. The principles laid out in this chapter should be viewed as *facts,* underlying principles that determine the pattern of human behavior in all contexts, whether we are referring to individual mental health, to interpersonal relationships, to culture, informal groups, businesses, or social change.

As these principles are grasped at deeper levels of understanding, we begin experiencing them in our own lives and observing their effect all the time in the news, in our work and in all of our dealings and our relationships to others. As this begins to occur, we start to learn more from everything that happens to us since we are constantly being provided with examples of these principles in action every day. This clarity in itself is liberating since it makes the world understandable.

We may not even know the details of the situation, but we can always see where the people are coming from (that is, their intentions, motivation, relative degree of ego or self-image involved in the situation, and their vested interest or position), and thus the direction we must take to maintain our positivism and well-being.

If this result does not occur, then what is happening is that the reader has understood these principles as concepts or as additional theories about human behavior, rather than as facts or insights about what is going on around us all the time. It is *beginning to notice* facts that brings a change in levels of consciousness because it is *per se* seeing the phenomenon we call human behavior from a deeper level of understanding.

We will start by looking at the principle of frames of reference to clarify the reasons why people live in separate realities and operate in a world of many separate realities without realizing this fact. We will then talk about ego and its relationship to frames of reference. The notion of wisdom or common sense will be introduced. This is a new dimension of which there is very little written or understood in the fields of psychology and human behavior in general. Wisdom is the answer, and the recognition of our own wisdom occurs when we start to realize what it is and how the awakening of this wisdom occurs. We have all had experiences of wisdom. When identified in the context of understanding separate realities, the role of the ego and the power of insecurity in shaping our realities, the experiences of wisdom introduce into our experiences levels of understanding based on facts rather than on beliefs. As a result, maturity, self-confidence and a high sense of self-esteem become more and more common, recognized and appreciated in our day-to-day lives.

A FRAME OF REFERENCE

A frame of reference is very simply an accumulated set of information used as a reference point to relate and to categorize what is seen as new information. The function of a frame of reference is to use what is presently known to direct the search for new information, to evaluate what is seen as new information, and to incorporate and/or integrate any explanation into the existing framework of knowledge.

The main fallacy associated with a referenced explanation lies in the fact that any such explanation must be understood by the existing frame of reference in order for it to be incorporated. Anything which is not understandable to a frame of reference is considered unexplainable, unamenable, and, thus by definition, unsuitable for incorporation. Simply, the old cannot see the new because the new is non-existent to the old. The known, as a set of information, cannot possibly capture the unknown within the boundaries of its understanding because it doesn't yet exist for the known. This does not imply that the truly new does not exist — it does. It merely doesn't exist for a set of information which does not, at a given point, include it.

For example, if a person functions within a frame of reference of mistrust and particularly sees the opposite sex as insensitive, manipulative and selfish, he or she will interpret all behavior in that frame of reference. The statement *"I love you"* would tend to be interpreted as *"What does (s)he want now."* Flowers would mean guilt or softening up for something one person wants to get from another or to get away with. Any behavior would be logically interpreted in a way consistent with that frame of reference. The thought that at least some people of the opposite sex are sincere, loving and honest does not exist in that frame of reference. Therefore, no one's behavior toward such a person would be interpreted that way. The thought or suggestion that people are to them as they think them to be would not even warrant consideration for it could not be understood within this frame of reference. The accompanying feelings of mistrust, loneliness, jealousy and so forth, as seen from this frame of mind, would function as both the reason for and the resistance to any change in our thinking.

SEPARATE REALITIES AND THOUGHT

All human beings accumulate and possess a frame of reference in life. This set of information is stored in the forms of what we call ideas, concepts, attitudes, beliefs, opinions, perceptions, experiences, reactions, and so on, about everything, including the relationships between the forms of information themselves. The information is experienced and retrieved via thought. The frame of reference itself, the specific information, and its experience through thought comprise a person's thought system. Even though there are similarities among some of the content of thought systems, for example, a specific belief, these similar units of information exist within dissimilar frames of reference (thought systems). Thus, these apparently similar beliefs are seen and held differently by different people and are not, in reality, the same: not all believers in anything believe the anything in the same way. Thus, each thought system is unique and separate from all others.

As a result, each and every human being literally sees and experiences his/her life unfolding in terms (for example, beliefs, issues, and so forth) of whatever they think is significantly real. Thus, if one individual thinks differently from another, he or she must see life differently. The only true identity is the ability to think about anything in any way. It is this unique aspect of every individual's thought system which is the basis for the separate realities in which people live. Even though as human beings we may share the same apparent names and labels for the world, we, nonetheless, experience the reality of our world. There are at least as many different realities as there are or have been people on earth.

The realization of the fact that we as human beings are free to think anything we wish cannot be found within the confines of the information comprising our individual frames of reference. In and of itself, a frame of reference has no power. It is a fixed, accumulated set of information which can be brought to life and seen as real only via thought. The experiences of our separate realities are real to us regardless of how non-existent they may be to others or how non-existent they are in fact. The fact that they are illusory realities emerging via thoughts from our very own thought systems is an insight which may or may not have been realized.

EGO

The aspect of our thought systems that keep our present frames of reference intact is what we are calling the *"ego."* Again, the name we give to it is unnecessary to understanding the actual principle of how this aspect of our thought systems function.

The barrier to the true understanding of life which brings the positive changes resulting in peace, happiness, and tranquility in our lives is ego. The ego is neither an entity nor a force which is independent of our thinking. Ego is an image of individualized self-importance — an illusory image emerging via thought from the individual frame of reference composed of stored information from the past. The ego condition is experienced as a feeling of insecurity due to the fact that it exists as thoughts of information contained in a frame of reference which is not only limited and circular, but is also unique. As a system of thinking, ego cannot see or seek beyond itself to the larger situation in which it exists. Ego as a reality is, therefore, incapable of explaining, proving, or changing its own existence. Ego loses itself in the content and the details of its own thoughts which it sees as *the* reality of life. As such, this image of self-importance exists only as an illusory creation of our ability to think. The thought (and feeling) of insecurity must be present for ego to exist.

In lower levels of consciousness, ego and insecurity are functionally related in the protection and for the defense of a thought system. Defending a thought system is important only when the maintenance of the particular set of beliefs is seen as essential or important; in other words, because of insecurity. Therefore, we have a process which is circular and self-validating in the sense that we are unknowingly taught to be insecure. We are taught to develop and to adhere ourselves to a particular set of beliefs by which we must live in order to protect ourselves from the feelings of insecurity. The ego or image of self-importance then comes in to maintain, defend, and reinforce our particular frames of reference (that is, our belief systems) and, therefore, our insecurities.

The situation of ego is not merely the information and the experiences stored in a thought system, which in and of itself is entirely neutral. The situation of ego exists as a lowering of the level of consciousness of an individual to a level where the true knowledge of what life is is forgotten and becomes nonexistent to the individual (ignorance). It is at this point that via thought the stored bundle of information takes on illusory importance to explain life — an explanation not to be found within the information storage of a frame of reference. The ego experience of its own importance to explain the happenings in life, positive or negative, in self or others, internal or external and thus creates the insecurity about maintaining its image.

MUCH ADO ABOUT NOTHING

The ego's inability to use a relatively microscopic set of circular information to figure out or to explain an experience becomes the insecure image which then seeks to constantly prove and/or improve something or other. In our dealings with others we clash, conflict, argue, defend, and fight unaware of the true, infinitely larger context in which all of this is happening.

With our egos in full bloom, our experiences cannot include the positive feelings that accompany the true experiences of trust, respect, or gratitude for anything beyond ourselves. For if we did, the very images of self-importance would be seen for what they are and the insecurities creating our egos and thus our egos themselves would vanish. Since, in the ego state we cannot think of anything beyond what we already know — ourselves — we are caught up in a cage of circular thought. As a result, we can never really listen and learn something truly new for if we did, the existence of realities beyond our own would be acknowledged and/or realized, and again our egos would be shown for what they are (our thoughts) and would vanish. When we are in a state of mind or condition where our common-sense natural self-esteem and wisdom about life is operational, ego is non-existent; or, more accurately, it has been neutralized or placed in a state of non-activity or non-interference with our daily affairs.

It is our own thought-created egos which must, at all costs, argue, defend and prove whatever they believe — whatever they think. In the situation of ego, our tendencies are to see and hear everything and anything as somehow already existent within our frames of reference and thus to judge our own worlds. We react with fear to anything we perceive as new (beyond what we know). The absence of conflict also threatens the existence of our egos. This is because with nothing to figure out, argue over, or deal with, insecure thoughts — the necessary ingredients for our egos — diminish to greater degrees. Thus, the deeper we go into the illusion of ego, the more we have to prove and/or improve, the greater the tendency to seek some form of conflict in which to prove ourselves. In other words, our insecurities are the negative feelings called ego created by our thoughts using the information (beliefs, ideas, and so forth) stored in our thought systems.

Since ego comes with a negative feeling, we can always recognize the ego state due to the negative feelings of anger, hostility, mistrust, suspicion, possessiveness, jealousy, and fear that are associated with ego states. In fact, any feeling of negativity must come from a state where ego and insecurity are activated and in charge of our perceptions and reactions to events.

Ego, via the feeling of insecurity and its misperceptions, is the cause of all negativity in life. It is our ego which we use to judge, analyze, and criticize ourselves via our thoughts of others. Since negative thoughts create negative feelings, the ego condition is a condition of ignorance of the fact that it is the thinker who experiences the results of negative thinking —

the hatred, envy, jealousy, anger, and other negative feelings. An individual caught up in ego does not use his own negative feelings as the clue to what he is doing to himself via thought. Rather, in this condition he uses these feelings to further justify and boost what he thinks he is already doing and seeing. Ego thus creates more of the same to keep its game going.

RELATIONSHIP OF LEVELS OF CONSCIOUSNESS TO EGO

The existence of levels of consciousness explains why, in higher levels of consciousness, we see the relativity of our stored information and experiences from the past; and, in lower levels of consciousness, we will fight, defend, argue, and create negative feelings over the same bundle of information which we think is absolutely factual. Put in another way, in higher levels of consciousness, we realize a clear, objective state of mind where information is used, via our thoughts, for our well-being. Past experiences, positive or negative, are recognized for what they are: memories of past experiences, which are no longer real, carried through time in a form called memory. In clear contrast, lower levels of consciousness are accompanied by feelings of insecurity where past experiences are of paramount importance. In these states of consciousness we do not see objectively, but live in a reality distorted by our own thoughts of the past. In this state of mind, we are imprisoned in the contents of our own thoughts which we think real and which, therefore, dictate our realities. This is our ego in full function. All problems which humanity has ever experienced stem from this negative perspective of life called ego, as manifested through lower levels of consciousness triggered by insecurity.

The theory that we need an ego to live or to succeed, to get ahead or to *know who we are* is false. Since our egos are actually nothing more than our images of self-importance, we only lose negative feelings when we eliminate or even soften our needs to prove and/or improve ourselves. From this perspective, the feeling and thinking state of the individual is totally different. We actually begin to live our lives outside of the ordinary ups and downs of life, the low moods, the misunderstandings, the conflicts and the *"working things out"* that we used to think were normal or natural.

When an individual is living in a higher state of consciousness, free from the distortions of individual ego, he or she will not react or become upset by others' beliefs, opinions, and reactions because he or she will see with extraordinary clarity how that person is caught up in an individual thought system at a lower level of consciousness and, therefore, is innocently protecting the reality seen as important for self-esteem.

It is only higher states of consciousness that enable us to see others with this understanding and compassion. It is also in these states that we are relatively free of needs and, therefore, do not place any demands on other people. In these states we have a high natural sense of self-esteem, enjoyment of life and involvement in every experience in such a way that the outcome of that experience or situation is not important to us in terms of our own senses of well-being. We are then able to see what is really happening in that situation with more clarity and maturity, and grant a deeper wisdom about what is appropriate than do others who may be caught up in lower levels of consciousness, that is, being less able to see beyond their own versions of reality.

This effortless state becomes so normal and ordinary in our experiences we begin to realize that this condition is the natural state of humanity. Since this state is so natural, we do not often recognize it even when it happens. It takes no effort, trying or act of will to get there; merely the stopping of trying to make it happen. We have all experienced these states to some degree at one time or another in our lives. We all have times when we are relaxed and not thinking about our problems, yet because we are not primarily aware of this being our state of consciousness, we may be amazed by or fascinated with how much enjoyment we seem to be getting out of such seemingly ordinary activities like sitting on our lawns watching our dogs play, or being with our children, or just enjoying whatever surroundings we happen to be in at the time.

When we are in these states of consciousness, we normally have no idea of and, in fact, we do not even think about how we got there. We only actually notice these states after they happened. We take ourselves out of these states as soon as we begin to think about our problems, worry about our businesses or our family affairs, or some other aspect of our lives that we do not feel is the way we want them to be. All of us are capable of experiencing these states of tranquility and intense enjoyment of our moment-to-moment experiences with an absence of worry or thought to much deeper levels than most of us have ever thought possible. It is when we are in these states of consciousness that insights come in the forms of what we would call wisdom or new perspectives in our daily affairs, whether these are business matters or social happenings.

UNDERSTANDING RESISTANCE TO CHANGE

The functional nature of these states is what we are calling wisdom or common sense. It is in these states that true positive change can take place to free people from their own negative frames of mind. Psychology today does not discuss or include this dimension in its theories or concepts. Within the present framework of the profession, people are pretty much seen as their personalities. Of course, this belief reinforces in people that they have styles, habits, likes and dislikes that will not change; the belief that the best they can do is learn to live with them and understand their effect on their lives.

As psychologists and as therapists, we tell people where we think they got their present problems. We label them with different forms of diagnostic labels and then we treat them as if they were irrevocably linked to these diseases of personality and malfunctioning. Through doing this we deny that people have the capacities to move beyond these learned or acquired ways of coping. We teach coping skills as if the individual were crippled for life and needed these crutches and coping aids to get by at a minimal level of functioning. Psychology, as people know it today, unaware of the facts that we are pointing toward in this book, reinforces the notion that people are emotional cripples. As a field, we profess to people our own beliefs about how hard it is to change and how many forces are affecting our behaviors. At the same time we wonder how we can help people change and accept responsibility for their behaviors and feelings. This belief is the biggest limitation the field of psychology has perpetrated on people. Patients can not see that they can easily change because they do not believe it to be possible. Therefore, they stop short of even recognizing the possibility — a sure sign that nothing new will happen.

In much the same manner as our personal frames of reference, larger frames of reference (for example, professions, societies and cultures) function identically with regard to problem-solving, change, discovery and innovation. Only because the information is stored in the form of theories, customs, traditions, protocols and the like is this not always noticed. Nonetheless, once a group, however large or small, begins to adhere itself to a particular frame of reference, changes are not easily received, regardless of how badly needed or beneficial they may be. This happens because we, as human beings, begin to function within specific patterns of thinking and rapidly become accustomed to functioning within the boundaries of the realities our thinking creates.

Therefore, each time something truly new is discovered and introduced into realities we are accustomed to, it is initially not understandable to the prevailing patterns of thinking. Attempts to explain such new discoveries follow and are usually characterized by increasing diversity and contradiction. This, in turn, draws attention to the obvious limitations of the existing frames of reference of our thinking. Consequently, controversy, intense scrutiny and/or an attack (all motivated by insecurity) usually follow any truly significant breakthrough. In time, however, the fact that a true breakthrough is of a higher order and, thus, brings a greater depth of understanding than previously existed, the controversy subsides and the breakthrough is recognized and acknowledged.

WISDOM

The thing that creates the ability to easily change is a fuller understanding of the state we are calling *"wisdom."*

Without exception, humanity has throughout all time sought knowledge, insight, or revelation that would result in the common sense and understanding to help it change from a reality of negative experiences to one of positivism. Wisdom is not information. It is the knowledge existing within every human being which, when realized, reveals to man the workings of his own thought system and thus life, and guides humanity towards the attainment of high self-esteem, peace, happiness, and tranquility which was beforehand non-existent within the reality of personal frame of reference. The particular information within any given frame of reference only sees itself. Wisdom, understanding or common sense is the realization of a reality existent beyond a frame of reference — and this cannot occur via thought using the information comprising the frame of reference. The realization of this knowledge is what brings the clear state of mind in which an acquired frame of reference no longer gets in the way to create, sustain and promote the illusion of its own ignorance where all its information is defended as real and then reflected in rigid, biased, prejudiced and negative manners.

The freedom from an acquired frame of reference on which all beliefs and value judgments are based is accompanied by what people refer to as happiness, clarity, objectivity, and security. It allows a human being a positive direction in life unobstructed by one's very own beliefs, attitudes, opinions, biases and prejudices which so often lead to conflict. This common sense is the experience which affords any human being the wisdom to avoid all the recurrent negativity of arguments, conflict or confrontation based on nothing more than people's thoughts, powered by the feelings of insecurity which serve as the basis of the image of self-importance we call ego.

This knowledge called wisdom, understanding or common sense rather than being another concept, belief or idea is the knowledge of what beliefs, concepts and ideas are: thoughts. This wisdom, therefore, is not something which can be proven, stored up or defended; it simply is a realization of the situation we call life — the human situation. Wisdom cannot be in any way dependent on ideas, concepts, attitudes, opinions, views, models, theories or their data because all these vary from person to person, theorist to theorist, profession to profession, specialty to specialty, culture to culture, society to society, family to family, *ad infinitum.* The variation in how people think differs within an individual's lifetime, family, profession, and so forth. Wisdom, therefore, is not to be found within the confines of any one or a combination of variables, but rather in the state of mind that exists before the creation of this variation. It is what we are calling wisdom that helps one see that all the particulars of life (the different ideas, concepts, and so forth) are all, in principle, variations of thought existing in an infinite arena of mind.

THE PUZZLE OF LIFE

The reason that no one can tell anyone else exactly what wisdom is is that there is really no content to wisdom. Wisdom is the impersonal principle or knowledge underlying all the *do's* in life. The wiser we become, the simpler our understanding becomes. The process of moving to higher states of wisdom is analogous to the way a jigsaw puzzle seems to come together. The more caught up we are in insecurity, the more important each piece becomes; the more pieces seem to be missing, the harder it is to find out where any of them fit and the less we know about our direction and goal. In this state we know nothing about the principle of the puzzle and, thus, do not have much of a direction or goal. Anyone's belief about what the puzzle is about is as good as anyone else's. On the other hand, the more common sense we obtain, the less pieces are out of place. Since more pieces are filled in, it gets easier and easier to see where the rest belong.

As this puzzle reaches completion, the picture it paints gives more of an understanding of each piece in relation to the whole picture. In states of wisdom, we have a clarity and a common-sense understanding of how thought systems and the human mind work that enable us to distinguish between facts and beliefs.

Breaking down the physical universe to atoms, all of which had a nucleus and electrons, greatly simplified our understanding of the physical universe. Characteristics of these atoms, of electrons and protons, were used by scientists to explain literally all physical phenomena since all things are made up of combinations of atoms, no matter how different the substances appear on the outside.

The same is true of the relationship of frames of reference, ego-insecurity and wisdom to all the different manifestations of human behavior. The deeper we go beneath the apparency of differences on the surface, the more we understand all human behavior with a simple, profound grasp of the connection of these principles to whatever any person is doing at any given point in time.

CHAPTER 10

The Mental Health Field versus The Route to Mental Health

Once we began to get an understanding of how the thought system and frame of reference work to generate experience, we realized that the normal form or process of therapy, addressing the problems and the issues in the client's life, figuring out where the problem came from and even taking the problem as real at all, all make the situation worse!

AN OPPOSITE FOR MENTAL HEALTH

The true route to mental health is not to address and to resolve problems, thereby leading to happiness or maturity; but the opposite. The true route to mental health is to go directly to wisdom and then with understanding to solve or eliminate the problem.

The state of mind that we are in when we are experiencing problems is one of fear, insecurity, anxiety, anger or pain. At the time these feelings seem real and compelling, or we would not be in trouble. Therefore, the reasons and justifications we have for being in these frames of mind also seem real. When a therapist or counselor also treats these versions of reality as real, he is cementing in that frame of mind. Much of this therapy involves talking about negative feelings and events and assessing the traumatic effect on the client's life. This is absolutely the last thing in the world to have happen if therapy is to be serious, yet most psychotherapy is very serious.

We are not stating here that therapists are consciously or purposefully adding fuel to the fire. There is no malice or forethought, merely an ignorance on the part of the field as a whole about how individual thought systems work each moment to generate perceptions of reality.

We cannot solve any problem when we are caught up in the situation, angry, or defensive. All we can do in that state of mind is to keep going back to the anger and the reactiveness that created the problem in the first place. When people talk about their problems and take them seriously, they are using the frames of reference that created the problem in order to try to solve it.

For example, when we are in depressed states of mind, we have negatively distorted views of how things are going in our lives. We see things in terms of limitations, hopelessness, and anxiety. In these states, we cannot really solve any problem; in fact, whatever we do in these states is likely to make things worse. However, if we jump to better frames of mind, those of more common sense, we will feel more positive and hopeful and then will see opportunities where we previously saw problems. A well known behavioral psychologist recently completed a five-year research grant from NIMH, the conclusion of which was that people cannot be happy and depressed at the same time. His new form of behavior therapy is now to tell patients to go out and to do things that make them feel good. The futility of this behavioral approach is that when we are depressed, nothing we do feels good. Whatever is tried tends to make us more depressed.

THE DIRECTION TOWARD MENTAL HEALTH

The route to mental health is through positivity, happiness and feelings of enjoyment. These are not ego-related feelings of gratification but sheer senses of happiness and joy just to be alive, and to feel grateful for whatever is in hand now, no matter how much or how little. If we attach our positive feelings to any particular happening on the outside, we immediately make our happiness contingent on our egos being satisfied. Even if that result happens, our egos must continually go back for more and even bigger doses of the same result to maintain our happiness. We are just like junkies hooked on some drugs.

Many current therapies espouse ego-building techniques or strategies to build a person's ego strengths. The goal of these therapies is to build up a person's self-esteem through having each develop traits that he or she can take pride in, or that can be used to better cope with areas of life that are stressful or upsetting to the person. These strategies are harmful in the sense that they give people another set of standards or behaviors to use to prove themselves, rather than to see past the need to prove themselves at all.

When we actually start to see the illusions of insecurity and drop these illusions, our common sense shows us the obvious consequences of proving. The proving is in terms of the constant vigilance and the resulting stress of continually evaluating and judging ourselves and others, of noticing how we are doing and what other people think about how we are doing and so on. The good feelings that accompany this common sense are natural and effortless, and not connected to proving anything about ourselves in relation to our self-images. It is from this state of natural self-esteem that we can live our lives the way we want, without our problems.

The only way to get to mental health is through good feelings. No amount of figuring out, intellectual understanding, or expressing negative feelings can do it. These good feelings often come to people spontaneously, when they are least expecting them, or when they are not even thinking about anything in particular. We may be walking to work, or just sitting in our own living rooms with our families watching T.V. Suddenly, for no reason, we are feeling a strong sense of well-being about life, of contentment, of being fine just where we are. It's a feeling that nothing can touch us and nothing needs to change to make us feel good. These are natural feelings that are there when our insecurities let their guards down a little bit and allow us to stop worrying and figuring out. At that moment, we may feel intensely alive and notice ordinary things as special, rare and strikingly beautiful. Our children seem precious and special and we may experience a stream of insights that are exciting and make all our problems seem simple.

While most people have experienced these feelings, they may not trust them as real since they do not constitute the ordinary or normal condition. Yet, these are the most natural and normal feelings in the world. All other feelings of envy, anger, fear, anxiety, doubt, guilt and stress are false feelings created by personal insecurities. Our egos attempt to give us ulcers, or at least heartburn, by taking on the world from this field of feelings.

The kinds of feelings that lead to true mental health are not attached to any result. They are natural feelings of joy and well-being that well up and come out when we begin to drop insecurity and allow our minds to quiet down and stop thinking about our problems.

THE POWER OF POSITIVE FEELINGS

Since these good feelings are not attached to the content or the details of the person's previous frame of reference, they have the power to take that person out of that state of mind altogether to a new, higher level of consciousness, from which he or she will see life differently. Rather than wading about in the swamp, the individual has been lifted out altogether and can see the swamp for what it is — merely a bundle of illusionary thoughts and feelings.

This fact about changing levels of consciousness is the reason why when we take a vacation from work, go on a holiday for a few weeks, we often return not only rested and refreshed, but also seeing our work from new perspectives. Things we were caught up in before seem more simple and not so serious. We find ourselves having fresh insights about problems that had us on the ropes before we left. In fact, if more people realized how this process worked, they would take more breaks from work and get more accomplished!

One of the authors taught management in a business school. In telling his students how to prepare for the final exam, he advised them not to go over and over the text or lecture notes to attempt to memorize everything; but to read, at an enjoyable pace, for insights, things that hit them as true. These realizations would then naturally come back to them in the form of common-sense understanding when they took the exam. He also advised them to watch T.V., to go to a movie, or to do something else to relax and forget about the test the night before the exam. Several students reported that they studied in a similar way for their other classes as well, including statistics and accounting, and received the best grades they had ever received in those courses. This approach is a much different way to studying than we learned in college: staying up all night before the exams, memorizing as many of the theories, concepts, formulas and techniques as we could handle, and then forgetting all of them immediately after the exam.

Learning math is a good example of what we are talking about. Math is merely common sense, a logical set of relationships between variables, put down in the form of equations and formulas. Without insecurities we see the underlying relationship or principle between the variables for any type of problem, and can then easily solve any problem in that set or category of problems. However, if we are insecure, the insecurity itself keeps us from grasping the logic of the relationships and we try to memorize the formulas and steps. The errors we make then are mostly lack of common sense. We had a friend who missed a problem on her graduate statistics exam not because she did not know the formulas, but because she forgot to divide her answers by the number of people in the sample. Insecurity invariably causes us to overlook the obvious. She had gone over the question many times, feeling that her answers were out of line, but never saw what she had forgotten. If she had been feeling good about her grasp of the logic underlying the types of problems on the exam, she would have seen it as common sense to divide by the number of people in the sample.

INSECURITY: THE ENEMY OF COMMON SENSE

The number one enemy of insecurity is the natural state of happiness, good feelings about ourselves and life that are spontaneous and free from an association with or from being contingent on any condition or outcome. Since they are non-contingent, they cannot be attained by doing anything in particular or through any technique or process. All that we can do is to allow them to come in and feel grateful when they do. They are much more likely to come when we have more of an understanding of the futility of trying to figure out or to solve our problems from insecurity, which leads to a compulsive search for solutions.

When we are in states of ego and/or insecurity, we can achieve feelings of satisfaction or high self-esteem through our endeavors, but only temporarily at best. Since the ego needs to prove itself to feel good, it only allows us to feel good when we have achieved that particular goal or accomplishment. For example, in prep school one of the authors found himself second in his class after the first semester. Rather than feeling pleased or satisfied for long that he had done so well, he soon started to worry and to think about whether he would make it to number one the next semester, or even be able to maintain the number two position. The whole situation suddenly changed from a good experience to primarily a stressful experience.

For most people, the outside successes and the external appearance of accomplishments, although socially considered to be a sure sign of well-being, maturity and stability, are never really enough to make them happy. We know an extremely beautiful, intelligent and charming woman psychologist who could be whatever she wanted in life and who has a wealth of attractive and desirable suitors. Yet every job she gets is cause for doubt and anxiety. Should she really be doing this, or get married and have babies? Should a woman with her academic credentials be in an even higher position? Should she have stayed with her last job longer? What kind of work is really important?

When she starts dating someone, she worries about how it is going to work out. Should she have stayed with her previous boyfriend? Should she find someone with more similar interests? What does it mean that he did not call her yesterday? We were told by one of her ex-boyfriends that the main reason he was an *ex-* is that she spent an entire evening with him talking about the pros and cons of all of her previous boyfriends and why perhaps she had made the wrong choice when she did not stay with each one of them. She is now thirty-five and has found no one with whom she is happy, nor has she found satisfaction in her work.

The route to positive feelings and thereby to mental health is not to even think of, dwell on, or try to solve problems. It is not to analyze and unravel the details of this situation, or that pattern, or any childhood trauma. The route is to gain a deeper understanding of how the thought system, the frame of reference attached to insecurity, works to filter and color experience not only in ourselves, but in everybody.

THE THOUGHT OF SEARCH

Every human being searches for whatever will guide him to a more effortless and positive existence — an existence free of the negativity and ignorance which has always plagued mankind in the forms of anger, hostility, prejudice, jealousy, and so forth; and which has led to such extreme forms as hatred, violence, wars, and killings. Thus, it is the *status quo* — what is presently thought, seen, and experienced — that every search hopes will improve, get better, or disappear altogether and be replaced by the new. If the origin of the search, however, is the very same frame of reference which creates the *status quo* being experienced, then the search will be fruitless. Although fruitless in terms of finding the solution via information, the individual's search has nonetheless put to use, albeit in ignorance, his thought system which brings to life the experience of a reality seen through the details of the search. Because such searching is circularly referenced to the existent reality, it takes the form of producing, changing, sustaining, or eliminating the details, conditions, events, or situations which are thought to be the underlying bases or causes of the *status quo*. Thus, life ceases to be the positive moment-to-moment spontaneous discovery of the new and, instead, becomes the stagnant experience of constant effort to overcome life's hurdles. In fact, part of the experience which one hopes will come to an end in such states is the searching itself.

For example, if someone lived within the frame of reference of beliefs that he or she was unlikable or unattractive, and/or felt that the opposite sex was in general untrustworthy and believed he or she would be taken advantage of, this person would continually have serious problems and stress in relationships, would continually be testing for motives and be suspicious of the partner's behavior. The search for solutions within that frame of reference to specific problems and incidents would merely create additional problems. In fact, the search for solutions within any given set of beliefs about who a person is and how others are cannot produce a new experience outside the boundaries of that frame of reference.

When the searching is coming from within the boundaries of the same bundle of information which created its need (the *status quo*), the effect becomes circular. All thinking within any frame of reference cannot be anything but circular since all the information is related to itself. Thinking, using the stored bundle of information which acts as a frame of reference, serves only to exhibit, demonstrate and reinforce what is already known — the *status quo*. Such thinking amounts to searching through the data of a past which is no longer real, but exists only as information in a thought system. In turn, such thought serves to contaminate the reality of the present, which is then seen in terms of an irrelevant past. Thought within a frame of reference seeks to explain itself, that is, the reality it is experiencing. It only knows of itself, however, and ends up running around in circles trying to prove itself. If the solution to a problem created by the existence and experience of a given frame of reference were to be found within its boundaries, then a search would not have existed to begin with as the solution would have already been included in the *status quo*.

SEARCHING AND LEVELS OF CONSCIOUSNESS

When we are in higher levels of consciousness, we are relatively happy, secure and naturally enjoy doing things with our families, friends and loved ones. We may feel like having a party or playing tennis, going to the movies or simply spending a quiet evening with a loved one. The activities we engage in, however, are really secondary to the positive feelings that prompted us to consider doing any of these things to begin with.

On the other hand, if we are in low levels of consciousness, we may find ourselves feeling insecure, unhappy, lonely and even angry at ourselves over these feelings. In such states of mind, the closest thing to happiness that we may be able to find is to conjure up in our thoughts the memory of something we did or someone we were with in the past when we felt happy and secure. From the perspective of such realities, we are very likely to think that these past conditions must be recreated in order to pull ourselves out of the pits. It is at such levels of consciousness, where the illusory power of rituals is experienced that our search for happiness becomes ritualized.

RITUALS AND CONDITIONING

Any activity in which we repeatedly engage on the basis of a belief that it is somehow the necessary route or method to our well-being or happiness is a ritual. Because the rituals we engage in were learned or conditioned at some point in our lifetimes, they are tailor-made to fit the conditions which existed at the time we incorporated them into our ways of thinking about ourselves and our feelings. In other words, our rituals are a result of levels of consciousness we experienced that resulted in our giving certain behaviors and activities sufficient significance such that we took them on and made them important and necessary to our well-being.

A good example of how an activity as ordinary as a sport can insidiously become a ritual can be seen from the following story. When one of the authors was in tenth grade, he attended a school which was highly competitive in terms of social activities. At this time, he was particularly insecure about his relationship to the opposite sex. Because of this insecurity he always hung around with what he considered to be the *"in crowd."* Dating among the in crowd, however, went far beyond simply going out to have a good time, but was rather a matter of going out with the *right* girl. Thus, he was only attracted to girls who, in turn, would date only *popular* boys. Needless to say, in this environment his insecurity was as subtle as a porcupine on a waterbed. He was constantly preoccupied with figuring out how he could make himself more attractive and popular.

One day, while being timed on a track for a physical education class, he accidentally found out that he could run very fast. All of a sudden he found himself in great demand and was encouraged by a coach to try out for the track team. This he did and became one of the best track runners in the entire city. Aside from enjoying the competition and comradery, he had also found an activity which would make him well-known and popular.

Although this activity brought him a significant degree of popularity and good feelings, his basic level of insecurity was unchanged. His insecurity became more and more attached to his running, his winning and the collection of awards in order to maintain his popularity and self-esteem with his peers, especially females. As this occurred, anything that interfered with practice, winning or recognition brought about instant bad feelings. Every new girl whom he met had to be educated on what track was and what a track athlete did. This would be followed by an account of his victories and why running was good for one's fitness and health. Practice time was spent thinking about how all the suffering would pay off in terms of his social life. What started out as an experience of finding a nice sport to enjoy became a ritual.

OUR ATTACHMENT TO RITUALS

The degree of adherence that any of us will ever exhibit with regard to any ritual is dependent on our particular levels of insecurity, rather than on any inherent quality of the ritual — anything can be a ritual. Because rituals are beliefs that must be utilized and incorporated in our thought systems before they are exhibited, they act as reference points to keep us in realities where we are insecure. Thus, the insecure realities we experience when we are in lower levels of consciousness not only create perspectives from which we attach ourselves to rituals of all sorts, but also the very carrying out of all such rituals serves to keep us at such levels. Likewise, the less insecure we become, the less we are preoccupied with methods or techniques on which to base our well-being; the less we are attracted to rituals.

The seeming paradox to all this is that there must always be insecurity attached to any ritual we truly believe to be the key to our happiness. The insecurity associated with a ritual can take many forms. We may experience anxiety, if we cannot carry out a particular activity. We may feel doubt as to whether or not we are performing it adequately, long enough or frequently enough to get the desired results. Most of all, we experience the fear that we will lose our self-esteem by acknowledging the countless times when our rituals fail.

RITUALS AND THE PLACEBO EFFECT

Because all rituals are essentially beliefs (thought patterns) we sustain in our own thoughts, they act to varying degrees as placebos — thought-created *middlemen* that stand between us and our well-being. Said another way, rituals represent our own minds' versions of obstacle courses to feeling happy. Like any other placebo, however, the effects of any ritual are totally based on the power that we give to that ritual in our own thoughts. Thus, placebos can never provide any lasting or permanent relief from our own unhappiness.

Within a frame of reference the attempt to use one's thought system to figure out anything in order to increase one's knowledge about life results in either an immediate question of whether the figured-out is truthful, real, useful, harmful, and/or wanted; or the instituting of some ritual thought to be the route to such knowledge. Thus, figuring-out becomes a way of life. Somehow we always seem to forget that life has existed long before our attempts to figure anything out. From creation on no intellectual concept, theory, idea or model has ever figured life out. This is a fact. The true understanding of life cannot come via the figured-out. Being only the intellectual product of a frame of reference, life simply joins the list and adds another piece to the puzzle.

Better understanding or insight can only come when we literally stop trying to figure things out, put our whole subjective frames of reference aside, quiet our thoughts and look with objectivity and through our common sense or natural wisdom. The answers then come to us in the forms of insights and realizations.

We have all had the experience of working on a problem, thinking about it until we start to get a headache or until we become frustrated because the same old thoughts keep running around and around in our heads. We may then take a walk or go out and play golf or racquetball. Suddenly, when we are not thinking at all about the problem, the answer hits us as a realization or insight. At that point we become exhilarated because the answer is so apparent and straightforward. This type of experience is the most normal thing in the world and could happen many times every day, if we would let it happen.

STAYING OUT OF THE WAY

As we or anyone gain more real understanding, we also begin to see our own insecurities, which leads to this endless searching. We see them with a clarity, an objectivity, and hopefully a sense of humor that we did not have before. We then begin to take our problems and lives less seriously, our insecurities vanish, and good feelings start to come in, leading to higher states of consciousness, which gives more clarity and understanding, which leads to more positive feelings. This process keeps going if we stay out of the way and let it happen. However, it seems difficult to stay out of the way.

The hardest thing for the human mind to do is to mind its own business. If we would merely stop trying to figure life out, to analyze and to understand our problems, there would be no problems. The trick is to stop using our present frames of reference to address our problems and to let our natural wisdom and common sense emerge! As our minds start to quiet down, we begin to live in the realities of what people normally call insights. It is when we really begin to quiet down and see the relationship of a quiet mind to insight, self-esteem and mental health that we begin to actually live every day in a world of insights and good feelings. We find that insights about how our minds work lead to good feelings, which lead in turn to new insights about our work and personal affairs.

CHAPTER 11

Insight in Relation to Mental Health

Insight is the experience of seeing beyond an existing frame of reference or beliefs. This only happens as the consciousness level rises and one's thought system assumes a silent role and is seen for what it is. Thus, the thought system, no longer busy figuring it out, gives way to a more tranquil, clear, and objective state of mind. Only in these increasingly positive states of mind does the experience of ever deeper insights and understanding come. These insights are, without exception, always new and positive.

Any experience which results in negativity or misunderstanding or which maintains these states is not true insight or understanding. It is merely the manifestation of a low level of consciousness using intellectual information to play a negative game. As was stated before, the information stored in the thought system is itself neutral and, thus, secondary to the level of wisdom, understanding or common sense. This is why true insight must, by very definition, bring greater understanding and positiveness. If this does not occur, what is experienced cannot be insight.

INSIGHT

Adding the dimension of insight or of wisdom to psychology is analogous to adding a third dimension to a two-dimensional geometry. Others have labeled this shift *second order* transformation or a shift to a more encompassing, more objective frame of reference. This higher frame of reference includes what was there previously, and more, in a way that what was experienced and seen previously is no longer given the same meaning or significance. As we discussed in Chapter 7, we could think of a *first order* frame of reference as being a belief system (a conditioned frame of reference) that limits and distorts our visions, generating habitual or reactive behaviors. The shift to a new first-order frame of reference would entail our dissociation from one belief system along with a new attachment to a second or different belief system. In fact, one well-known author in the field of social psychology in an article about attitude change called this whole process *unfreezing-refreezing.* He then talked at length about how to get this change to occur. This process or the attempt to get this process to happen is also what is popularly called *"brainwashing"* of *"reconditioning."*

We were fascinated in graduate school by learning of a study carried out almost twenty years ago by a Harvard-based anthropologist, Rosabeth Kantor. She found that every *utopian* community she studied that had existed in America since the revolution to the present used exactly the same *commitment mechanisms* to gain the attachment of would-be converts to a particular ideology or belief system. These mechanisms included fear; embarrassment; emotional catharsis; physical isolation from the rest of the world; putting people through a physically and emotionally draining experience that made them feel special or different in becoming a member of that group; the sacrifice of personal property, time and energy; the fostering of an in-group *we-they* mentality between that group and the rest of the world; and a constant pressure through threats of punishment and ostracizing to conform to that society's behavioral, moral and attitudinal norms. In fact, we have seen all of these processes used to one degree or another in fraternities, graduate schools, personal growth organizations and even to a lesser degree in businesses. The content of the belief systems or ideologies are widely varied, yet the process of *conversion* from one belief system or first-order frame of reference to another is always similar.

On the other hand, the shift to a second or higher order frame of reference merely involves insights about or the realization of the existence and the nature of self-limiting first-order frames of reference. This new, higher, frame of reference in itself involves no content, but merely the realization of and ability to operate responsibly and naturally from principles; impersonal principles that clarify the facts behind the workings of separate realities. From these higher order frames of reference (that is, higher levels of consciousness) there is no insecurity, as the thought of insecurity itself is seen for what it really is. Therefore there exists no need for individuals to attach themselves to any particular group, ideology or movement to follow a particular leader or to base their self-esteem on belonging to any particular group.

The difference, in our experience, is similar to a child in elementary schoool learning addition first through practicing and memorization; then, at some point, realizing the principles behind the process of addition, which then enables the pupil to add all kinds of numbers not from practice, but from seeing the logical relationships involved in each problem.

A second-order frame of reference is one in which these insights become clearer and clearer. We realize the principles of the psychology of separate realities, of the conditioned realities in which we live and react when we are not aware of what is really going on. In these higher states of mind, the detailed contents of our thoughts and others' thoughts become less important, and we see each situation in terms of these deeper principles and the interactions among the various thought systems involved. The principles of these second-order frames of reference are impersonal and objective and do not make any judgments about the content of anyone's thoughts.

When an individual finds himself in an unhappy life or with problems that seem beyond his or her capability to solve, he or she often seeks guidance from someone who is, supposedly, wiser — someone who sees beyond the problems. Such a person possessing insight would never engage in methods, techniques, and/or rituals which analyze or utilize negativity and the externally perceived causes or elicitors. Such methods, rituals and techniques originate and are of relevance only to a frame of reference which created the problem to begin with. In essence, all these rituals, subsumed under the label of *therapies,* represent the counterproductive use of a thought system attempting to use information to figure out the causes and contingencies of its problems ignorant that it is all thought. In all such situations, such solutions for man's problems never include dropping the thought of the problem. A solution which involves dropping a thought pattern which created the problem could not be called a method, technique or therapy because the moment the thought creating the problem is dropped, the problem would not exist in thought. There would be no problem to think about, figure out, solve or treat in any way. A problem simply would not exist.

This result occurs only when we have insights about the role of our first-order thought system in creating our habitual reactions and ways of seeing things. There have been innumerable articles written about self-acceptance and mental health. The facts are that true self-acceptance occurs after we realize the illusionary or made-up quality and nature of all our self-judgments, guilt and feelings of inadequacy. This is another way of saying that as one goes up levels of consciousness, the realization of our true responsibilities becomes a fact. The so-called external world or environment then becomes more understandable, controllable and compliant. Even the manifestations of lower levels of consciousness in our worlds are understood to deeper and deeper levels. The more we realize that what we see in life are the manifestations of our thought systems, the more perfect our worlds become.

THE LIMITING NATURE OF A THOUGHT SYSTEM

These insights keep on coming, if we do not close down our minds. Because we have previously not realized what thinking is or what our thought systems represent, we all have tendencies to want to grab on to new realizations and to develop them into new conceptual frameworks, or new frames of reference from which to view life. As soon as we realize something new, our egos get excited and want to go out and show the world what they have discovered. This taking credit is crazy because the way we managed to have these insights was to drop ego for an instant. Yet the ego quickly comes back in to build a new limited conclusion around that insight. As soon as we have developed new concepts, our thought systems then, like the older versions, continue to limit and determine our experiences of life.

We then use these new thought systems to evaluate what is right or wrong about the world, to judge other people, to defend our own positions and behaviors, and to prove our egos. We are then right back where we were before. That is why we are saying that a conceptual or theoretical understanding of what we are learning is of absolutely no value.

It takes some courage to look at the sum total of what we think we know now and to keep letting it go, to keep going back to innocence and a condition of openness or not knowing. However, the rewards from this courage are tremendous. Once we honestly realize we don't know anything and relax, we get a new feeling, which brings with it a deeper understanding of life, of the mind, and of the power of thought. We then begin to actually experience that our thoughts of what is real are like the electronic beams that make up the picture on a television screen. These thoughts, projected outward, form totally the picture of our lives, what we see, how we respond to what we see, and how that picture changes. Once this realization occurs, we can never be mentally ill or emotionally disturbed again. We have gained a deep wisdom and common sense that allows us to see clearly how every person on earth is caught in subjective frames of reference or beliefs — the very sources of all mental health problems.

THE IRRELEVANCE OF CONTENT

In looking at our mental health, the content of what we believe we are (that is, our particular frames of reference, including the details of our beliefs) is not the point. We could think we are Napoleon Bonaparte or a better parent than our families and friends think we are. It is the strain of defending any system of beliefs about our images of self-importance that causes our emotional stresses. Normally, the more bizarre or out of the normal our frames of reference are as seen by others, the more mentally ill we will be considered by others. All mental illness stems from the thought of insecurity. The stronger the thought of insecurity, the more we feel paranoid about defending our frames of reference, irrespective of how negative or distorted those frames of reference may be. People will even become violent at times, if someone contradicts their beliefs and realities.

The more we begin to let go of the thoughts of insecurity, to allow ourselves to settle down and be ordinary, the more easily and quickly we see the relativity and illusionary quality of our subjective frames of reference. All of our defensiveness and bad habits then drop away naturally. We personally know hundreds of people in all walks of life in all parts of the United States who have without any effort or trying stopped drinking, using drugs, consistently losing jobs, fighting with their spouses, having nervous breakdowns, enduring chronic episodes of paranoia and depression, and who have lost all their psychosomatic illnesses merely from deeper understandings of the power of thought and of insecurity. We could easily produce any or all of these people along with their medical and psychiatric records, showing a dramatic change from their pasts compared to their present conditions of life. In fact, we are presently responding to interest from the National Institute of Mental Health to design and to carry out such a study.

The key and common element in all of these results is an understanding of what insecurity is and how it works before this feeling of insecurity begins to manifest itself into any particular form of neurosis, compulsive behaviors, fears and self-doubts that could be labeled as symptoms of emotional distress or stress.

CHAPTER 12

The Many Faces of Insecurity: Looking Past the Disguises

Understanding the power of insecurity not only allows us to release our own natural good feelings and high self-esteem but also gives us the freedom to be gentle, to have empathy and to be patient with other people. When we honestly understand and start to drop our thoughts of insecurity ourselves, we can see where other people are coming from, how much they are ready to hear, and when and how to help them gain a deeper understanding that shows them the route to mental health beyond their insecurities.

Levels of consciousness or levels of clarity, wisdom and common sense do really exist. We are not talking about a theory or any technique. People caught up in negative, hostile and judgmental frames of reference are in lower states of understanding or ignorance. People who are happy, content, get along well with people and can laugh at themselves are in higher states of understanding. We feel that we ourselves are only beginning to learn and that even though our own lives have already changed tremendously, there is no limit to where we can potentially go.

People in negative and judgmental frames of reference would probably not agree with what we are learning. They could not agree because their insecurities are the very things creating that lostness and it is these insecurities that feel a need to defend those realities. More and more recently, we have realized that it is a waste of time to argue or to debate. The insecurities of those people's minds will not allow them to listen to what is being said, but they will rather be looking for ways to refute or disagree based on a logic they make up that fits with their frames of reference. Their insecurities will not allow them to look deeper, to see that we are talking about frames of reference and thought systems, and how they work, rather than offering an alternative thought system.

FEELINGS OF LOVE VERSUS INSECURITY

We cannot really know what the experience of love is until we drop our own insecurities. Until that time we may feel gratification or attachment or need, but not the deeper, purer feeling we call love. True love is only experienced in the absence of self-consciousness, without attachment or wanting anything other than the enjoyment of that feeling. In a condition of love we have no desires, needs or demands, but merely a deep appreciation for the beauty we see in the person or object toward which we are experiencing those feelings. It is a mistake to say, *"I do not know what love is."* Everyone knows what love is — it is a feeling that comes totally on its own when we drop our insecurities. Insecurity and ego cannot experience love, because their only basis in reality is proving themselves or judging others in relation to our self-images. The feelings that are generated are fear of or gratification for our own desires.

The feeling that most of us call love is perhaps most commonly experienced within the context of a relationship. At some point in our lives we meet someone and attribute to them one of the nicest, most beautiful feelings human beings can have: love. For the most part, people who fall in this state of love usually know little to nothing about the other person. Initially, the feelings of aliveness, excitement, and novelty are so strong that the details of each other's beliefs, lifestyles, backgrounds, and so forth are irrelevant. We may even ignore beliefs we have long ago established, being much more interested in the present feelings. We may stay up late night after night, or drive miles out of our way to be with our beloved. We will beg to do things for each other that we previously would not have considered. We will volunteer to do dishes, go grocery shopping, sweep, mop, babysit, or anything to be together.

People in these states of consciousness act as if they are immune to the problems and the tribulations of the so-called real world. A dingy apartment becomes the garden of Eden. The job that once contributed a meager salary is suddenly seen within the same feeling and now feeds a flourishing relationship. People in love do not care where they are or where they go as long as they are together. Silence and quietude, the enemy of worry, are welcomed and treasured. All search is at a standstill. These realities are so beautiful that we hope such feelings will never end.

Most of us are familiar with this or something very close to this experience. Unfortunately, we are also familiar with the events that follow the re-emergence of our insecurities along with our caravan of beliefs, opinions, rituals, and so forth which bring our egos into play. Thus, the willing and effortless devotion exhibited by people in love is replaced in behavior and in feeling by the contingent mechanical behavior of two people analyzing and evaluating each other from the perspective of nothing more than insecurity.

We have seen beautiful, loving relationships destroyed because the insecurity of one of the partners led to feeling that the other person was not really loving the other when not directly paying attention to the first. We have seen divorces because one partner would not get into health foods or yoga, because the husband's career was not as important to the wife as he wanted it to be. We can produce an endless list of reasons why we are not compatible. Compatibility, in producing good relationships, is irrelevant. Compatibility is judging the other person's beliefs, lifestyle and habits against one's own thought system. All that compatibility can tell us is whether our belief systems can tolerate the other person's belief system, given the level of insecurity we both have now and assuming that neither will ever change.

INSECURITY AND RELATIONSHIPS

The source of all conflict in relationships, marital or otherwise, is insecurity. Insecurity in relationships is manifested when partners attempt to impose their thought systems on the others, without an understanding of the others' frames of reference. When couples first meet and are falling in love, they do not notice the other person's habits or behavioral patterns; these are not important because the good feelings are more enjoyable. As soon as couples start to settle back down into their own habitual routines, the differences in their habits, life-styles, beliefs and what they like and do not like start to become more important. It is at this point in relationships when people begin to analyze and to evaluate the details of why they like the other person, their looks, habits, beliefs, how reliable they seem, how much they can be trusted, and which qualities might get in the way. It is as a result of this preoccupation with figuring it all out that the beautiful feelings begin to disappear. The greater the insecurity of the individual, the more he or she will react to the partner when the partner does something out of line with what is considered appropriate behavior in a particular thought system.

In relationships, when insecurity is present a person's imaginary thoughts and fears can lead that person to interpret and react to the partner's behavior in a thousand different ways, usually fearing the worst. We have seen couples fighting over the craziest things for years because those things have a different significance for each person's thought system. We have seen parents disillusioned from holding on to an image of what their children should grow up to be. Through this vehicle, they keep their relationship to their children stressful, unpleasant and tense for most of their adult lives.

Once either partner in a marriage or any relationship starts to get some common sense, he or she will see the craziness of judgments, reactions, impatience and fears. The person will see the conflicts for what they are: illusionary thought systems clashing. One of the authors, for example, had many recurring patterns of conflict with his fiance in graduate school. One of their major battlegrounds was around the area of giving advice. He had the belief that if people gave him advice, they actually felt that he was incapable of running his own life. She felt that giving people advice was the best way to have your friends want to keep you around. Since they were both insecure, both reacted automatically as if their lives were at stake to a conflict around giving advice. Typically, she would give him advice, he would get angry and defensive, she would get afraid and upset, and they would be well on their way to a good fight about nothing!

We aren't aware of many relationships that do not have these recurring patterns of conflict. While in lower levels of consciousness none of us can see what is really going on, so we get caught up because of our own insecurities in blaming the other person. The truth is that no one is to blame; both people are innocently caught up in their particular forms of insecurity. They are judging and reacting to their partners through their own perceptual filters, filters that keep them seeing blame and negativity.

The only way couples can produce any lasting positive change in their relationships is to drop insecurity, to see the other person from the positive, loving and appreciative frame of reference that they started the relationship with in the first place. Our insecurities are more often and more intensely taken out on our partners because they are more accessible and safer and because they are usually more important to us than our other friends.

Family counselors and marriage therapists who attempt to go back into the past and try to help couples solve specific problems are missing the boat altogether. All we can do as therapists for families and couples is to help people realize that their own reactiveness comes from their own thought systems (their judgments and fears) and would be inflicted on anyone in the position of their family members, unless, of course, that their behaviors fit the others' beliefs and standards exactly. In that case, they would probably be upset because they feared the others were too wishy-washy and did not have minds of their own.

As people drop insecurity, the enjoyable, exciting feelings of love normally begin to come back to the relationships of couples and between family members. We then see that their habits, reactions and insecurities are as innocent as ours had been. These behavioral patterns then become less and less relevant and, in most instances, drop off entirely after a while like leaves off a tree, without effort, by themselves.

Imagine receiving unconditional love and regard from your partner. This feeling coming from that person would soon make all our insecure games seem unimportant, certainly irrelevant. In addition, the things we would normally fight about no longer work, particularly if only one person is fighting. The most natural, normal state of relationships is love and appreciation, which if left alone will naturally grow deeper and more loving all the time. Again, this only changes when we bring in our egos and insecurities to start judging and reacting to our partners in negative ways from our own thought systems. Once we begin to realize how this result occurs, we merely stop the judging and find the feelings we want coming back into all our relationsips.

Therapies that teach methods of fair fighting or that involve expressing any negative feelings are crazy. These therapies merely validate and authenticate individual judgments and thoughts. It is only these thoughts that create personal negative feelings. Again, we must go one step deeper and eliminate the sources in our own insecurities of these thoughts and their importance to our own senses of self-esteem.

We have known hundreds of couples who have sought help in the personal growth arena and then started fighting about whose trip was better, who was more *out of touch* with their feelings and on and on. We can attach our insecurities and needs to prove ourselves to any form that exists. Couples cannot get to happiness by addressing or even talking about their problems. Therapists who have begun to realize this fact are having far better success with their clients. Rather than teaching them better ways to communicate or work on their problems, they focus on the positive side, on the loving and tender feelings that people want to experience in relationships. Once these feelings come alive again, all the problems seem to dissolve themselves.

It has been nice for us and for our friends and colleagues as well to know that the natural and easiest course in relationships is to start with attraction and love, to just enjoy the person and allow these feelings to get deeper and deeper.

Parents who constantly experience these types of feelings of love and respect for their children will naturally guide their children to wisdom and maturity with little effort or trying, without attempting to impose their beliefs or neurotic patterns on their children. We know couples who have ten- to twelve-year-old children who are so wise they can look at any adult and know immediately what is going on with that person. They are wiser than most psychologists while at the same time full of playfulness, joy of being alive and having a rich enjoyment of all the activities that children of that age normally get involved in.

The secret to relationships of any form is not in learning techniques or theories of parenting, communication, or behavior modeling. All we need to do is to drop the thought of insecurity and our natural warmth, understanding and clarity as human beings will take over. We will then know how to raise our children and to make our marriage happy with the same intuitive wisdom that all animals have about mating and rearing their young. Again, like everything else, the secret in relationships is simplicity, not in looking at or figuring out the complications. This simplicity begins to happen when being happy and in love becomes more important than being right and defending our egos.

THE FREEDOM BEYOND INSECURITY

With a truer, deeper wisdom about people, their states of mind or frames of reference will not affect us because we can see how innocently they are caught up in whatever they are caught up in at the time. With real understanding we know that it is a privilege for us to be able to offer a stability, a confidence and a presence that assists others to calm down, even a little, and to see that they are merely caught up in reacting to something that has triggered their personal insecurities. If we are truly, at that time, in a deeper state of wisdom, our presence itself with that understanding behind it will often be all we need to offer, and may have an affect way beyond any words.

In addition, if we are honestly in a higher state of wisdom than the other person at that time, we will have less attachment to a particular outcome or to how they are with us. In other words, we will more easily be able to do whatever works to help them feel comfortable and safe than they can do. The difference in levels of insecurity causes them to want what they want with more of a feeling of need. In fact, whenever anyone says that he or she has certain needs all that person is really saying is that he or she is insecure, and having certain things happen will temporarily alleviate that feeling.

In another instance, it may be that person or someone else assisting us to realize that we have slipped into a low mood and are seeing things through the filters of our insecurities. No one can tell anyone else what to do to really help someone in any given situation. The only thing that can help us see what to do is our own wisdom. Our wisdom, if operational at the time, will naturally assist us in knowing what is appropriate, what is the most helpful, whether it is listening or a dose of common sense or something else. No technique or method will work. It is only when we can say or demonstrate something true that that person is ready to hear or see that we can be helpful.

PHYSICIAN HEAL THYSELF

The most important thing we can do to become responsible and effective therapists is to become happy. The truth of this statement is also found in the old cliche, *Physician heal thy-*

self. It only makes sense, after all, if we do not know how to be happy ourselves, how can we teach others?

We have had psychologists literally say to us *"Well the point of therapy is not to make people happy; it is to make them well-adjusted."* If we ask what *well-adjusted* persons look like, we are told that they have learned to live with their problems. However, they are already living with their problems. Most therapists can make clients more expert at living with their problems only because they have many of the same problems themselves. In fact, we were told by more than one psychotherapist that they weren't ready to get rid of their *garbage* because they still felt comforted by it!

When people in therapist roles actually do drop insecurity, they can see how insecurity works in their clients. These therapists will see people acting out or dealing with their insecurities in a myriad different ways; some by overeating, some by drinking, smoking or using drugs, some by picking fights with their friends or families and others by becoming depressed, paranoid or by exhibiting other forms of coping mechanisms that involve reactivity and fear. The therapists will then naturally see how to bypass all of these symptoms to go more directly to the sources; to show their clients, more impersonally, what insecurity really is. If we as therapists are insecure ourselves, we cannot do this with our clients because we too are caught up in taking the details of our lives seriously. We are in the same boat as our clients.

Most of what is now offered under the labels of therapy or personal growth counseling consists of insecure professionals alleviating the gnawing of insecurity by having others look up to and depend on them. The clients temporarily relieve their insecurities by asking someone else what to do. Both sides play their respective roles to continue to feed the game of insecurity like junkies feeding their habits.

We are not saying this to put down therapists. Everyone's insecurity emerges in a different form. People who feel insecure as parents come down on their children harder if the offspring do not always live up to the parents' standards.

People who feel insecure about work blame their bosses or start militant worker movements, or perhaps drink too much, use drugs or take it out on their spouses.

REALIZING FACTS ABOUT OUR MIND VERSUS A CONVERSION PROCESS

As we have repeatedly noted, everyone lives in a separate reality from everyone else. Each reality is the result of unique conditioning and acculturation or socialization throughout life. Anyone's reality, however, can be changed through a variety of types of experiences to a new conditioned reality. This type of process is what we would call a *conversion process;* that is, a process in which an individual is conditioned to a new set of beliefs without being aware that conditioning is occurring and/or without knowing what a belief is. Such conversion processes do not involve any real change in our levels of understanding, our insecurities are simply given other systems through which they can be manifested.

Realizing facts about the workings of our thought systems, on the other hand, involves insights about how the acculturation or conditioning process works in the first place; in other words, realizing facts about what a conversion process really is. True insights give us the clarity and understanding of how we as people move from one belief system to another and allow us to free ourselves from the effect of any particular set of beliefs, conditioned or acculturated reactions to events, situations and people. We have found that these impersonal insights about the functioning of separate realities (or separate thought systems) in all human beings, free us from living with the effect of our own insecure thoughts, fears, and conditioned or habitual behavior patterns. We then become free to choose the lives we want to live and to be happy regardless of the beliefs and opinions of the people around us.

Normally, once people begin to see how insecurity works and go to new levels of understanding to see beyond their previous frames of reference, every aspect of their lives will begin to change effortlessly and naturally. They will go to work with more confidence, maturity and with a greater appreciation for other people's frames of reference. They will see their spouses and children with love and gratitude, giving them the wisdom to become good parents and to enjoy their partners. Bad habits will drop away since they were born of insecurity which leads to boredom, depression, fear, and resentment, and on to behaviors aimed at getting rid of these feelings. As they drop insecurity, all these feelings disappear, and are replaced by maturity, insights, and a new excitement about life.

All we can do as therapists is to understand and start to drop our egos and insecurities and then to share our wisdom, excitement, and good feelings. Once our insecurities drop away, we begin to stop relying on our techniques or methods and concepts, and use our common sense. We start to realize that all of these tools of therapy are merely *Linus blankets.* We need them when we are insecure to give us something to do, when we really don't know what to do.

When we ourselves start to see deeper, to realize what is going on beyond the specific form of that client's insecurity, we will then find the best way to share that understanding with our clients in a manner that makes it most likely that they will actually hear something new. Each time we do that, it will come out differently. Each time we do that we will learn more ourselves, and the next time it will come out differently again.

Often, when we talk with people now, it feels to us as if we ourselves are hearing for the first time what is coming out of our mouths. This happens probably because insights are not possible to plan in advance. All we can do is to be living in the frame of mind where insights are the stuff of our consciousness, rather than any specific frame of reference.

Often at our conferences, people will say *"Well, what you are saying makes sense, but what do I do when the client says . . . ?"* No one can answer that question for anyone else. If we try, we are just pretending to know something we cannot possibly know until the time comes. When the time comes, we even then will probably do something different from what that person would do anyway, because we are different persons, our relationship to the client is different, and the emotional state of the client may be different.

It is a nice, even exhilarating feeling to know that just by being ourselves and pointing out what we see, we can always be helpful to others. We don't have to prepare, to use a technique or worry whether it will take; all we have to do is drop our insecurities about our effectiveness as helpers, stop worrying about whether we are good therapists, become happy ourselves, and honestly want to help others.

SUMMARY

In previous chapters we have introduced the functional characteristics of how an information frame of reference composed of thought works. We have pointed out how this process manifests itself at the levels of our own individual understanding to create whatever realities we see and function in. We have also noted that in the relative absence of what we are calling common sense or wisdom, there is a corresponding relative tendency for our frameworks of information to assume an illusory image of self and importance: the ego.

Accordingly, the lower our levels of understanding that our images are imaginary, the more we innocently get in our own ways of appreciating what is actually occurring. Instead, we seek to prove, impose and defend these images of ourselves to others; a task which can never end and only serves to bolster our insecurities. Quite understandably then, we increasingly become insecure and begin to more dogmatically adhere to whatever system of beliefs, assumptions, attitudes, and so forth we have accumulated from the past.

As the problems associated with such realities are experienced, all of our attempts to analyze the causes in order to arrive at solutions become circular and counter-productive by virtue of our already lowered perspectives. Furthermore, the results of such problem-solving is that we are further removed from the true sources of our own realities. Thus, true change and innovation (that is, insights) become more and more difficult since they fit less and less with our ever-increasing and present insecurities and rigidities of thought. The end result is the loss of our direction toward a deeper and more truthful understanding of ourselves and the adoption of an offensive/defensive system of detailed explanations with which to protect our insecure and stagnating images.

The field of psychology, in the way both research and therapy are currently carried out, contributes to this process rather than helping people see for themselves the way out of this downward spiral. In the next four chapters, we will explore in more depth how what we are discovering about the facts of separate realities and levels of consciousness relates to current theories and research in psychology; in fact, to the frame of reference within which these theories are developed and tested.

SECTION IV

THE RELATIONSHIP OF PRESENT DAY PSYCHOLOGY TO OUR EVOLVING UNDERSTANDING OF THE MIND

CHAPTER 13

Today's Psychology in Theory: A System of Thought

Knowing what we do about how the human thought systems operate relative to levels of consciousness, it is not difficult to understand why the field of psychology today functions within a self-limited framework. It was inevitable that our own desires to understand ourselves psychologically from intellectual systems of thought would result in the production of an immense quantity and diversity of ideas. It was also inevitable that we would categorize and finally organize these ideas as a discipline, which in turn would be used as a reference source for what people have thought about human behavior. What has further developed, however, is that we now look at this collection of ideas about ourselves (our array of theories) as if they were actually a set of facts about our mental and emotional functioning as human beings.

All of our theories, concepts and models, however, are themselves thought systems that are self-validating in the way that any belief system becomes a self-fulfilling prophecy. If, for example, we as therapists think that people's problems come from traumatic events in their early childhoods, we will unearth events that could be seen as traumatic and show a consistent relationship between these events and present behaviors. For most therapists the theories have been learned by them from their teachers and are passed along in a mechanical or automatic fashion to their clients or students. Therapists then develop their own methods or techniques for helping their clients based on whatever theories they were taught and have accepted. As we have spawned more and more schools and specialties these techniques have become highly differentiated and more and more complicated.

Thus, present-day psychological training, consulting and therapy usually consist of professionals teaching others to follow something that they strongly believe to be true without really knowing this for themselves. In other words, they have been following someone else's ideas in place of their abilities to see and to understand what is actually occurring. The professional helpers consequently never really experience their own responsibilities for what they tell or suggest to those who come to them seeking help for their own lack of understanding.

THE EGO WITHIN PSYCHOLOGY

The principal point we wish to develop in this Section is that the illusory condition we have called ego is not limited to us as individual people, but also exists and operates in an identical manner in any group or organization of people. That is, relative to the prevailing levels of understanding, all frames of reference of thought function in fundamentally the same manner. This is evident if we consider that any group or organization of people in reality represents a collective bundle of ideas, concepts, beliefs and values, which are themselves thought systems. Thus, if not for the prevailing wisdom of its units, any group or organization sooner or later will become lost in a self-serving image of its own making — even to its own eventual disadvantage.

BREAKING THROUGH A SYSTEM OF THOUGHT

In writing this section of the book, we often make what will be considered to be very strong statements about the field of psychology. Yet in order for the field to truly help itself, there is no doubt that we must be willing to take an objective look at ourselves with the same degree of honesty and directness we ask of those who look to us for help. This requires that we as a field break through the barriers of our own thinking.

It is understandable and predictable that every field of study during the course of its evolution will begin to stagnate or to limit itself within its own specific conceptual framework. The signs of this happening are a further and further refinement of what it has already known, or a breaking down of existing categories into sub-categories with finer degrees of specialization and differentiation between each school or specialty. A breakdown in objectivity follows and is reflected in the formations of many different schools of thought, each defining its own interpretation of the existing data.

When a new breakthrough to a deeper level of understanding occurs, it serves to integrate and to clarify the relationship of all existing data, regardless of how fragmented they may seem, into newly recognizable principles. Again, however, we must emphasize that such breakthroughs do not result from the experimental manipulation of what is usually misunderstood data. Quite the opposite — breakthroughs occur at the level of someone's understanding and are only later incorporated experimentally. The experimentation simply verifies the new insight.

When Einstein discovered relativity, the new insights and principles came prior to any experimental attempts to document the results of these insights. As a matter of fact, much of the experimental verification of Einstein's principles came years and decades later when the experimental technology was finally available. The same is true with any field of study. New insights lead to new approaches to experimentation that further clarify how these newly discovered principles work. For example, the insight, concept, or idea of television must have existed in someone's mind before televisions could be built and finally mass produced.

What we are attempting to say to the field of psychology is that in order to grasp new insights it must be willing to break through perhaps even the most basic thoughts about human behavior, or at the very least begin to question the validity of the context in which it views these assumptions now. We have seen from our own personal resistances to taking responsibility for our versions of reality how difficult it really is to walk into the unknown. Yet the rewards from actually doing this are tremendous. Each time we honestly see what we are doing, we go to new levels of consciousness. Each new level of consciousness is always accompanied by greater wisdom, more humor and stronger feelings of happiness and high self-esteem. Thus, while we as a field evolve in our real understanding of separate thought systems, we must ourselves become models of the type of mental health and enjoyment of life toward which we honestly, truly want to help our clients move in their own lives and affairs.

AN EVOLUTIONARY CONTEXT FOR THE STATE OF THE ART

In order to fully comprehend and appreciate the larger context to which we are pointing, it is helpful to first understand the present *state of the art* of the psychological professions and the nature of the frame of reference to which it is now tied. The reader, however, should keep in mind that plateaus of understanding characterized by circular reasoning are not in any way specific or particular to any field of study. Rather, it represents a level of evolution, a level of understanding at a given point in time.

Throughout the known history of humanity this situation has occurred in every culture, society, institution, science, family, and individual. In fact, the end of any such era of circularity is when the *status quo* finally gives way to the new; this new is known as a *discovery* or a *breakthrough*. There are countless examples in our history such as Columbus, Galileo, Pasteur, Einstein, Edison, and Ford to name only a few. What we are presenting, therefore, should be looked at in the light of the continuing evolution of a culture, science, profession, and individual toward a clearer understanding of what people are doing to themselves.

PSYCHOLOGY: THE STATE OF THE ART OF ITS LOGIC

The field of psychology today is looking for answers within

a frame of reference where certain assumptions, key assumptions in fact, are fairly well taken for granted. Yet today, within the present frame of reference of the field of psychology, we have not really found any answers. The majority of psychological studies are primarily descriptive in the sense that they first posit a particular theory or model that connects in a causal fashion certain events and results in terms of personality traits in a person's life. Secondly, they attempt to verify through some kind of documentation that such a connection does indeed exist.

These connections invariably take us back into the past to analyze how these connections started or became ingrained or conditioned into our habitual ways of seeing ourselves in relation to the events and experiences of our lives. Describing these connections, however, has nothing to do with understanding the principles of how and why we activate and use these acquired thought patterns now to evaluate, judge, interpret and react to events and people; why we sometimes do and sometimes do not get caught up in reacting or using our conditioned filters (perceptions).

THE SELF-VALIDATING NATURE OF CONCEPTS AND MODELS

The most basic problem with this level of reasoning is that every person's thought system is an internally consistent and self-validating reality. What this means is that each of us operates on the basis of a specific framework of beliefs. Furthermore, we do so at a given level of consciousness or understanding about the reality of those beliefs. Accordingly, we then experience situations in a manner consistent with this reality; that is, we make certain interpretations of situations we experience and arrive at certain conclusions about our lives. If we remained at that same given level of consciousness, we would continue to re-experience the same patterns over and over again in various detailed forms throughout our lives.

What today's psychological studies and research actually

accomplish, then, is to validate the fact that each of our thought systems is internally consistent and that therefore there are similarities throughout time in our experience; that there are certain predictable meanings that we give to events, relationships and problems in our lives. What psychology has not fully realized is that it is only these meanings that we ourselves give to our pasts or to our present experiences that determine the states of our mental health at the moment. It is the present level of understanding of the field of psychology that prevents it from recognizing this fact. Psychology today will not learn anything new until the field as a whole begins to break through its own thinking to a deeper understanding of the fact of separate realities.

When Einstein realized the laws of relativity, one of the new principles which physics had to deal with was the fact of relativity itself. Einstein realized that any measurement, whether of time, speed, distance and even mass, is affected and altered by the relative position or perspective of the viewer. The realization of this principle led to a major redesign of all the experimental procedures in the field of physics and a major reconceptualization of the relationships between bodies in the physical universe.

Psychologically we as people are all the same in the ways that we trigger our insecurities to move in and out of different moods and perceptual states. The details of our perceptions will differ because we are different people with differing backgrounds, yet we are all the same in terms of how and what results occur when we activate our habitual thought patterns.

As the field of psychology begins to more fully understand the facts and principles of separate realities as individual thought systems, there will have to be a major reconceptualization and reorientation of the frame of reference of psychology. Until such a time, all that psychological studies will continue to do will be to document the internal consistency of each particular type of thought system operating at a given level of consciousness. The documented data will be used to categorize similar types of thought systems into different forms of diagnostic evaluations. However, throughout life every person develops a belief system that will always include predictable types of events and problems along with whatever significance is attached to these events, culminating in an individual state of mental health. Epidemiological studies in psychology in terms of how they are normally used merely verify that a particular level of consciousness makes these connections and therefore has the internal consistency that is characteristic of all thought systems.

PSYCHOLOGY: THE STATE OF THE ART OF ITS SCIENCE

As a result of our present misconceptions, we have yet to realize the circularity of our theoretical reasonings. Objectivity has been interpreted as consistency and reliability in the interpretation of its research data. As a result, the use of what is known as the *scientific method* in psychological research has been unable to bring objectivity to the field for the simple fact that the very data of psychology are theoretical. That is, we are assigning a quantitative value or scale to some psychological force, entity or process outside ourselves which is believed to be the cause of our behaviors. Thus, the fact that quantitative or numerical values are assigned to something which is based on theory has been interpreted as a sign of the objectivity. Nothing could be farther from the truth, however.

The fact that this situation has been up to now overlooked by the field is reflected in the present situation where researchers design and carry out their research in line with their theories. In most cases each researcher finds support for a particular view. Very few theories have been discarded from the accumulated collection. These theories and their conclusions are then used as the conceptual bases for further research, and thus become incorporated into the frame of reference of psychological literature.

THE SEARCH AND THE RESEARCH

In order to begin to grasp the principles of separate realities, present-day psychological research into human behavior must be objectively seen as an example of the circular reasoning to which we are pointing in this book. Research, as is presently being carried out in psychology, emerges from and is directed by the current framework of psychological theories which guide the thinking of the profession. The validity of such theory-based research hangs on the validity of the existing and accepted set of theories of testing and measurement.

To further complicate matters, the theories of psychological testing and measurement are themselves based on theoretical assumptions concerning human behavior. What, when, where, who, why and how psychological testing and measurement is carried out is symbiotically tied to theory. The reason for this relationship is that all present-day psychological tests and measurements in some way were developed to meet the need to prove, validate or substantiate some theory of human behavior. Simply stated, the rationale or basis for the existence and use of psychological tests is to establish the connection within a given framework between specific theoretical psychological explanations. As they stand today, psychological tests and measurements are validated by using some forms of cross-validation with some other established tests or established theories of behavior. While the established theories of behavior are considered open to question, they are tested using established methods of testing and measurement, which are themselves fundamentally based on these theories.

For example, if we correlate some human relations styles in business managers with the extent to which their parents punished them as children, we will usually be able to make such a correlation. Yet, we are pounding another nail into the belief system that we are products of our pasts. The managers may then be told that they need long-term treatment to understand why they get impatient or deal with employees' questions in certain ways. Within this frame of reference there is no way that the underlying assumptions of the testing, therapeutic diagnosis or therapeutic ritual would ever be questioned.

These people are being dealt with within the existing frame of reference of the field of psychology, an internally consistent belief system about cause and effect.

The recycling of results from the study of the internal consistency of each person's thought system is, therefore, of no value in bringing something new or more efficacious to the field of mental health. Any treatment program based on these results must also serve to reinforce and to maintain the client's current self-image. All theories now accepted in the field are based on certain assumptions of cause and effect, and are tested on the basis of hypotheses developed from the same underlying assumptions. The assumptions are that people do have real problems that come from somewhere in their pasts or in their physiological makeups. Given this frame of reference the job of psychology now is to surface more problems and ascertain their causes, within the existing theoretical framework.

These assumptions assure that we will not look more closely at the dynamics of what occurs as we move, moment to moment, from one frame of mind to another. These assumptions in themselves have acted as barriers for us as psychologists in terms of our understanding of how our thoughts are related to our experiences, and the underlying principles of how we actually change our minds (our thought systems) in our evolution to higher states of consciousness.

As a result of these misconceptions, the formal results of present-day psychological research are fed back to society in the forms of new disorders to look for, tests to uncover them, and new therapeutic techniques and methods to deal with an increasing list of problems. The results of research into the success of these therapies usually show mixed and uncertain results. Most psychological research usually ends up explaining the lack of results in terms of individual differences or variances among human beings — and our inabilities as psychologists to accurately measure and control them. We say this but do not follow what we are saying to its logical end. Instead, we typically recommend more searching because of our inconclusive results.

This picture is complicated by the placebo connection many of us make between thinking that something will work and at least will give the temporary experience of relief from chronic negative habits. In the following chapter, we will discuss these phenomena as they are manifested in the practice of psychology today.

CHAPTER 14

Today's Psychology in Practice: The Search for More Problems

Although psychology as a field is admittedly somewhat unclear about what it is itself doing, it has nonetheless become accepted within society as a health care provider. The field has defined itself as a provider of psychological aid. It has gone ahead and developed tools which can in theory identify those in need of such services. However, due to the fact that there exist so many divergent theories, a consensus as to who needs help for what or how to render such help has never been reached. As a result, each theoretical orientation has developed its own version of diagnostic tools. Even though psychological research continues to be inconclusive, thousands of psychological tests have been developed and are now routinely used as the basis of directing people's lives in this society. Since these tests fit the logic of people's insecurities about themselves, they lead to people continuing to look outside themselves for the solutions to what they think are problems. These products of inconclusive research have put the field of psychology itself in an inconclusive light in the eyes of society.

THEORY AND PSYCHOLOGICAL TESTING

The development of psychological tests provides another example of how a field can unknowingly self-limit its own scientific evolution by developing technological products which are valid only inasmuch as they are consistent with a particular theory.

Most psychological tests used today fall under the categories of what are referred to as *objective* or *projective* tests. The labeling of these tests as such, however, is misleading. Contrary to what most people believe, the designation of a test as objective or projective refers to the format of the test itself and not to any objective quality of the test logic or results. For example, if a test requires that the person taking it interpret pictures or designs, the test is considered to be projective. That is, the person's interpretations are considered by the examiner as a projection of an internal psychic state. On the other hand, if the test format consists of multiple choice questions or true-false questions in a questionnaire form, it is considered objective in nature.

What many people do not realize is that regardless of the test format the interpretations given to both types of test results are just that — interpretations. For in fact, how these tests are clinically interpreted has nothing necessarily to do with the condition of the person taking the test; it depends on the theoretical orientation of the psychometrist. As such, all these tests are theoretical and subjective.

The fact that all psychological tests are actually subjective by virtue of the fact that they are based on the theories of the testor is not always apparent since some tests have been standardized with regard to the interpretations given to a particular test pattern or response. This, however, does not change the subjective theoretical nature of the final product. All that is accomplished by standardizing a psychological test is that most of the professionals following a particular theory agree on a certain interpretation; that is, they are consistent. We often forget, however, that prior to Columbus, the vast majority of the Western world agreed that the world was flat — this belief was standardized in the culture and was consistent with the theories and the data of the times.

In essence what most psychological tests do is translate obvious human conditions (for example, retardation, criminality, anxiety, depression or anger) into complex psychological terms that theoretically explain problems we do not see for ourselves. As a result, many people have become life-long consumers of therapies or programs for conditions which are assumed by some theory to be the remedy for a problem that a test supposedly uncovered.

We have ourselves seen hundreds of clients who have developed long-lasting clinical self-images with complicated explanations as to why they exhibit certain behaviors and feelings. This all serves to keep them living within those versions of reality. We know mental health professionals who assert that they themselves will feel guilty or exhibit certain reactions the rest of their lives because of the type of parents they had or because of what the Minnesota Multiphasic Personality Inventory says about their personality styles or what some other test they took in graduate school revealed about their personality traits.

Such offspring as intelligence tests provide another example. A person's ability to memorize and repeat relative information pertaining to cultural literature, history, geography, vocabulary, and arithmetic is considered to be *verbal intelligence*. Likewise the ability to duplicate and/or complete different varieties of puzzles is considered to be the *performance intelligence*. Test scores depend on the time it took to answer and whether the answers were right or wrong. The results of such tests constitute what psychology has labeled *intelligence*. This has led to the common ironic situation where people of equivalent test *I.Q.*s do not act equally intelligent — the discrepancy may, in fact, be almost funny. As the old saying goes, *"He/she is really intelligent, but they cannot tie their own shoelaces."*

"High intelligence" as presently defined by psychology, does not guarantee us that we will not produce the feelings of anxiety, depression, insecurity, stress, delusions, prejudice, anger, hate, hostility, jealousy, or envy in ourselves which often lead to such destructive behaviors as suicide, killings, fights, stealing, hostagetaking and war. In fact, this so-called *high intelligence* doesn't even pretend to guarantee anyone a good marriage, a nice family life, a successful career or a peaceful and fulfilling life. The only thing these tests do predict is how well people will do on tasks similar to the I.Q. test.

We as human beings must at some point take a clearer look to see that there is a more profound and true intelligence than what we have previously recognized; an intelligence that can guide us to more creatively and positively use information for our own benefit and that of our society. Information, regardless of how voluminous or sophisticated, in the absence of the deeper intelligence we are calling common sense, wisdom and understanding is of absolutely no use toward helping us in our evolution. Information by itself can in fact be used to create and spread more superstitions and the negative rigidities which guard such ignorance.

STRESS AND THE FRAME OF REFERENCE OF PSYCHOLOGY

Recent newcomers to the arena of psychological inventories are the stress scales. These scales are actually lists of events such as birth, marriage, job promotion, and so forth with an associated numerical value representing the degree of stress thought to be inherent in them. People are supposed to add up the points associated with recent events in their lives. The sum total of points is assumed to tell persons how much stress they are under that perhaps they did not know about! If the subjects' total scores on these stress assessment surveys exceed certain criteria, they are told that they are in a high risk to experience some sort of mental, emotional and/or physical breakdown in the near future.

All life events included in these surveys are assumed to result in some stress. Some examples of these stressors are birth and death, marriage and divorce, job promotion and demotion, moving to another city or job — the list goes on. Stress, then, is considered to be a component of even such positive events as marriage, having a baby, getting a promotion and so forth. The more basic underlying assumption here is that stress is an unavoidable part of living. In essence, these types of tests point people in the direction of thinking and viewing their own lives as if they were composed of or made up of a continuous series of burdens or stressors which threaten their very well-being and survival. Thus, the presence or absence of stress is not the question in these surveys — just how much. It is often that we run into people whose tranquility has been disturbed by someone who unknowingly suggested to them that their lives added up to major risks. The effects of these psychological surveys on a society are, at best, stressful.

All of these stress scales again are developed from descriptive studies of those events that are stressful for people living within the confines of certain conditioned belief systems at given levels of insecurity or levels of consciousness. None of these theories or approaches to stress takes into account the existence of separate realities or the principles of levels of consciousness; that is, how we move in and out of separate realities. Therefore, these theories do not take into account the fact that a certain event can be less stressful or not at all stressful to an individual, even an individual who may have experienced that event as having been stressful in the past.

We personally have observed hundreds of individuals who are now easily carrying out jobs or succeeding in professions in situations which three years ago would not have been possible for them to manage without a high degree of stress. We have worked with nurses in intensive care units in hospitals and have seen the stress level drop from extremely high levels to almost nothing over a six-month's period with no change in personnel or other external variables. We have worked with law enforcement agencies and have seen police officers start to handle delicate situations with more mature judgment and calmness, merely as a result of their beginning to realize that each situation is only as stressful as it is interpreted to be.

Thus, we are realizing even more deeply that an identical situation exists in the case of personality and/or psychopathology tests. There is an ever-growing list of these tests being developed. All depend on each other or some established theory in order to be admitted to the established list of accepted tests. Once people take one of these tests, they are labeled as certain personality types. They are then, more often than not, stuck with these labels in relation to society. Many of these tests are used as a basis for directing the lives of children, adolescents, and adults based on the relative power of the labels which they apply such as *"schizophrenic," "psychotic," "neurotic," "feminine," "masculine," "hypochondriacal," "compulsive,"* and so forth.

Every time we assign a stress level to an event, or assign a label to a person, or a certain score on a psychological test, or a certain type of past, or even certain physiological characteristics we are literally making it hard for that person and people in general to become anything else but products of those causes. This occurs because most people who seek out psychological help are insecure to begin with and are looking for someone to tell them what is happening to them. In this sense they are very suggestible to any proposition that fits with the frameworks of their problems. In fact, many such people are unaware of their own roles in creating their problems and are receptive to some explanation that places the responsibilities for their experiences outside the boundaries of their own controls. As a result, we are inadvertently making it harder for them to understand for themselves principles of separate realities which could free them from their experiences of stress or emotional trauma and recurrent behavior patterns.

Psychological therapy that is carried out on the basis of such explanations serves to validate whatever diagnosis has been applied by finding causes and symptoms in the person's past and present life. The result of this process is that it keeps both the therapist and the patient at levels of understanding that are consistent with viewing their own lives in terms of someone else's theory of human behavior.

PSYCHOLOGY: WHAT IT DOES FOR PROBLEMS

All present-day psychological therapies have been derived from two major theoretical traditions: the analytical and the behavioral. The analytically derived theories in psychology (that is, Jungian, Adlerian, Gestalt) can be traced to the tradition initiated by Sigmund Freud. Although a great variety and number of combinations of these theories exist today, all share the same methodological direction introduced by Freud. In fact, many of the founders of subsequent therapies were students of Freud himself or were initially trained in Freudian thinking.

The dynamics of all these analytically derived systems deal with the *hypothesized* causes of behavior in the form of psychic entities and forces, along with a storyline from the past to the present in terms of how each of these factors relates to each other. The nature of the story about the past determines the category of problem and, in turn, dictates the detailed nature of the therapeutic ritual. Since it is considered impossible to deal directly with the causes themselves (for example, id, ego, archetype, and so on) or how they interrelate, these therapies focus on explaining the compulsive nature of present behaviors by pointing to causes from the past. Various techniques may then be explored to purge these behaviors and feelings from the person's psyche. These therapies, then, dissect and analyze people's past and/or present problems, emotions, viewpoints, fears, and reactions from the perspective of some theory which is used like a cookbook.

The behavioral therapies, on the other hand, have as their origins the learning/conditioning theories and concepts of theorists such as Ivan Pavlov and B. F. Skinner. Although fewer in number, when compared with the analytically derived theories, there are nonetheless a large variety of learning theories. Acknowledging that the theoretical constructs (causes) of learning could not be observed or measured, the resulting methodology focused exclusively and strictly on behavior. Behavior was measured, however, within a framework similar to the analytical approaches. The behavioral assessment includes the description and the analysis of the so-called present problem. This is followed by the assessment of the problem using the causal terms of learning: how long, how strong and how often the undesirable habit manifested itself in the past. This, it is thought, sheds light on the history of reinforcement as well as the past and present stimuli which contributed and/or contributes to its present elicitation and maintenance.

The resulting therapies then fall into the same pattern of dissecting and analyzing people's behaviors found in the other therapies. Which of the many variations of behavioral therapy is used, of course, depends on when and where the therapist was trained. However, in both the analytically derived and the behavioral therapies, there is a focus on the past (either conditioning or significant events) as being the cause of a behavior pattern that is now locked into the person and out of personal control, requiring the use of some external mechanism (re-conditioning, catharsis, analysis, or others) to purge or to alter the behavior. Thus, the fundamental assumptions underlying both classes of therapy, minus the details, are identical.

When these learning-theory based therapies reached the clinical market place, the emphasis was to seek out and uncover new and old negative behavior patterns with which to validate these therapies. Although initially hailed as the objective alternative to the subjective analysis of problems, the behavioral approaches merely introduced the conditioned analysis of conditioned problems.

A ROSE IS A ROSE

In addition to the major theoretical schools of thought mentioned, there are innumerable combinations and permutations of other theories and psychotherapies programatically packaged under a host of labels. By whatever name these programs are labeled, all are fundamentally the same in their assumptions, directions and results.

Once again, the reader should keep in mind that it is not the specific details or context of any theory that is right or wrong. Rather, we are simply pointing out how the very essence of any method or technique directs people to accept, to some degree, the fundamental assumptions of whatever theory they are associated with. Thus, although there are hundreds of theories and therapies which differ totally in content and detail, all are the same with respect to their fundamental assumptions.

All present-day psychotherapeutic practices, then, take a dim view of human potential. All feel that the way people behave now is determined by their pasts, out of their present controls and subject to change only by some outside manipulation done to the clients by the therapists, which often must be constantly repeated over long periods of time for it to have any effect at all. So, thus far, the effects people have been able to measure of any therapy have been inconsistent, inconclusive and often contradictory.

ACTIONS SPEAK LOUDER THAN WORDS

Some of the newer approaches such as rational, reality, responsibility and cognitive therapies would claim that they are operating from or adhering to the principles presented in this book. Yet, when we look more closely at these, we realize that what they are doing is contradicting what they are saying. For example, to get people to take more responsibility for their own thought systems, the therapists may hypnotize them or recommend some technique such as a positive validation or relaxation techniques or other ritualistic kinds of behaviors. As soon as the therapists do this, they are in effect stating that the ritual, technique, or method imposed on the patients from the outside will change their realities. This is never the case. Only each individual can change his or her own reality through a deeper realization of what that reality is. The use of any technique, no matter toward what enlightened state it is proported to lead, can only create another placebo or conditioned connection in the mind to that behavior or situation being responsible for whatever good feelings develop.

In one sense it is the insecurity of psychology about its ability to get the results desired that weds it to techniques, irrespective of theoretical orientation. We are known as the experts and therefore feel that we want to do something to help people. What we fail to realize is that the very doing of that something is in itself making it harder for us to really help people. Techniques create a barrier to giving people a deeper common sense about what they are doing themselves, moment to moment, via the vehicle of their own thought systems and their levels of consciousness, to create and maintain the unique versions of reality in which they live and experience all of their problems.

One key aspect of this unfortunate situation that psychology has failed to realize is that by thinking in this framework the potential psychology can possibly see in people is severely limited. The clients of the therapy system are then convinced by the powers that be of this limited potential in themselves. Faith healers know that they do not heal people, but that the people themselves believe strongly enough that they will be better, so they get better. They in essence heal themselves, although the faith healer would never want them to know this fact since it would ruin his business.

WHEN THE SHOES FIT, CLIENTS TEND TO WEAR THEM

There is no doubt that there are many people who are in need of guidance. As a field, however, we must begin to take a more compassionate look at the predicament of these people and realize that, due to their troubled states of mind, they are attracted to or actively seek out explanations which fit with their experiences and expectations. Many such people will accept a label and a treatment which appears to be consistent with their perceived troubles, not knowing that at the same time they are accepting more problems — problems that happen to fit the need of a field seeking acceptance in the health care marketplace.

The whole issue of psychology's tests of psychopathology, personality and intelligence, as well as its therapies has now prominently surfaced as people in society have begun to question their validity and utility. These issues have attracted society's gaze as it begins to realize the circular tendency of present-day psychological thinking and explanations. Unless we as psychologists begin to honestly look at these issues from a fresh perspective to see their validity, we will be acting in essence to promote the institutionalization of societal irresponsibility on the part of our own profession and will ignorantly label others who then become the chronic consumers of products which must be used continually in order to keep one's well-being in life.

CHAPTER 15

Today's Psychology in Effect: The Price for Treating an Illusion

Over the last several years we have realized that it is not necessary to look at problems or to go back in the past in order to help people. However, the state of the art of psychology today is to look at the problems, take them seriously, and try to do something with them. This tradition, as we have stated, has been handed down in the field of psychology since the early work of Freud and has continued as an almost habitual approach regardless of our espoused theories.

The lack of long-term results from any set of techniques has prompted us to take a fresh look at the field of psychology. We have realized that, contrary to Freud and most of psychology since his time, there is absolutely no value in going back into our pasts even one minute to figure out or to analyze or to do anything with the behavioral patterns we have picked up over the course of our lifetimes. All of these experiences and all of our present attitudes, habits, reactions and insecurities are only memories. They are thought patterns that we have decided for whatever reason to keep around from our pasts.

The way to drop these thought patterns is to realize that they are now only illusions made up in our own thoughts. Most of us have not realized this fact because we have grown up thinking that the way we see life now is unchangingly real. We give credence to our judgments, biases and memories, the neurotic patterns and the beliefs we have accumulated. This is the reality we see and, just like Archie Bunker, it makes sense to us. It is our *"Linus-blanket"* in life and whatever it is it has gotten us this far even if we are still insecure and suffering.

THE DISADVANTAGES OF PSYCHOLOGY FROM THIS FRAME OF REFERENCE

The counterproductiveness of how psychology is now practiced must at some point be recognized. Psychology, as it is today, keeps these memories, the bundles of negative thought patterns, around by getting people to analyze them, learn to deal with them, express them, re-experience them, and so on. Freud pointed psychology in the wrong direction by focusing on the garbage — the fears and reactive behavior from our pasts. In essence, he institutionalized them in the name of mental health.

Our research, trainings and consulting experiences during the last ten years have shown us that everyone has the capability of rapidly and directly developing innate common sense or wisdom about life to the point where the craziness of keeping these patterns around can be recognized and these patterns are forgotten.

It is unfortunate that today's psychology, via its theories and rituals, points people in a direction opposite to that which would allow them to realize for themselves the role that their own thinking plays in their perceptions of life. This is unfortunate because the real key to our mental health is when we start to see the power of our own thoughts. When we start to notice that, whatever we are thinking, *we are*. The world we see, from our subjective frames of reference, creates the world we live in. No matter how bad that reality is, it is still a fact that what creates our experiences of life is the sum total of our judgments and the perceptual biases that we have picked up and instituted in our thinking. Everyone is the same in that respect, until he or she begins to become aware of what is happening; to begin to actually recognize how this process works in each person.

Contrary to many assumptions within the field of psychology today, gaining the ability to change one's mind for the better is natural. As soon as we get a glimpse of the fact that we are creating what we see and that everyone else is doing the same thing, we gain the power to change our realities.

Everyone innately knows how to be happy. The only thing we can accomplish using exclusively our intellectual information is to get in the way of our natural wisdom, intuitive understanding, self-esteem and spontaneous enjoyment of life. We start to believe what people tell us that we need; or have to have to become happy, successful or free from our neurosis, our recurrent problems in work, in our marriage, in other relationships and other areas of our lives. Every school of therapy has its own theory, whether it is to express feelings honestly, to be assertive, to learn relaxation techniques, or whatever ritual that particular theory tells us we need to become happy.

THE TRAP OF TECHNIQUES IN GENERAL

The fallacy and the dangers of psychological techniques exist only because they perpetuate more problems by assuming the problems are real and that we must search into our pasts in order to find the causes. Most of psychology today as well as personal growth organizations who offer seminars on human relations, motivation and stress use some technique or mehod to get people to change bad habits; to work through their negative feelings; to work on, to deal or to cope with their stresses and insecurities; to practice skills in the form of techniques for relating, communicating, problem solving, goal setting, listening, alleviating or resolving conflict.

All of these techniques lead to the same trap. First, they take seriously what we now perceive and feel, thereby literally validating and justifying our fears, insecure thoughts and distorted beliefs, and giving them even more power. Secondly, they tell us that we cannot go directly to the sources of these thought patterns, gaining a deeper understanding of our own minds to see the illusionary quality of these bundles of memories, judgments, and fears. Rather, we must rely on some outside mechanism to relieve us temporarily at best — of the constant experiences of these feelings and behavior patterns. These mechanisms now popular in the field range from yoga, meditation, cross-country skiing, mountain climbing, expressing feelings, rolfing, rebirthing, getting angry at parents to understanding all the games we play, or learning skills to become assertive, a good listener, centered or more relaxed. Every one of these is, in actual fact, counterproductive.

Therapies that teach methods of fair fighting or that involve expressing any negative feelings are themselves forms of insecurity. It isn't hard to see how these therapies actively validate and authenticate our judgments and thoughts. It is only such thoughts that create our negative feelings. Again, we must go one step further and eliminate the sources in our own insecurities of these thoughts, and their importance to our own senses of self-esteem. We have known hundreds of couples who have sought help in the personal growth arena and then started fighting about whose trip was better, who was more out of touch with their feelings and on and on. We can attach our insecurities and needs to prove ourselves to any form that exists. Couples cannot get to happiness by addressing or by even talking about their problems.

THE EMPEROR'S NEW CLOTHES

All methods and techniques are bound in direction and principle to the thought patterns creating their needs. The rehearsal of a preconceived, prechoreographed ritual promotes the existence of the very problem it was designed to eliminate. In much the same way the wearing of garlic or a bone of a deceased temporarily gives the feeling that one is safe from vampires and evil spirits, the very ritual literally validates the illusion. The final product is a human being whose pattern of behavior is a ritualistic, noncreative therapeutic plaster which is bound to a problem-oriented existence. There are numerous examples of such ritualitic behaviors that are so stereotypical it is immediately possible to tell what type of therapy they have been through and what problems they have encountered. Such people are as helplessly bound to their therapeutic rituals as they were to their problems. Woody Allen and Bob Newhart are two American comedians who most accurately portray this dilemma in their comedy routines.

SEEING THE PLACEBO EFFECTS OF TECHNIQUES

The best that any of these can accomplish is to have a placebo effect because *what we think, we are!* If we believe something will work, it will have some effect. However, since we do not realize that our own thoughts about the relation of that *sugar pill* to the result are the sources of the change, we keep having to go back to the technique over and over to get even temporary relief, or to go on to some new technique — which many people do when the old one stops working.

THE TRAP OF INTELLECTUAL UNDERSTANDING

What anyone of us has gone through in life, accomplished, experienced or think we have learned has absolutely nothing to do with understanding or gaining back our deeper common sense about life. We know plumbers, pipefitters, housewives, real estate salesmen, personnel specialists, managers, businessmen, paraplegics and quadraplegics who have a more profound understanding of people than many psychologists or personal growth leaders we have met — and we have met and worked with many of the best-known people in the field.

It has been of great interest and benefit to our learning over the last several years to witness the reaction of mental health professionals to what we are presenting. To begin with, each individual initially asked questions which were directly related to whatever theoretical system he or she had adopted and/or was trained in. The answers the majority of these professionals would consider were those which in some way kept valid or supported their particular theoretical beliefs. The majority of these individuals — all in some manner stated they did not understand what we were presenting or even its applicability to mental health — queried if the theories they were listening with differed from what we were addressing.

In yet other instances, we know many professionals who tell us that they are in total agreement with us and with what we are saying. Many have attended our seminars and conferences over the years and have pledged their support. Yet in the next breath, the very same people will tell someone about their latest experience of being rebirthed back to the womb or to the state where they experience their *"spermatozoic" mind,* floatation tank meditation, talking to empty chairs, and so on. These people honestly think that they fully understand the power of thought, while they are at the same time giving power to these external placebos to create new experiences.

THE BLIND LEADING THE BLIND

It is not surprising that mental health professionals and personal growth leaders are the ones who initially actually have the most difficult time grasping what we are attempting to demonstrate to the field. We can understand and empathize with their situations since these are the people who would naturally feel they have the most to lose particularly if they are basing their livelihoods on the methods or processes in which they were trained.

They may feel that they have to deny years of training and the development of their techniques or therapies. Most are actively involved in living out their own techniques, which have become integral parts of their lifestyles, their ways of relating to people and the sources of their own self-esteem. These are the people who espouse releasing anger and become enmeshed by doing this to their friends; use it so well as the source of their self-esteem, and actually become immersed in this belief-system as a way of life. There are the people who use megavitamins and see all change in themselves coming from that source; people who believe in psychic energy actually experiencing the illusion of this energy emanating from their pores.

Over the last few years we have begun to appreciate more the early frustrations Einstein must have had in attempting to get Newtonian-trained physicists, who had built their careers on what they had been trained to do and look for in their work, to see what he was trying to show them.

PANDORA OPENED PANDORA'S BOX

The more we examine and observe the results of what we are doing, the more our own understanding deepens, and the more we see the limitations of the state of the art today. Psychology as a field is perhaps worse than most because there are so many divisions, specialties and schools of thought, all of which are in competition with each other for patients. Everyone is caught up in the details of his own area, looking at the nature and manifestations of those specific kinds of problems and, therefore, cannot see the bigger picture where all the answers lie! The result of this focus and searching for answers in techniques means that each sector will continue to surface more and more problems.

Many of the problems psychology has been surfacing and labeling over the last twenty years are literally made up. This creates a new field or specialty, which then, in turn, gives people trained in this specialty a way to make a living. *"Mid-life crisis"* is an example of this phenomenon. People now specialize not only in categories of problems, but also in different age, sex and ethnic groups in terms of clients. We know specialists in the sexuality of physically handicapped women over 55, specialists in assertiveness training for middle-class boys between the ages of 15 and 17, and specialists on smoking problems of teenage girls between 13 and 16.

HURTING THOSE WE WISH TO HELP

A clear illustration of how this process works to create and institute new problems can be seen in what has resulted as a function of officially sanctioning the past as the cause of present problems. The mental health professions have just attached themselves to the concept of Post Traumatic Stress Disorders to explain our present problems on the basis of our past negative experiences. In doing so, they have unfortunately reinforced the illusion that the past has some kind of force independent of and beyond our present control. This force then has the power to affect our emotions, our behaviors and our lives.

As people in the field incorporate this concept into their practices, they are doing so in the context of the specific populations they are working with and the theoretical orientations they presently hold. Thus, for example, those specializing in psychological problems of women have focused on what they or their clients presently perceive to be past significant traumatic experiences particular to being a woman. Those specializing in specific ethnic groups stress the past in terms of traumatic events having to do with ethnic racial problems. Likewise, those using this concept as a vehicle to help military or ex-military personnel have sought to explain this particular group's present problems in terms of past negative experiences particular to being in the military.

This latter example has led the government health facilities to focus on Vietnam as a past traumatic event which could be causing the problems. Accordingly, the label of *"Post-Vietnam Syndome"* has surfaced as a new disease requiring specialized treatment by specialized staff at specialized centers. This disorder is, by definition, suffered by the ex-Vietnam veteran. This new syndrome allows veterans to lead normal lives most of the time (even up to approximately ten years) until some day, some unspecified stress triggers off a mental breakdown which may take the form of craving for excitement (learned from the war), anxiety, depression, or acting out hostile behaviors. In turn, this may lead to problems in marriage, job, or with society. The therapies recommended for this syndrome include discussing past Vietnam experiences, reliving and analyzing their experiences to get out their hostility in order to deal with or rechannel it.

The creation of this new syndrome is now finding its way into court cases to explain and to defend the behaviors of veterans who have attempted robberies, murder and other antisocial behavior. The use of diagnostic labels to prove legal irresponsibility is certainly not new. This topic has been debated for years. Perhaps it is time, however, to simply recognize that this merely represents another variation associated with the existing framework of thought found in mental health professions today. Then we can go one step further to realize the societal implications that go along with this level of help.

This is not to imply that people who went to war did not experience stress. On the contrary, war is stressful. We are merely pointing out that the stress experienced in war is not the cause of any present hostile, violent or disturbed behavior. Any present problems being experienced by such veterans are products of their present states of mind. The obvious and most common-sensical way to help such people out of their problems is to simply offer whatever help and assistance we are willing to provide and give it now. To invent and display diagnostic labels only serves to validate and to foster people's attachments to their pasts, their insecurities and their problems.

We have spoken to literally hundreds of World War II, Korean and Vietnam veterans who have already noticed how these programs are in practice counterproductive. They can see that we are merely blowing something out of proportion and giving it more power than it deserves. Ironically, we have also talked to thousands of Vietnam veterans, many of whom had significant combat experiences, injuries and disabilities, who by virtue of their common sense have been able to place their pasts in more proper perspective. Many of these people, in turn, have let go totally of many problems they once thought to be caused by *"Post-Vietnam Syndrome."*

This situation is a beautiful example of how we can connect or associate anything with something and come up with a new theory, even a new mental illness instead of simply helping those who are in need and want to be helped. We could literally, if we want, manufacture a theory that children watch action-adventure shows on television and develop a craving for excitement, which leads them as adults to steal cars, rob banks, beat up their wives and do other nasty things. Since most people now have watched these kinds of shows on television when they were young, we could do research and show a correlation. We could then make a fortune defending and treating people who might otherwise be considered criminals.

RECOGNIZING INSECURITY

The truth is, however, that every problem we have now stems from our present levels of insecurity. Insecurity creates fear and boredom, which is merely the ego's need to be keeping something happening to make it feel special. The drug of excitement is just like any other substance we take to deaden our insecurities. We know people who drag themselves from party to party every night with a hangover from the night before because they are afraid of being alone.

The insecurity that leads to any form of destructive behavior never rests, but manifests itself in different ways. If we cannot go out drinking, we fight with our spouses, or gamble compulsively, or engage in destructive affairs, or pick fights in bars. This insecurity then spills over to our children who may smoke, drive fast cars, use drugs or alcohol and join movements or other groups to cover their insecurities. The insecurity of a child may take a very different form than that of the parent, but this insecurity is what the parent is really passing along to the child.

It is vitally important to understand more deeply than psychology has to date the dynamics of how insecurity works prior to its emergence in any particular form and context. Insecurity triggers insecurity. Yet the form in which it emerges in one person may be, and usually is, quite different from the form it takes as a result of another's acquired thought system. Once we truly begin to recognize what insecurity is and how it works at this deeper level, the form becomes secondary. Only then can we truly teach others to drop their insecurities the way that will allow them to change at will their maladaptive behaviors.

In Oregon a nationally funded experiment on behavior

modification for acting-out children was attempted with the parents of these children. While the classes were going on and the observers were in the home, the parents were able to remember the techniques of positive reinforcement. However, within a few months after the observers left, the parents reverted back to their old habitual patterns of reaction. This happens with all techniques because the underlying insecurities of the parents have not changed.

A parent who is not insecure will pass on security, will share good feelings with the children and will know what to do when upset. Patterns of acting out will never get started. Any techniques with any client, family, or group must end in failure because the underlying insecurity is not altered.

The attempt to make the techniques work will cause more insecurity; since we worry if we are doing it right, we blame ourselves when we forget and react from our conditioned responses and insecurities. Insecurity only vanishes when we decide to stop creating insecurity. We begin to stop creating insecurity when we see that the bundle of insecure thoughts is an illusion, something we are making up. It stops when we see that this bundle of insecure thoughts is the source of all our stress, bad feelings and upsets. We see how crazy it is to keep doing it. The back and forth nature of these thoughts is endless: *Am I a good enough lover? too passive? too aggressive? Am I strict enough as a parent? too strict? Why didn't I marry my high school sweetheart? or take that other job? Couldn't I have gotten a better deal on my car?* and on and on and on.

As the illusionary quality of these thoughts starts to be realized, the thoughts become less important. Then they start to come less often and our minds begin to quiet down, letting our common sense come in and show us the easy way to handle life by understanding it rather than by trying to figure it out. Once this change occurs, we often get a laugh out of how we were running around attempting to find answers to questions we made up and to solve problems our minds were creating.

CHAPTER 16

Today's Psychology In Essence: The Self-Fulfilling Nature of Its Orientation

When we watch Archie Bunker on television, we see that Archie thinks he would be happier if Meathead would quit raiding the refrigerator or stop disagreeing with his politics. Yet if Meathead actually stopped these behaviors, we have faith that Archie would find something else to react against. We laugh when we see Archie and Meathead raging at each other on the T.V. screen; but if we could honestly take a look at ourselves and see how deeply and completely we are the same with our own versions of reality, we could laugh at ourselves in much the same way we laugh at Archie and Meathead. Most of the stimuli in our perceived environments are just like Pavlov's bell — they bring out conditioned reactions which we then allow to control our behaviors at that point.

All techniques in psychology are basically the same as well. They act as placebos or sugar pills, providing an association that gives temporary relief. Others are downright destructive since they attach our mental health and well-being to the craziest rituals such as being re-birthed, rolfed, or sitting in an uncomfortable position. Some techniques are aimed at building up the ego, in fact, a destructive thing to do to anyone. We have seen group leaders tell people to yell or to scream at someone they envy in order to boost their self-esteems. We have seen people in personal growth seminars harrassed, put down, intimidated and embarassed by leaders. People pay horrendous sums of money to be degraded, to be shoved under water, to stare at the wall for twelve hours repeating *"who am I"* or to release their primal screams. All of these activities would be funny and are funny except that they are perpetrated on ignorant people searching for some relief and sanity while all they are getting is more insanity.

In more traditional therapies, if someone gets depressed or upset and goes to a therapist, the therapist will find associations from past and present behaviors to validate a diagnostic label of *"chronic depressive"* or some other category of problem. Convinced of being troubled, the person really is neurotic or paranoid or whatever the theory and diagnosis happen to be from that therapist. We have seen different therapists tell people that they have totally opposite problems from the last therapists' diagnoses, yet no professional told them that they did not have problems serious enough to warrant therapy.

HOW TO ACT SANE IN AN INSANE PLACE

In an experiment we mentioned earlier that was carried out in 1973, normal people — mentally healthy professionals — were admitted as patients to various mental institutions. The staff were unaware they were not real patients. They were diagnosed as being psychotic even though they exhibited normal behaviors on the ward. Each person mentioned that they were closer to their mother when young and closer to their father when they were older. This was sufficient evidence for them to be classified as having some form of psychopathology. One patient was told he possessed an ambivalence in relationships that was characteristic of his form of schizophrenia. If any patient arrived at the cafeteria early for lunch, this was evidence of the oral acquisitiveness nature of the syndrome; in other words, another symptom of schizophrenia. Attendants could do just about anything they wanted with a patient since any irritation or anger was invariably diagnosed as a symptom of the patient's illness.

None of these normal patients was diagnosed as not mentally ill except by other patients.

One of the main points made by the psychologist who carried out this innovative study was that, based on our present-day level of thinking, the diagnostic labels that the mental health field bestows on people are, in fact, themselves negative in nature. These labels endure even after people leave the mental health setting. They are not only incorporated into the patients' thinkings, but also into the perceptions and expectations of relatives, friends and society. These labels are most often eventually accepted by the patients themselves due to their insecurities. All of the varied and excessive meanings that these labels carry become the guiding principle for the lives of people who accept them.

Throughout all the many studies that have been carried out of why people end up in institutions, the only statistically valid predictor of whether someone has a good chance of going to an institution is whether he or she has been there before. If the person has been institutionalized, there is greater than an eighty per cent chance that that individual will return. In the eyes of society, family and friends, what can be expected from a person who is *schizophrenic* or who is supposedly a psychological time bomb because of *post-traumatic stress disorder?* Is a happy life anticipated that includes beautiful family and a good job; or is it abnormal behavior, imminent breakdown and rehospitalization? We as professionals must begin to see that we have been supplying ourselves with our own clients in a roundabout manner that, up to this point, we have not recognized.

WE REAP WHAT WE SOW

Eighty-five per cent rescidivism rates in state and federal hospitals are normal for most inpatient care programs. In fact, the only program anywhere we know of that lowered this rate to any significant degree was a program carried out experimentally through the University of Wisconsin. Rather than doing any of the traditional forms of therapy or diagnosis, they moved a group of chronic schizophrenics to aids' quarters on the hospital grounds. They taught these people how to live independently, to shop, pay rent, cook their meals, collect welfare checks, apply for jobs, do budgets and clean house. After a few months, the patients were moved into apartments outside the hospital and lived on their own. Everyone (landlord, shopkeeper, social worker and others) who dealt with these patients was told to ignore any behavior that seemed unusual, and to always maintain the belief that these people were just as capable as anyone of making rational decisions and handling their own lives.

The rescidivism rate for this group was under thirty per cent, and over eighty per cent of those who stayed out of the hospital got and held regular jobs. The reason that this experiment worked was because there was a profound truth in the statement, *"what you see is what you get."* Since the authors of this study held the hypothesis that what these people lacked were basic living skills, rather than being crazy, these patients were merely unable to do certain things. Thus the program spent time coaching and teaching them very practical things.

If we look one level deeper, we can see that what mostly occurred was a re-conditioning from one set of learned responses to another set, with no real understanding given to the patient about what was going on. The underlying insecurity of the patient has not changed that much, it merely changes form.

Extreme forms of disorganized behavior patterns which can be manifested in the conditions presently labeled functional psychoses (schizophrenia), neuroses (anxiety, phobias), personality disorders and situation reactions all represent the experiences of varying degrees of insecure feelings and emotions. Such feelings and emotions of insecurity can include any degree of fear, panic, anger, jealousy, envy, suspiciousness, paranoia, helplessness, and hopelessness. How, where and towards whom or what (including oneself) these feelings are associated depends on the existing associations stored in the acquired frame of reference of a person's thought system.

MENTAL ILLNESS AND LEVELS OF CONSCIOUSNESS

These severe emotional and behavioral disorders, then, exist to all degrees and levels. When people are so-called *crazy,* they are caught up in a world of insecure thoughts. These experiences reflect the circular disordered thinking which is relatively, and to degrees, devoid of understanding. Due to the fact that these realities exist at low levels of understanding or relative ignorance about the role that one's own thought plays in the creation of feelings and overall well-being, people attempt to think their way out of themselves. As a result, nothing really provides satisfaction. The more the insecurity, the less we think that we can handle all the perceived demands, pressures, people and details of our lives. If we go to a therapist and he or she provides evidence from our pasts that we are mentally ill, we may feel embarrassed; but mostly in that state of mind, we feel relief. Our insecurities have found a form to attach themselves to on the outside, again with no different an effect from alcohol or drugs, a form that temporarily relieves insecurity or makes it more manageable.

The longer we are in therapy, the more we learn about our symptoms, the causes and the true seriousness of our problems; the more we step into that act or role in life. This role becomes familiar and comfortable. If we end up in a mental institution, we are then provided with higher level educations in becoming better patients, just as people who go to prison learn how to become more hardened criminals.

In the early seventies, the National Institute of Mental Health led a drive in most states to deinstitutionalize mental patients; that is, to move them into halfway houses in community-based day treatment programs in an attempt to dramatically reduce the population of state institutions. One of the reasons behind this drive was the finding that the only statistically valid predictor of whether someone will end up in a state psychiatric hospital was the fact that the person had been there previously. Many community mental health center outpatient programs feared this change because therapists already had client loads of 85 to 100 clients, many of whom had been clients for over fifteen and sometimes as many as twenty years. We are not pointing out these facts to judge or to put down the mental health field. We realize that everyone is doing the best that can be done, yet the facts do speak for themselves and cannot be explained away. The facts are that the field is not getting the results that we as professionals would like to see. We must be willing to take an honest, open look at what we are doing now and why it doesn't work. Only then will we be able to look in new directions for what really might help.

The mental health system unknowingly creates and perpetuates its clients. If patients in the studies and programs we have previously mentioned saw what was happening themselves, they would have realized that they were being taught to transfer their insecurities to other forms, which then were continually reinforced in them by the people around them. Once they became used to these new forms, they became accustomed to these new routines and pretty much stayed close to the behaviors they were taught. These people will continue to live outside the state hospital — which is nice — but will not likely marry, buy homes, get promoted, eventually own their own businesses or evolve in their maturity throughout life, until they become aware of the sources of their insecurities and how these insecurities are related to how they experience their lives.

Throughout the course of all the experiments discussed above, the question of whether any of the patients were themselves happier or more at ease never comes up; nor is this criterion normally considered in any therapy model as a useful standard for evaluating the results of any program. Behavior modeling or behavior modification programs are the worst in this respect since they are only concerned with whether the behavior has changed. The client could feel even more miserable carrying out the new pattern of behavior and no one may even know it. If a patient is insecure in a lower state of consciousness, he or she will experience negativity in any situation.

We have a friend who became depressed during graduate school at Cornell when he started to question the purpose of getting his Ph.D. (This kind of feeling is probably experienced at one time or another by every Ph.D. candidate we have ever known, including ourselves.) He then went to a counselor who found out from our friend's past the reason he had to be depressed. He took a series of tests and was diagnosed as a chronic depressive personality. He was convinced of the truth of this diagnosis, and his depression became longer and deeper. He eventually spent time in a state institution, still depressed. He came out to live in a halfway house, still depressed. He continued to see three therapists weekly; he went to a Freudian, an Ericksonian and a psychiatrist who prescribed psychotropic medication. He had an affair with his Freudian psychiatrist, a woman who was very unhappy in her marriage; was hypnotized by the Ericksonian therapist; and was constantly moved from one medication to the other by his doctor, without result. He was still depressed.

At this point in his life, he was seriously considering jumping off the Golden Gate bridge. From a brief phone conversation made to tell us that he was about to end his life, he heard something that stopped him. He started to see that his chronic low mood was the result of all the thoughts, beliefs and theories he had accepted. His self-image, his world, was one of hopelessness. He was not even trying to make things work, knowing beforehand he would not be able to hold a job, that he could not make any relationship work. He had become unkempt and slovenly, not caring how he dressed or looked, which of course reinforced the impression he believed would be created in others. He woke up a little and saw the illusionary quality of his reality.

His life has turned around 180 degrees since that time. He now has his own apartment, a regular job and is applying to graduate schools. He has lost weight, and the last we saw him was almost totally unrecognizable as the same person he had been before. This person is no different from anyone on earth.

We all, in terms of our personalities, lifestyles and beliefs, are walking around in illusionary realities, worlds we keep recreating every day from our thought systems. It is only when we begin to realize this fact for ourselves that we can begin to change the quality of our worlds. We can move from one city to another, from one relationship to another, from one job to another; but if our levels of personal insecurity remain the same, the quality of our lives will remain the same. We will continue to have similar problems and patterns in relationships, the same difficulties in work, the same physical problems.

We have seen people, who can afford it, go from Greece to India to the Himalayas or to the Carribean looking for answers. However, the only time their lives really change is when they raise their own levels of consciousness and begin to see their lives from more positive feelings, common sense and higher self-esteem.

It is an interesting paradox that in lower levels of consciousness we only really experience one reality wherever we go. At higher levels of consciousness, we can literally walk in and out of separate realities, richly and deeply experience that culture, lifestyle, and the lives of people in that setting, without being caught up in the seriousness, judging, reacting and upsets that come from being immersed in those realities. As we move to higher and higher levels of consciousness life becomes richer, fuller, and much saner.

WAS THE EARTH REALLY FLAT BEFORE IT BECAME ROUND?

There is absolutely no doubt that what is being put forth in this book is difficult to understand within the existent frame of reference of psychology today. Psychology as a field has had a hard enough time dealing with itself as a collection of conflicting theories. The answer to this dilemma is not more analyzing, synthesizing or integration of existing theories. Neither will it be fruitful to introduce another theory as has been done so frequently in the past. Rather, we as scientists must see that we are in the same predicament as a person who seeks an answer to a problem, but at the same time lacks understanding and therefore adheres, defends and promotes the patterns of misunderstanding which stand in the way of the knowledge sought. As a profession we must realize that our theories are thoughts, products of the very thought systems we wish to understand. The memorization and the integration of our theoretical products merely add up to the recycling of our own pasts, albeit in various and diverse patterns. We as behavioral scientists must realize that we thought this theoretical diversity into existence and that diversity cannot explain itself; it can only attest to the creative power of mind.

As a field, mental health today stands in a self-made predicament: we have fostered an illusion where life is seen as complex, serious and in need of more theory to explain it. We have created puzzles which, theoretically, people must put together with the aid of mental health professionals before mental health can be realized; without knowing, however, we have done the same to ourselves.

IT IS TIME THAT WE IN THE FIELD OF PSYCHOLOGY WAKE UP

In order to truly help people, we as mental health professionals must literally turn around and look in the opposite direction. We must realize that the tradition initiated by Freud has led us to follow negativity; and the longer we muck around in the garbage, the longer we will stay in the garbage, even though we can describe it beautifully, where it came from, how we picked it up and how it smells.

We must stop and take a hard, searching look at what our effect has been on society. If we really took an honest, hard look at the results, we would see that we are unknowingly doing more harm than good. Most theories, techniques and methods used in the field of psychology today are at the least counterproductive and at most actually harmful to people because they keep people's focuses on their distorted fears, problems and insecurities. In addition, there are almost as many methods around in psychology today for doing this as there are practitioners. Every new technique attracts a new set of followers, often many who have tried other techniques without success, or who have fallen into what we call the *psychotherapeutic* or *personal growth* lifestyles. None of these methods does any more than change the form through which we act out our insecurities.

The first thing that we as a field and a profession must start to realize is that it really, honestly does not matter what the details of our emotional patterns or reactivities are, nor does it matter where they come from. What is important to realize is that we all live in separate realities; subjective psychological sets or frames of reference through which we uniquely interpret and then react to life. The subjective perceptual field is the sum total of our conditionings, beliefs, patterns of behavior from our parents, peers and past socialization, training and education, cultural backgrounds and significant events in our lives.

However, it is totally unnecessary to delve into the details of this frame of reference. All that is needed is to recognize that this frame of reference is to a large extent now an illusion, merely the way we have been programmed in whatever ways to view the world; and how this illusionary or distorted view of reality is kept in place by our egos — our definitions of our personal identities and images of self-importance, our thoughts of insecurity, NOW. Realizing this fact in itself releases our natural potential to develop our own maturity and natural understanding of life by ourselves, letting go of our attachments to our pasts and to our problems.

Freud and most of us in the field of mental health since Freud have literally kept ourselves and others in the dark ages about mental health. All we do is develop a finer and finer understanding of where our problems come from or of the garbage or mental illness which is itself the ignorance, darkness or lostness of each of us in our own pasts, in our own distorted and biased beliefs and perceptions, attitudes and fears. The answer lies outside or beyond this whole bundle of thoughts, feelings and reactions. However, we cannot get out of the swamp by digging deeper into it. All we can do is to see this whole bundle for what it is, and how we are operating psychologically now to keep it around, and then to stop keeping it around!

It is ironic, but nonetheless true, that initially we have had more success in dealing with ordinary people and business executives, with non-mental health professionals and people who do not have any particular investment or interest in a particular theory about human behavior. In our consulting work with managers, we have found that businessmen are grateful for gaining new perspectives; to step beyond their present frames of reference; to see a wider range of forces affecting their situations than they had previously seen; to see other people's frames of reference with more clarity; to more deeply understand how they sometimes get caught up in patterns of insecurity or reactivity to situations and to people in a way that clouds objectivity and the ability to make confident decisions based on clear, unbiased assessments of all the forces and variety of perceptions acting on those situations. Similarly, our experiences with individual clients and fellow colleagues in other health professions have become simplified and more reflective of the value of what we are sharing.

In summary, we realize that what we are sharing and the results we are observing constitute a major breakthrough for psychology and for people in general gaining access to a deeper common sense, self-esteem, tranquility and wisdom about life, beyond their bundles of fears, neuroses and insecurities. However, up to now we in the field of psychology have been busy trying to find ourselves and have been unable to understand these results. We feel that it is terribly important in these times of stress, social changes, and with more and more people becoming clients of the mental health system, to release this knowledge to the general public. Once the general public begins to pick up this wisdom, then perhaps the whole field of psychology will have to take a look. Then we as mental health practitioners will really be able to begin to do the job we are trying to do, and to help people who really need help.

Psychology as a field must begin to look for knowledge with more humility. If we already knew, we wouldn't be looking. In the next section of this book, we will explore in more depth the implications of what we are learning for the future evolution of the fields of therapy, mental health education and human relations training; and for the direction and practice of psychological research; and for our evolving understanding of human behavior.

SECTION V

A NEW DIRECTION FOR THE FIELDS OF PSYCHOLOGY AND MENTAL HEALTH

CHAPTER 17

The Evolution of the Helping Professions: The New Direction of Therapy

The principal route to mental health is to go as straight as possible in the direction of positive feelings and wisdom. We do not and cannot, contrary to the basic tenets of today's therapies, follow our problems or solve our problems to get to mental health. We must first develop our understanding and happiness, then the problems we had will themselves be taken care of easily. They will end the way nightmares end when we wake up; we will stop being immersed in, and taking as real, those illusionary realities.

As we go to higher levels of consciousness, we can easily see how our previous reactions and habits have gotten us in trouble. We can also see more clearly how others' conditioned views of reality are getting them in trouble without blame, judgment, guilt or anger. Thus, from higher states of consciousness, we are our own therapists. We see through our own problems and are aided by natural senses of self-esteem and good feeling that bring humor to previously stressful situations. Yet the art or the understanding of moving to higher levels of consciousness again has nothing at all to do with anyone's specific set of problems. Those are the results of whatever level of consciousness the person was in when those problems were created.

THE DIRECTION OF PRESENT-DAY THERAPY

Unaware of how levels of consciousness work, present-day

psychology applies therapeutic rituals to clients when they are in lower levels of consciousness; that is, when they are distressed. This cannot possibly be of value because the clients can only understand from those levels intellectual concepts about how to be happy. Traditionally, even when the client is temporarily relieved, he or she is encouraged for the purposes of assessment or treatment to in some way relive, confront and dredge up negative events from the past to talk about, discuss, and/or share. In reality, the therapist is (without knowing it) directing the patient to leave their well-being behind and to increase their self-consciousness — this is exactly the opposite of a therapeutic process.

These misconceptions have resulted in the wide array of therapies, treatment and self-help approaches that are now marketed, most with ambiguous results. The state of the art of psychology today is much like the field of astronomy in the days when all of the equations and models describing the movements of the heavens were calculated using the earth as the center point. This misconception generated very complex, often conflicting models and theories. In much the same manner, psychology as a field has used the past and the notion of prior experiences or conditioned patterns of learning as a starting point. When these assumptions are used, it is impossible to begin to understand the principles that determine the moment-to-moment activation of our habitual thought patterns because we are looking at the result not the cause of our experiences.

WHAT THERAPY SHOULD DO

It is in the higher states of consciousness when people are relatively happy and free from their own insecure thought patterns that therapy can help. True therapy is for the therapist to share personal knowledge and common sense about how thought relates to life. All people, regardless of whether or not they are labeled schizophrenic, paranoid, phobic, depressed, anxious, or distraught in the past, at some point have had the experience of having fun, being happy, or feeling gratitude for something. It is at these times when people are not caught up in the details of their thought systems and are relatively open that they are able to listen to and to realize deeper insights about the real sources of their problems. Any attempt to bring up past problems, to analyze assumed negative tendencies, or to share negativity is sharing ignorance. How can a negative experience be labeled therapeutic when the purpose of therapy is to guide people away from their own negativities and not toward them? It is through allowing more and more natural feelings of well-being to exist by not creating interference with the habitual insecure thought patterns which brings the lasting results everyone seeks.

MOVING CLIENTS AWAY FROM NEGATIVITY NOT INTO IT

When a client enters a therapist's office seeking relief from some problems, he or she is invariably in a low state of consciousness, caught up within the reality of a subjective frame of reference. A person caught up in such a reality will be experiencing the pain, confusion and stress we all experience when we are searching and re-searching in circles through the details for causes and explanations for our feelings. What such an individual sees from within the context of such a reality determines that they will experience their distress as being caused by the details of a life situation (for example, mate, job, height, race, personality traits).

The obvious reason why anyone experiencing problems would seek the advice of a mental health professional is to learn how not to become lost within one's own negative tendencies; how not to create such negative experiences to begin with; and finally, how to find the knowledge which will enable that patient to get these results. The reason, however, why these obvious facts are missed is that the patient becomes insecure and begins to function on the basis of acquired habits and reactions thought to be needed under such conditions! Thus, although seeking help to change, the client defends his condition using acquired information to explain the causes in terms of external forces beyond his control, and ironically misses the fact that this level of explanation is the problem. This person is thinking, seeing, feeling and reacting in opposition to himself.

It is quite natural for a troubled client who is caught up in the feelings of insecurity to want to talk about personal troubles and what he or she thinks and sees to be the causes. This is precisely what is of no value for it is this very frame of reference which is creating the problem. This is a fact that must be understood and realized for any therapist to get results. With this understanding, the therapist can point to principle rather than getting side-tracked with details. From this understanding the help is clear and compassionate and yet unbending in its positive direction, not out of method but out of the evident and the obvious.

THE THERAPEUTIC PERSPECTIVE

These statements have strong implications for the process of therapy particularly as it is carried out today. One implication is that we as therapists or consultants must first look at ourselves and begin to see how our own insecurities keep us locked into our upsets, reactions and views of other people. We must then begin to drop enough of our own egos to realize that our training and education has tricked us into thinking that an intellectual memorization of concepts, tests or techniques is of value in gaining insights or new experiences to others. The actual seeing of levels of consciousness has nothing to do with anything the intellect does or can possibly do. This clarity comes from a state of high self-esteem, a lack of self-consciousness and from objectivity. In this state we are not as involved or attached to the client's seeing us a certain way or changing because of what we do. In this state we have less judgments about the client's behavior, nor are we drawn to commiserate with the bad feelings or problems of the client. We have a natural compassion for the distress and the discomfort of being caught up in a negatively distorted frame of reference and the insecurity attached to that *stuckness*.

We honestly want to help that person see more clearly what he or she is doing, knowing it is always the individual's choice.

In this state of clarity, the therapist is not inclined to commiserate with the client's problems because he or she sees that not only is it harmful to take on these negative feelings, but also that it would be harmful to the client as well. Yet, at the same time, we realize that the client cannot change those feelings because that person is at that time a prisoner of a reality not yet recognized as created by thought habits.

THERAPY: THE WILLINGNESS TO CHANGE

In our experiences we have found that not everyone in some form of psychological trouble is ready to change. This is also quite natural. We as individuals or groups of human beings have the freedom to believe, assume, opine, view and thus see life any way we want — whether we accept this or not. This realization is up to each of us as individuals.

Our choices in life may be to live in realities where beliefs, theories, opinions, views and assumptions are of grave importance. We will have no choice but to conform to what goes along with such realities. Well-being will depend on defending opinions, beliefs and views of self and others. There will be insecurities, judgments and reactions in self and others based on the prevailing beliefs, opinions and interpretations. This is not wrong in a judgmental way; it is wrong in the same way as screen doors would be on a submarine — it simply doesn't work. Thus, there is no value associated with a judgment or complex theoretical explanation about someone's inability to listen. All behavior at any given level of consciousness makes sense for that level.

BEING RIGHT OR BEING HAPPY

Unless we are honestly willing to seek happiness and tranquility over sustaining beliefs we will not listen with open minds; we will hear with our acquired frames of reference. We will attempt to argue for the justifiable existence of our problems or positions. We will not be able to sit still and listen to the facts because facts will not sustain our views of the problem. An ego trip at its best.

Proof about well-being, happiness, understanding and psychological facts does not exist for us when we are in lower states of consciousness. The only substantial proof comes when an individual's level of consciousness rises, revealing the connection of thought to whatever negativity is being experienced by that person. This is what we are calling an *insight*. This proof cannot be given away to anyone via words, concepts or rituals. Words and behavior are only a direction giving reflection to higher realities to those open to change in themselves. We all have the capacity to see the implications and the evident possibility of positive change in ourselves without limiting such change to a specific detailed form. It is then that we will change.

When people are unhappy, they really don't know what they are looking for. They are looking for a way out of their problems, yet they are caught up in their problems and can't see their way out. We have found in our experiences with therapists and in our own consulting work that giving people a common-sense grasp of how levels of consciousness actually work in practice enables them to begin to take more relative views of the realities in which they are immersed.

THERAPY: A SHIFT IN VANTAGE POINT

What we as therapists are really looking for in therapy is the ability to assist our clients out of feelings of being overwhelmed by or immersed in their worries or bad habits to the extent that they cannot find a way out. We want them to be able to shift their perspectives to see possibilities, solutions and opportunities that did not even exist in their previous views of their situations. We want to assist them in experiencing greater degrees of well-being, happiness and high self-esteem than they had previously experienced.

These results will always occur once people begin to realize that first, their previous views of reality are relative and illusionary views, distorted negatively by acquired patterns of thinking; second, their egos, with the accompanying insecurity of needing to be proven, are what create their needs to defend their realities; and third, what the condition of mental health is as a natural state beyond an illusory ego's need to prove itself. Since these principles or insights are impersonal in terms of our recognition of these dynamics occurring in everyone, they can also be applied and related to anyone's experience, irrespective of the form or symptoms that are a result of personal insecurity.

In our work and that of our colleagues, therapy sessions have become more and more impersonal. When the principles discussed in this book are related to a client's personal experience, it usually happens in a humorous way. Every therapist with whom we have consulted to date has told us that therapy sessions get shorter, lighter, with less commiseration, and more experience of real insight leading to a lasting shift in vantage point on the part of the client.

Another way of putting it might be that the therapist ceases looking for or dealing with the wrong vantage point, but rather talks to and therefore points toward a new vantage point. Since this new vantage point is more natural and even more effortless than the old one, the client also begins to recognize the difference and to move toward a higher vantage point.

In most cases, before the client has even realized that a change has happened, he finds himself taking things less seriously, seeing situations from a new position or point of view and being less gripped by situations or events which would have paralyzed him previously. It is only as this process starts to occur that the person can build on the recognition of the fact of conscious states or separate realities. We have appropriately ourselves become unavailable as much as we possibly can to clients when they are in lower states of consciousness. As input or information or knowledge provided at that time is of less value to the listener and is met with higher resistance and stronger argument, we would certainly prefer (and most therapists will find this to be true) that people come in when they are feeling better rather than worse. We often recommend to our clients that before they see us, they take a short break from their work or do whatever they might enjoy to lighten themselves up.

Feeling good and safe, to whatever degree possible, creates a condition of more openness — a greater willingness to consider or to realize something outside of what is already thought or believed about the situation.

CHAPTER 18

Therapy Beyond Techniques: The Principle of Listening

When we can feel secure enough not to conjure up an ever-detailed and -vigilant evaluation of everything, but are willing to be ourselves and to listen in the same way we listen to our favorite song, we do not use our frames of reference to work against ourselves to eliminate our well-being. Listening is when we stop assessing what is being said by someone else using stored information from the past and simply *listen*. When we are thinking while another is talking, we are not truly listening; we are talking to ourselves. The object of listening is not to memorize what is said or to relate it to the details of our specific problems. Neither is it worthwhile to try and apply what is said or to synthesize a new view. Willingness to change is the strength of our wish to move from a known reality to another which is more positive but, until realized, unknown. This listening is what some would call humility and it is the channel to true change.

THE BACKWARD UPSIDE-DOWN WORLD

When people are in lower states of consciousness, troubled and negative, they invariably and directly think and behave in directions opposite to their own well-being. This is due to the fact that in these states of mind the negative qualities of reality are not seen as products of thought systems. They are seen as externally real situations, events, and details happening independent of our thoughts. Thus, when we are in these negative states of mind we will judge these happenings as if they are causing the negative feelings we are experiencing. Wishing to rid ourselves of these feelings, we react with negativity and try in some way to force or effect changes in the details. All of our hostilities toward our environments, however, is felt by us; it is the content of our thoughts and thus we are stuck with the appropriate feelings. Since the true sources of our problems are our thoughts, we push-pull on ourselves.

Thus, it is not unusual for people to think that problems take time to resolve; the more complex (severe) the problem, the longer. People neither expect nor believe in fast resolutions of problems they may be experiencing. They think it takes time, so it takes time. Since most people feel the details of their lives, as they think them, are the causes of their problems, it is not difficult to understand why they also think resolutions would take time.

Accordingly, many people erroneously think that *Time heals all wounds.* This is not true. This is an illusion that is perceived because in the past we produced — without knowing it — negativity which we sustained by thinking. Then, at some point, we began to drop some of these cumbersome thought patterns and began to feel better. As we felt better, our feelings of interest in the positive side of life were re-experienced and eventually this habit pattern to rerun our creature-feature horror matinees in our thoughts subsided; yet due to the ignorance about the roles of thought in all this, we perceive time to be the healer. All thoughts such as these only result in our thinking we want relief, but we don't want it now. For when we are in lower levels of consciousness, thinking negatively, we cannot possibly think of being happy at the same time! The truth is we can stop the horror shows any time we want, now or whenever, because they are our thoughts, they are our shows.

This is the so-called paradox of why people in trouble with marriage, drugs, alcohol, bad temper, stress and insecurity wish to better their conditions and at the same time justify their states of mind and behaviors to some degree by pointing to external causes which are supposedly out of their controls. This is no real paradox when we understand what a level of consciousness is and its relation to thought and the ego.

COMMISERATION: MISERY LOVES COMPANY

Therapy based on any presently accepted theoretical, methodological, or conceptual framework has no option but to deal with, to relate to and to reinforce the details of a client's past life situation and complaints. This quality of therapy is *commiseration*. Commiseration will make the client's frame of reference and thus the problemmed view of life more real, thereby prompting the person to become more entangled in the details of a negative reality. Thus, such therapeutic ritualization reinforces the illusion of ego which keeps the person thinking at an insecure level of consciousness where the realization of insights is impossible. As mentioned earlier, commiseration is harmful to both therapist and client.

PLAYING WITH THE SYMPTOMS

Treating psychological symptoms as if they are meaningful entities in and of themselves worsens people's problems and postpones the realization of relief by pointing the clients in the directions of their already cumbersome realities. We cannot help anyone by conceptually relating symptoms to what we perceive to be external life events. This amounts to trying to dispel their present illusions by substituting others. Present-day theories and rituals in psychology are placebos for they have no power in and of themselves; they are not the sources or facilitators of change.

Many of today's therapeutic rituals only appear as facilitators or necessary conditions for change when we are in lower levels of consciousness. At such levels we view our lives from increasingly insecure and irresponsible perspectives. As this happens, we have tendencies to think that changes in ourselves, our moods or our experiences in general are dependent on external changes, which are seemingly out of our direct reach, such as the external behaviors and emotional conditions of people around us. We subsequently seek out rituals that we have been told can help us change what we were unable to change: ourselves. The lower our levels of understanding goes, however, the more problems we experience, and the more we attach ourselves to a world of placebos disguised as rituals.

Accordingly, much of present-day psychotherapy is involved in exploring the relationship between symptoms and patterns of symptoms, symptoms and external events and conditions, or symptoms and past experiences. However, when we look deeper we realize that all such concepts and rituals are themselves symptoms — symptoms of our scientific levels of understanding.

If psychology and the helping professions today more deeply understood the dynamics of how our minds sustain these connections and give them whatever significance we give them in our own views of reality, psychotherapy would change so dramatically it would be unrecognizable to its present practitioners and followers. Therapy, rather than talking about or categorizing problems, would explore with the client the relationship between ego, insecurity and separate realities that has been discussed in this book. Seeing the relationship of these principles and underlying dimensions of how our minds work as human beings is the beginning of our finding mental health, high self-esteem, natural maturity and common sense in how we conduct our affairs.

Rather than relating events or experiences to each other or to our personalities, the true relationship that these external life events have in common is that they are created via thought from an acquired thought system. Thus, when the relationship between thought and what is called life or reality is realized, we find our moment-to-moment relationships to what is called the world. In principle, the true existing relationship of any experience in life — be it positive, negative, external, or internal — is to ourselves and our thoughts.

THOUGHT: A COMMON DENOMINATOR FOR MENTAL HEALTH AND MENTAL ILLNESS

A common denominator cannot exist as content because everyone's content is different. The common denominator only exists at the level of principle or impersonal facts. It is the fact that we have the power to create the thoughts that underlies the diversity of content we see, and not vice versa.

It seems at first that to state that thought is the vehicle which creates reality is an oversimplification. Nothing can be simpler, and this is precisely true. This is a fact that most of us have overlooked or forgotten because we have become confused by our own power to think and create content which we assume real and objective, seemingly independent of our thinking. How can a response to anything be independent of a person's thinking? A difference in thought is a difference in reality, and the differences between reality are what the field of psychology is struggling and trying to explain.

Most of us have lived our lives wrapped up in the contents of our own thoughts, operating within the details of our beliefs, attitudes, opinions, fears and judgments. We have missed the fact that we ourselves create these thoughts to begin with. Since many of us have grown up thinking we cannot control our own thoughts or certain categories of thoughts, we cannot. For instance, there are many people who think that some of their opinions are hard to drop without insight into the fact that it is these very patterns of thought that are holding them back. The moment they begin to realize they are living in worlds of their own thoughts in which only they have the ability to change, they are on the road to easier lives.

THOUGHTS AND FEELINGS: THEIR TRUE RELATIONSHIP

The source of all feeling is thought. Thoughts are feelings. Thoughts, whether positive or negative, create the contextual experiences we call feelings. Among these feelings are included all emotions which are different detailed names for positive and negative feelings within the context of present frames of reference. What is called well-being in people is another way of saying that people experience positive feelings. These feelings can be love, appreciation, esteem, gratitude, and so forth. The feelings that people produce make up the values their lives will be seen as having.

One of the misconceptions prevalent among people today is that in order to be feeling persons they must entertain all feelings, positive or negative. This happens because they think that exhibiting all feelings, positive and negative, is somehow connected to genuineness. The fact is that we create feelings. We have the power to create any feeling we wish. If this is realized then the futility of coping with, working through, and getting in touch with feelings will be seen; they will be seen for the empty rituals that they really are.

Once we have created the thought of blame or judgment or fear, it is too late; we already have the feeling associated with that thought. Whatever we do with the feeling after that point does not matter. In fact, anything we do to relieve the feeling actually keeps it around longer by taking it seriously.

Feelings are not stored up in a personal psychological warehouse. Negative feelings are created via the thoughts of insecurity. All people in trouble can do is to stop producing the negative thought patterns which are creating their negative feelings. By dropping these patterns, the relief and positiveness they seek will be uncovered for it already exists. Positiveness does not have to be produced. Positiveness is already there, only the negativity of people's thoughts in the forms of insecurity obscures this natural state. Children do not go around purposely thinking positively. Yet they enjoy life because they have not yet covered life up with patterns of thought about who, what, when, where and why based on insecurity.

There will be those who disbelieve that it is possible to be truly happy in life. For these people all we can suggest is that they listen honestly to what they are saying and the implications such thoughts have for their lives and those they wish to help.

THE ROLE OF FEELINGS

Another misconception which often comes up in therapy is that all feelings are natural and therefore cannot be ignored. This is true, but not in the way that most people think. Feelings simply tell us with an uncompromising honesty what we are doing in life and the direction in which we are going. A feeling is what tells us whether our levels of consciousness are positive or negative. If our feelings are negative, they are natural guides to telling us that we are misperceiving life due to the negative directions of our thoughts; signals from ourselves to go the other way. Thus the feelings of insecurity can be of help to protect us from hurting ourselves through becoming blinded by our own egos for when we are immersed in negativity we lose our common sense. In ignorance, we use our own feelings of negativity as justifications to blame something or someone in our world in some way. In actual fact, we are blaming no one but ourselves.

Feelings are simple. If we feel negative, it is our feelings, our states of mind and our thinking which is in error. If we hate someone, we are stuck with our own creation, a feeling of hatred. If our thinking leads us to feel sorrow for someone else, we experience sorrow in our own lives. In an identical manner, if our thoughts are such that we love someone or something, we will live in these feelings. Whatever the feelings we experience, whether positive or negative, they are created from our thinking.

FEELING: THE PRINCIPLE VEHICLE TO COMMON SENSE

Feelings point or direct us to our inborn wisdom and common sense, to a deeper insight into our condition. No human being requires any training or formal education to know whether he or she feels good or not. Our natural feelings of well-being are every human being's inborn wisdom and common sense in action. As the constant insecurities brought about via our egos begin to fade, we begin to realize that our feelings are our natural internal compasses which can be utilized to by-pass the pitfalls of life, regardless of the details or conditions existing around us. We begin to see and learn from our feelings rather than turning them on ourselves by blaming this or that detail or ourselves. As we experience higher levels of understanding and insight, our abilities to live happily become easier, more stress free. We begin to enjoy the beautiful feelings which in turn allow us to appreciate and to feel gratitude for what we have found; we become less drawn to producing negativity that obscures this clarity.

What brings people to seek psychological help, regardless of the details of their problems, is the loss of positive feelings and the presence of negative ones. Thus, the direction of therapy must be toward good, positive and healthy feelings. Since such feelings are present to some degree when we are not caught up in desperate attempts to figure out how to get one up in our lives, the direction of therapy must be toward these feelings and not toward unraveling the psychological confusion.

As we begin to experience higher levels of understanding, free from negative thought patterns, it becomes easier to see that all negative feelings are, in principle, the same. It becomes more evident that to classify different negative emotions is useless. What determines the classification are the contexts in which negative feelings occur. All negative feelings are insecurity dressed in the clothing of a situation. Insecurity in a relationship may be classified as jealousy, resentment or boredom; insecurity in a job may be stress, tension and job dissatisfaction. The moment a therapist or client begins to classify negativity, he or she is going in the direction of psychological confusion.

It is not difficult to see why the principle, *"What you give is what you receive"* is applicable to the direction we can point out to clients because in fact what persons put out via their thoughts never really go anywhere. What persons put out come as results of the perceptions they have and results in feelings which they give to themselves. The particular thoughts depend on their particular thought systems. Until people begin to awaken to this insight, they must conform to states which imprison them in whatever belief systems they acquired in life.

For example, when it becomes clearer for people to recognize that their anger, for instance, is based on thoughts which create unpleasant pictures of reality in some way and at the same time go along with unpleasant feelings called anger, they will then find it easier to cease using such patterns, even in the presence of others who may or may not be creating anger. Once we can learn to use our minds in positive directions, we will find that the well-being created from our understanding will protect us from any habits we formerly had which prompted us in the past to create negativity in ourselves.

The psychological confusion caused by people's negative habits takes care of itself since all habits attached to insecurity go into neutral with the realization of the deeper sense of well-being which accompanies a rise in our levels of consciousness. All habits are associated with states of mind and realities in which we feel insecure. The habit is our placebo ritual we think is necessary in order to become happier in life or to maintain ourselves at some level of functioning. The details of all our habits, no matter how different, are in principle all the same.

As people become free from the states of insecurity which feed their habitual patterns of thought and begin to enjoy life more, the needs for the habit wither. The essential principle is that instead of people seeking an external rearrangement of the detailed conditions they think necessary for happiness, it is the recognition that it is the thoughts of those habits which have placed them in the realities of placebo existence. We can have the happiness anytime we want. What we do with our thought systems is merely block that happiness by connecting it to an endless chain of theories, concepts, beliefs, conditions, and details which we must handle. The irony is that the power of mind, via our thought systems, is so potent we can even accomplish this feat.

Precisely because our minds are capable of attaching any event to any reaction via the power of our own thoughts it is impossible to achieve real insight from any external process, method or technique. All we can do is to listen and to start to recognize the facts about our experiences as human beings. We could say that the value of a philosophical discussion with someone who actually sees and understands separate realities and the power of thought is far more valuable than any technique or model of therapy that has ever been invented.

CHAPTER 19

Recognizing the Placebo Effect in Mental Health and Mental Illness

The power of thought has not gone unnoticed in the area of mental health. In fact, the utilization of the placebo effect has even been suggested as a specific form of treatment in mental and/or emotional disorders, including psychosomatic disease. Thus, the recognition of the powerful influence that thought has on the therapeutic effect of psychotherapy has long been recognized as a placebo component. The fact is that an individual's thoughts in the form of beliefs, expectations, attitudes and opinions literally underly the effect of any psychotherapeutic ritual. There are already people in the mental health field who have suggested that all psychotherapeutic effects are placebo effects by the very definition of what they are treating.

THE PLACEBO EFFECT: ITS IMPLICATIONS

The *placebo effect* is a situation where a change in any aspect of personal experience is attributed to some object, ritual or condition which has no direct relationship to the particular change other than in the individual's thoughts. That is, the actual source of the change is the person's thoughts about the object, ritual or condition. The necessary ingredient for any placebo to have effect is the individual's thinking regarding the relationship of the placebo object to the desired change. The more doubtless the thought, the greater the effect.

The effects of a placebo can range from minimal to quite pronounced. The most commonly known situation in which placebos are used is one in which a person wishes relief from some negative conditions experienced (that is, pain, anxiety and so forth). In such cases an inert sugar pill, water injection or ritual may be presented as being the remedy. The patient is usually told that what he or she is being given is the medicine for such a condition. The individual taking treatment has no idea that it is a placebo. The two crucial aspects of this phenomenon are that first, the individual expects, creates and attributes any relief to the placebo object and thus, in the case of pain, for example, a pill (the object) can actually be experienced as reducing or eliminating the pain; and second, because all placebo objects or rituals are connected to an identifiable form (that is, the therapist, the treatment ritual, the session, the pill) which has a discrete beginning and an end, the effects are temporary and do not really provide the knowledge to eliminate the problem at its source. A patient in such a reality earnestly requests and awaits the next dose of this remedy once the previous dose wears off!

One interesting aspect of the placebo effect is that it can occur regardless of what may be believed is the source of the negative condition. For example, pain relief using a placebo can occur even with pain associated with surgical operations as well as with cases where there is no identifiable source of pain. The illusory quality of the placebo effect is not the effect (the change) itself, but rather what is thought by the person receiving the placebo.

THE IMPLICATIONS OF THE PLACEBO EFFECT
IN MENTAL HEALTH

The harmful result of using placebo rituals to try and guide people out of negative mental and/or emotional states of mind is that their uses perpetuate the illusory framework of thought which creates such disturbances. Stated simply, the problems which we acquire are themselves negative placebos which are given power via our thoughts; that is, we attribute our disturbances to some external object (wife, husband, situation, and so forth) which appears to us as being the cause of our emotional reactivity, but which in actuality did not create this condition. When therapy involves anything other than pointing to the real source of the disturbance, it does nothing to help the client realize the actual source of mental and/or emotional upset.

What is the harm with a technique that gives someone a nice feeling? The answer to this question is simple. First of all, it is not true because a technique *cannot create* a feeling, be it positive or negative. Secondly, it may well lead the client or patient to accept as factual an illusory reality that a technique is the cause or necessary condition for a nice feeling to exist. This would further remove anyone from realizing that thought is the true power underlying any and all feelings. This perpetuates the very illusion that creates the problem to begin with — not knowing where feelings of well-being come from. Thus, even if relief is experienced as resulting from the use of some technique, the client is very apt to attribute the relief to the technique and thus go out into the world in a similar state of mind that got him into trouble in the first place. This is why, at best, problems are never eliminated; they are merely relieved by psychotherapies. New or different problems, however, always come up. The effects of all these rituals do nothing to help us realize the knowledge that will allow us to eliminate our tendencies to create problems.

REALIZATIONS VERSUS PLACEBO EFFECTS

Realizations are experiences of actually observing one of our own thoughts becoming a fact in our reality. Within the context of the present discussion it is the experience of how our own thought patterns create the separate realities we call our lives. The realization of this fact is not an intellectual conceptualization. It is the actual experience of change from one reality to another as a result of a change in our thought processes rather than a ritual or technique which differentiates a realization from a placebo effect.

A realization of a psychological fact is what is commonly referred to as an insight; that is, sight into the fact that we are creating or producing whatever given reality we may presently be living in. Such an experience takes us from one reality to another, a new reality characterized by a new and more objective state of mind.

In relation to a problem, an insight takes a person from a reality of problems and negative feelings to one where such problems and feelings do not exist by virtue that he or she realizes how such conditions were created. In the midst of a problem a person may have the thought of not having that particular problem. When that reality changes to one where the problem no longer exists, a new reality has been realized. If the person having such an experience of change realizes how this is connected to personal thought, he or she has realized a higher level of conscious understanding.

With a higher understanding of oneself, the thought process becomes successively free from patterns which were ignorantly used against the person and led to the feelings of insecurity and, thus, mental and/or emotional disturbances. The effective direction of therapy, regardless of its actual form, must therefore always be in the direction of the realization of principles rather than of details.

THE PRINCIPLE OF DIRECTION

The true function of a therapist is to point people directly toward positive feelings. This can only be done when a therapist knows the difference between principle and details. Principle is what is applicable regardless of the specific details of any situation. Details are the units of confusion which differ from one situation to another. A confused individual who is caught up in a personal frame of reference of details may find it difficult to sustain or even experience a good stable relationship, job, friends and self-confidence. The individual may be prone toward argument or defensiveness. Depression may be experienced or anxiety about the future. In such a case, the details of each of these situations in life would dictate that that person engage in five or more different therapies to cover relationships, job stress, anxiety, assertiveness and on and on. All these therapies in some way would involve dealing, coping or communicating with others. They would give a person ways and means of manipulating others more effectively, even if by controlling himself or herself.

Principle, on the other hand, would dictate that such a person put aside the present frame of reference which is producing the present view of life and realize that he or she is the source of the problem. It makes no sense to produce a problem on the one hand and to try and deal with it on the other, since the person is both the source of the problem and the cure. The cure is to stop producing the problem by recognizing and eliminating it from the mind. The details of what it is do not matter, once it is seen as only thought. Any thought, regardless of content, is no more or less than any other thought. The detailed content of any thought is the problem only inasmuch as it is forgotten that it is only thought.

Therapy, when focusing on the details of any person's problems, is counterproductive not only because the details are irrelevant, but also because by taking the details seriously the therapist is actually reinforcing the level of insecurity or self-importance that was the driving force behind the client taking these details as seriously as he has up to this point in time. Our insecurities as clients leading to our present images of self-importance compel us to want reasons, justifications and external solutions to our problems. Therefore, interacting with clients by seriously engaging them in discussions of their problems at given levels of insecurity is of absolutely no value.

For example, if a woman goes to a therapist because her husband traveled more than she liked on his job, leaving her lonely and fearful about their relationship, most therapies would teach her techniques or methods to better cope with her loneliness or techniques to get him to change his behavior. On the other hand, once this client sees the fact of her insecurity creating these fears and frustrations, the fears and frustrations would no longer exist. This client would then do naturally and easily whatever she feels she really wants in that situation without even defining it as a so-called problem in therapy.

GIVING THE CONTROLS TO THE CLIENT

Thus, in our example, the traditional therapies would enhance the illusion that the person is not the source of the problem, but the mediator of a problem. Traditional therapy would assume that she does have control — but that it is limited control. That is, that she can reduce or relieve her problem. Traditional therapies however, would not assume that she created her problem and is capable of eliminating it altogether.

Therapy that entails keeping anyone caught up in the illusion of looking at details will only pass on whatever misunderstanding that illusion dictates. A good example of this is the many theories today which postulate that pain and suffering are useful, worthwhile, helpful or even necessary for growth to take place. Thus, the theories feel it worthwhile to discuss, face or work through these feelings and emotions. Many people actually go to therapists to help them bring out negative feelings they have supposedly locked inside of them and which are causing their problems, thinking that it is healthy to exhibit anger or hateful feelings. This is a belief that could be no farther from the truth. Pain and suffering are what naturally prompt people to seek release from such states of mind. The aim of help is to guide people out of such states. To direct individuals to those states is to direct people toward what they are hoping to rid themselves of.

Such practices are demonstrative of our own innocence as therapists, not knowing that to help clients eliminate negativity in life by asking them to entertain, produce or seek negative emotional states is to first direct them toward lower states of consciousness in which they utilize their thought systems to create more emotional distress. Oftentimes in our past we would direct clients whom we thought were not acknowledging or dealing with their negative emotions to face honestly how serious their conditions were, explaining how they could help themselves if they let it all out. We got what we asked for! The clients, however, did not.

States of pain and suffering are what create the reactivity which plagues humanity in the forms of negative emotions, thoughts and behaviors. When the direction of positiveness is adopted out of insight it is easy to see that, if a troubled individual experiences even five minutes of relief where his/her troubles do not even exist as considerations in thought, this is the state which the patient seeks. Such a state does not and cannot include the attraction to negativity found in lower states of consciousness.

230

CHAPTER 20

The Direction and True Role of the Therapist: Beyond Our Theories, Beyond Burnout

As we have already stated, when an individual seeks help for a problem in his or her life it is most common for that person to verbalize the scenario which is seen as the cause of the problem. This is quite normal; we have all done it. People in trouble, however, are the worst authorities about what, how or who are causing their problems and ill feelings. This is because, in truth, no one is creating or causing their ill feelings but themselves. We should perhaps remember the advice given in *Aesop's Fables* to never accept the advice of someone in distress. A therapist with some common sense will know this. Furthermore, the therapist will understand that the client is not in a reality which includes such a fact or that client would not have the problem in the first place.

Therapy, if it is to be truly therapeutic, requires that the therapist understand and act out of his or her own knowledge of what is happening. The professional will not commiserate by accepting the client's details as having any factual reality knowing that, if that person felt better, the particular story would have little or no importance. The therapist would not act in a way which would reinforce, promote, or support the personal view that something external is the cause of ill feelings or problems. Rather, they would gently guide the patient away from such a pattern of thinking and the troublesome feelings created. As was stated in Section IV, this is the underlying principle of why all psychological rituals used as preordained techniques are bound to the problem or condition hoped to be eliminated. They are bound in principle and direction.

THE THERAPIST'S OWN WISDOM: BEYOND REHEARSAL

Many people, fellow psychologists, graduate students and other mental health professionals often ask us how what we are sharing can be applied, conveyed or given to patients in place of whatever they are presently doing. The answer is that what we are presently doing is not a technique or method to be applied. It is simply that we share the facts we have realized in the course of our lives by just interacting. There are no magical words or rituals. There are no special effects to be set up in advance. We simply, to the degree we know ourselves, share with our clients what we know about life, mind and thought as honestly and directly as we can.

Thus, the questions, *"How do I pass this wisdom along to my clients?"* or *"What techniques or methods can I use?"* are impossible to answer at the level of understanding out of which they are asked. We cannot tell our clients how to live their lives or interact with their spouses, families or friends. We also cannot tell therapists how to interact with clients. All we can do is point therapists in the direction of the principles we have found underly our experiences in the hope that they recognize these principles for themselves. When we as therapists are in the state of clarity and objectivity where we can see the illusionary quality of separate frames of reference and observe the level of consciousness of the client, our own wisdom will tell us what to do. All we can ever really do is to be ourselves. Sometimes what we might feel is right is to be quiet and merely listen, feeling that the clients at some point will begin to hear themselves. We may feel humorous, see the funny side of things and respond in such a way that the problem starts to seem less serious and compelling. Alternatively, we may offer a strong dose of common sense, or we may offer a totally different version of reality than what the client is experiencing now, which may or may not have anything to do with the content of the perceived problems. Whatever we do will have the quality of sharing our own common sense, while always respecting the client's level of understanding about the validity of a present view of reality.

What we are really saying is *"Physician heal thyself,"* and work will become easier, more enjoyable and rewarding. Every reality we then come across is fascinating and full of learning for us as well as for the client. Our days seem full of experiences, surprises and new insights. We learn to notice when our own intellect comes in and wants to hold on to an insight or to some form and make it into a technique or intellectual construct.

INTELLECTUAL COMPARISONS AS A BARRIER TO LISTENING

We often get the reaction from people along the lines of, *"Say, isn't what you are saying like Dr. So and So's Theory?",* or that we are talking about a new version of some present form of therapy, or that we are saying the same thing as a person who has written about a psychological method for treating psychosomatic illness. These reactions occur because the reader identifies with something, some part of what is read, and immediately connects that recognition to something already known or heard about.

We particularly get these questions and reactions with regard to the responsibility and the gestalt therapies that focus on present pay-offs people receive for maintaining negative behavioral patterns. Yet all of these therapies continue to focus on details and ask people to work on or deal with their negative patterns as if they were real, and in a way that conceptually relates whatever technique the therapists use to their specific patterns of behavior. Yet, even talking about what we are learning in this book in a conceptual manner and relating it to our present views of reality in a theoretical or an intellectual way is of little value.

The intellect is something that we all develop, and is something which we are taught to be proud of. We are taught to look for more information and to compare theories or concepts. In this same vein, we love to discuss theories and concepts about the power of thought and how our thought systems are related to life. Yet what is happening is that we are talking about something theoretically or conceptually, while it is in fact happening right there within each of us while we are attempting to clinically conceptualize about it.

The only thing of real, lasting value to any individual is to begin to recognize and to identify or notice what is actually happening now, and then talk about what we see. This process involves sharing our own common sense; not sharing the details of what is seen, but recognizing a deeper grasp of the way that this process actually works in all of us.

It is only when the recognition occurs of how our own thoughts generate our own versions of reality to determine our moment-to-moment experience that our minds begin to quiet down. At this point we stop trying to impose our individual wills on life; taking what our thought systems believe should be true about life and attempting to make the world, including our own feelings about what we see, conform to that set of standards and beliefs. When we are not insecure and our minds quiet down to observe with more clarity what is really going on, we see the variety of thought systems in the world and how they interact to create whatever is happening at the time. As our minds quiet down, we begin to walk through life in meditative states that are natural and not connected to any technique nor to what we are doing at the time.

When we stop trying to control life and make things work the way we think they should, life becomes easier. We have gained a deeper wisdom about how things actually do work, rather than how we think they should work. We can use this understanding to create what other people would call minor miracles, changes and accomplishments they consider impossible or extremely unlikely in our lives including our work and personal affairs.

When we stop trying to control life, we are able to enjoy it as being much more. Our thoughts, worries, doubts, resentments and guilt drop away. We begin to experience richer, deeper and intensely alive enjoyments of each moment. Every day becomes an adventure of new experiences, insights and beauty that we had not been able to appreciate before that time. To describe this experience in words is impossible. It is similar to a manufacturer of a television with brighter color and a clearer picture attempting to demonstrate the difference by showing a picture of its television screen through an ad on T.V. The picture seen cannot be any better than the screen we already have.

The way to obtain a better screen — one consisting of increased objectivity, clarity and common sense — is not through analyzing the details of the picture, but rather moving closer in our understanding to the source of the picture itself in our minds; that is, to see more clearly the dynamics of how our thought systems are projected outward to form the details of a picture of our life.

LEARNING THROUGH IMPLICATION

There is the illusion of two sides to human experience. One is the thought of the experience itself; that is, that which is observed to be occurring quite aside from any explanation. The other is what is thought about the experience; what it was, whether it was real, what is it called, what caused it, whether it was caused or did it seem caused, and on and on. Of these two sides, the common-sense understanding is in the direction of the experience; the details of a frame of reference creating the experienced insecurity of the ego situation in the other.

Common sense and/or wisdom cannot be approached from the side of intellectual questions or answers because both are forms trying to explain a reality. Common sense or wisdom can be realized and does exist; but it is so factual it cannot be understood at a level of understanding where questions and answers are rigorously defined for this is the level of unanswered questions, the complex and circular use of intellect.

As we stated in Chapter 18, learning to listen is perhaps one of the simplest ways to realizing one's own common sense and wisdom. Listening is understanding through implication rather than explanation; that is, experience functioning in a positive mode without questioning or explanation. People presently think positiveness in any form must or can be explained in order to help those who are in realities or mental and/or emotional problems. The problem that mental health faces today is that happiness is a natural condition that cannot be intellectually created or explained. Any attempt at explanation immediately takes us out of that natural condition. However, happiness is what our ego is attempting to cope with by its use of detailed explanations. As with all true knowledge, the more knowledge is manifested and experienced as a reality, the less explanation needed. The hardest thing to explain — in fact, the only thing that cannot be approached with questions and explanation — is what *is*. If it were known, there would be no question about it. If questions exist, no answer can possibly be eliminated. Explanations are lesser than that which they attempt to explain. The more complex the explanation, the further away it stands from that which is being explained. The more simple, the closer, until no explanation is necessary, it is known.

Based on the principles set forth in Sections II and III, it is possible to relate in a simple manner the implications of these insights to what is called *psychotherapy*. Although we cannot tell a therapist or anyone else how or what to say in any situation in life, we can direct a therapist to seek the understanding of principles. In a psychological sense a principle is a compass-like guide in life which implies a logical direction regardless of the details of a situation. A conceptual guide which deals with details and whose direction giving accuracy varies with the details on the other hand would be of little or no use as far as directing people toward mental health.

The principal attribute that a therapist makes available to an individual in need and seeking help is his or her level of understanding and well-being in life. This is the sole determiner of how clearly, objectively, and unbiasedly anyone will understand the right use of the mind and its role in the creation of a unique reality. Thus, the realization of principle is the understanding a therapist speaks from. How effective any therapist is depends entirely on how successful he or she is in seeing past the frame of reference in which a client may be embroiled.

Perhaps the most fundamental principle we can direct the reader toward is the fact that no one can change anyone else. Likewise, no one can tell anyone else how to see life, how to live it, or what to do in any situation. Since everyone lives in a separate world of individuality, it is impossible to standardize details. It would be laughable to try and teach people how to taste food or how to see beauty. How each of us sees life is no exception.

DIRECTION RATHER THAN DETAIL

The way to help those honestly seeking help is by sharing direction in life rather than by relying on agreed upon rituals and codes of behavior. A positive direction will naturally lead a person toward what is wished. Specific advice will not make sense to someone in a troubled state of mind because in that state of mind the details are seen as the trouble. The therapists must see this positive direction for themselves before they can help their clients. Once this result occurs in the therapists, it is impossible for them to experience professional burnout, a topic that is popular among therapists today.

Some stress and insecurity is good, it is said, in keeping people motivated in jobs. Not so. The same has been said in the context of marriages with equally bad results. Novelty is another thing. But novelty, the unexpected, is different from insecurity — the negative expected.

What keeps any of us locked into our present versions of reality are the fears and insecurities of what would happen to us, if that reality changed in an unexpected manner. But all these fears and insecurities are in themselves parts of those realities that we are afraid to let go of. As we actually move to higher levels of consciousness, those fears drop away as well. Higher levels of consciousness must be accompanied by more security, certainty and safety in the form of maturity and increased common sense about life.

BURNOUT: KEEPING THE THERAPIST SANE

One great disadvantage facing those attempting to help psychologically disturbed people from a level of understanding which shares the importance of detail and past history is the negative effects this seriousness has on them as therapists. The use of psychological theories and rituals which we have intellectually memorized, rehearsed and practiced has put us, still ourselves insecure people, in the role of therapists. Although we seemingly are protected by our techniques or rituals we soon begin to experience the frustration and stress that go along with a lack of understanding of what we are doing and our low percentage of successes in therapy. Thus, we as mental health professionals begin to perceive the details of our profession to be a source of problems.

The term *burnout* in the context of mental health refers to the negative mental and/or emotional reactions experienced by therapists presumably as a result of the nature of their job. This burnout reaction can be manifested as any one or a combination of symptoms such as feeling sorrow, anxiety, irritability, over-reactivity, depression, job dissatisfaction, lowered productivity and illness. The only reason burnout exists is that the therapist is functioning at a similar level of consciousness as the patient. At lower levels both the patient and the therapist believe that problems are caused by this or that external situation and so forth. Furthermore, by thinking these problems are unavoidably real, a therapist is also reacting to such happenings or problems in his or her own past or to the possibility that what could happen in life is factual.

For therapists in such a state of understanding to be put in a mental health setting is not only a detriment to those seeking relief, but also a detriment to the therapists. It doesn't take long for such therapists to begin to identify with their clients' problems, emotional distresses and the perceived helplessness of people in such predicaments. When the professionals experience problems themselves, they have the added burden of hiding the fact they are in need of help. Such therapists may either struggle ineffectively to mimic sanity or may end up in therapy themselves hearing the same basic routines they dispensed to others.

For most professionals it is hard to see a common-sense alternative to either becoming emotionally embroiled in their clients' problems and having these negative feelings affect their own lives, or becoming emotionally insensitive which further leads to automaticity in their own lives.

The key to a third alternative involves an honest understanding of the difference between commiseration and compassion. Understanding this difference enables therapists to appreciate the common principles underlying human feeling in clients without taking on the pain implicit in the details of the clients' situations by relating these to the therapists' own fears, biases and hang-ups. This change in the therapists feeds back into their personal lives. In turn, as therapists become healthier, these changes feed back into their work and make their practices more successful.

The only real way for us to keep ourselves as therapists healthy is for us to find out what we are talking about to begin with. The principles of maintaining one's well-being are the same for therapists as for clients. In other words, we as therapists must learn for ourselves what happiness and well-being are and the relationship of these states of consciousness to our own thought systems and experiences — no one else's! This is why a therapist's level of consciousness, and not a method, is what directs the results in therapy in much the same way that the level of insecurity would direct the results in a relationship. The therapist's level of consciousness is the same degree to which he or she learned how to live a successful, stress-free and understanding life, including how happy to be in job, relationships, family, friendships, emotional states and other areas of life.

It is in the reality that we actually live from which we ultimately talk. The more clear our reality is to us, the clearer we can share this with others who must then seek this in themselves. The therapist merely points to the fact that such a reality exists, a reality where the details are not thought of as mistakenly crucial and complex so as to take away from seeing and experiencing life in a positive, creative and productive manner. The client must then go beyond the details of specifically thought conditions into the direction of a reality possessing those qualities but within personal life: family, wife or husband, job. This cannot be done intellectually. It can only be accomplished through self-realization of an insight.

CHAPTER 21

The Process of Therapy: Guiding Clients to Their Own Mental Health

The way to guide a client to better mental health is definitely not to categorize, to test, to examine or question the client in any way about present or past habits, symptoms, or problems. All these can possibly accomplish would be to convince that person that he or she has serious problems and that the present frame of reference or thought system must be taken as a given. The fields of mental health and therapy today still feel that people are prisoners of their own styles, personalities or pasts. Yet whatever a therapist does in any way to perpetuate this illusion is harmful.

THE KEY TO TRUE RESPONSIBILITY

If we push people and attempt to get them to do or attempt to do or feel things they are not yet ready to accomplish or feel, we are creating new standards that clients may feel guilty or inadequate about not living up to. They would feel the same way they are feeling guilty or resentful about the way things are going in their lives already. It is only when we begin to take responsibility for life that things get better. But we cannot be forced or told that we should be able to do that when we are not yet having that experience.

This paradox is the reason why the best way to use our wisdom as therapists is to talk impersonally and objectively from principle without attempting to get the client to do or to experience anything. If people honestly want to change, they will listen and begin to recognize the common sense of what the therapists are saying. This recognition will occur more quickly the happier and more stable the therapists are themselves. Clients report to us that they often walk away from sessions feeling lighter, noticing nice things happening around them, yet not knowing why they are having these nicer feelings. When they get home and their spouses or children want to get them into old patterns of negativity, they do not have the same old urge to jump in and mix it up the way they did in the past. They may even be surprised by their responses to situations by what they say or see going on. They are often surprised the next day at work to see how problems that were overwhelming the day before have obvious, more simple solutions; solutions that had not occurred to them previously.

THE ACTIVE INGREDIENTS IN CHANGE

The most helpful aspect of any therapeutic or consultative relationship is to share with the client the key to realizing wisdom. Then the client will use that wisdom to see beyond the limitations of previous experience and perceptions of problems. Often, it seems like a difficult process for us as therapists and consultants because we want to be seen as the expert or the source of understanding, while the client, who is caught up at the time in personal upset (seeing things through the perceptual filters created by insecurity), wants advice and is asking for solutions to specific problems.

THE NATURAL PRINCIPLE OF SEPARATE REALITIES

When we as therapists raise our own levels of consciousness to the point where we see with some clarity the illusionary quality of separate realities, we realize that no one can do anything that is not natural in their individual reality. If, for example, we are at a certain level of insecurity about relationships not working out, we will naturally develop coping styles to protect ourselves from being disappointed. This also results in keeping our relationships at certain distances and supposedly will help us in handling the trauma of relationships ending, or of people taking advantage of us which will continually happen within those frames of reference at that level of consciousness because of our expectations and stances in relationships.

If a therapist gave us any advice or techniques concerning what to do about the relationships in our lives at that moment, it would only result in attempting something unnatural and uncomfortable in that frame of reference. This would inevitably have a different effect than that intended. We would then probably feel worse because we could not do it right or make it work.

Alternatively, when we point clients directly to an increased common sense about insecurity, those clients may drop a little bit of insecurity, moving to a new level of consciousness from which to see people differently. Then most of the issues and the patterns dealt with previously in relationships would naturally disappear by themselves; they are no longer relevant (natural) in light of the new level of perceptiveness and understanding, of self-confidence and comfort with intimacy.

The power of actually dropping insecurity through realizing that insecurity is only an illusionary thought is far beyond the efficacy of any attempt to learn better ways to deal with, live with, understand our problems; or any form of therapy, personal growth or technique for change we have ever observed, read about or experienced. The results of this realization are predictable. If we drop some of our insecurities, we must see things differently. Without the filters of the irrational fears we do not focus as exclusively on our own needs and concerns. We do not worry as much about what people are doing in relation to us. We see their behaviors more objectively — not how it relates to our realities, but what it means to them in their realities.

WHAT WE CAN DO AS HELPERS: WHAT WE SEE IS WHAT WE GIVE/GET

All that can be done is to share what we know from personal experience about the route to a state of increased clarity. The client must then take personal responsibility for getting there. For example, a popular theory in the field of motivation is McGregor's *Theory X, Theory Y* dichotomy. Managers with *Theory X* have a belief system that employees are lazy and must be driven in order to work. *Theory Y* managers, on the other hand, have the belief that people derive intrinsic satisfaction from their work and respond to consideration, attention and opportunities to exhibit their initiatives and proficiencies. The fact is that people get what they expect; people who expect lazy workers get lazy workers. The concept of *Theory X* versus *Theory Y* managers does not tell people anything about changing their minds. Yet it is when the manager himself takes responsibility for how he sees and reacts to his employees and begins to see and treat people differently that the results he obtains in his management of people change.

The managers we know who have developed their own common sense understandings of separate realities have no theories about human behavior; they merely see what is going on within the framework of each of their employees' separate frames of reference. Therefore, they naturally know what motivates each person and how to manage or supervise that person to get the best that that person or that employee has to offer. These management situations are the most practical applications we have seen to date of a common-sense understanding of separate realities in organizational settings.

It is only when we gain a perspective of the bigger picture beyond the subjective, illusionary reality we are now trying to maintain and defend that we realize how everything we are doing, reacting to, trying to straighten out and manage is all a product of that same illusionary thought system. We then realize how much of the effort, negativity and stress we experience comes from attempting to maintain that thought system and to clean up the messes created from that thought system.

USING OUR PERSPECTIVE

If the therapist or consultant sees a situation with more perspective than the client and points out what is seen, this in itself may give the client more perspective, but only if the client realizes that he or she is listening to pick up a perspective rather than a list of detailed solutions to specific problems. If the latter is the case, then the immediate situation may improve; but in the long run the client will keep needing the consultant or therapist to come back, to solve the same or different problems, as from the same frame of reference and level of insecurity he or she will continue to make similar messes and complications. If the client experiences a new level of clarity, he or she will see more of what the consultant or therapist sees and run his or her life or business with more confidence, success and ease.

Rather than passing along specific advice or solutions to specific problems, the person who is acting as a consultant or therapist wants to give people something more; a perspective, a realization of the underlying principles of how the mind works because it involves looking in a direction and noticing things that have not been noticed before. The more we drop our insecurities as consultants or therapists, the more we are able to share this new perspective without compromising it to fit with the frames of reference of our clients, and without reacting with judgments to a lack of understanding or agreement. Because the intellectual mind gets involved and wants the security of linear cause and effect (do X and Y will happen), it seems like a world of opposites. The less we need the clients to change, the faster things will happen. More understanding may result when what we are saying makes little sense in the present frames of reference of the clients. Yet what we say has to make enough common sense that the truth in it cannot be denied, even though it may be different from what the clients see as true about those situations now.

The direction in therapy and in consulting that we want to take with our clients is away from a focus on the external situation and the details of how it appears to them now. The route or direction we want is to assist the clients to achieve states of clarity that make these details irrelevant because of the new insights they have to the point that they cannot wait to go back and to enjoy their new freedom and new feelings about the same situations that they saw before as intolerable or depressing.

We know lawyers, for example, who dropped out of their profession altogether because they were afraid to go to court and were intimidated by the intellects, presence and seeming unapproachability of senior lawyers and judges. They gained new levels of common sense and saw the opposite happening, that the insecurities of many lawyers trapped them in long intellectual harangues and arguments, posturing and protecting their own territories. These people are now some of the most successful lawyers in their area, respected by their colleagues and appreciated by judges for their ability to cut through the rhetoric and details, to point out the essential elements and relevant aspects of the case. Other lawyers are amazed at their ease and the naturalness of their courtroom manner, how they stick to the point and do not get rattled by courtroom tactics. They are effective, comfortable and love their work. These changes came not from training these people in law, but from their own realizations of their own common sense.

THE IMPLICATION OF SPECIALIZATION

Another strong implication for therapy of what we are learning is the fallacy of becoming a specialist in certain types of problems or categories of disturbance. The specialist in sexuality, for example, becomes an expert in the variety of sexual dysfunctions, the history of people who have these dysfunctions, and also develops more and more specialized techniques to treat each different problem. Yet any sexual problem is the result of insecurity. Without insecurity, people at any given time are either appropriately sexually aroused or not. When they are, they naturally know what to do, when and how, without thought. It is only when they start thinking that they get into trouble. Any technique or attempt to analyze a particular problem will only serve to increase thought (*Am I doing it right? Is she comfortable with this?* and so on).

When we start to drop insecurity, every area of our lives where there is a behavioral manifestation of our insecurity has to change. Our sex lives get better because we are not as anxious and will be there to enjoy it rather than to perform. Addictive or compulsive behaviors will change. We no longer feel compelled to create a high or to deaden our anxiety and discomfort with drugs or alcohol, or by constantly creating excitement and activity in our lives. A *workaholic* is someone who transfers personal insecurity to work, basing an attachment of self-esteem to how hard he works. Any compulsive behavior is an attempt to cover up or to deaden insecurity, and only works until the drug or alcohol wears off.

We have observed people who have stopped using alcohol or drugs by not focusing at all on their so-called addictive behavior, nor talking about their pasts, how they acquired their habits or why they think they do it. All that happened was that they heard someone who was talking common sense, and it hit home. They then began to relax, to feel less insecure and to enjoy life more. The alcohol or drug use then died away by itself without any attention. We have seen the same results occur in people who are trying to lose weight, to become better parents, to stop smoking, or to change any and all types of addictive or compulsive behavioral patterns.

As we recognize a deeper level of understanding about insecurity, we can laugh at the craziness of our behaviors in the past; at our attempts to ingeniously cover them up, throw them at other people; how we let them affect our physical health, even our sex life, eating and drinking habits; even how comfortable we felt around other people.

A glimpse of a life without insecurity, realizing the intimacy, ease and enjoyment of life that are accessible, is enough in itself to erase a compulsive search for relief and for solutions in specific treatments. Once we begin to see the dynamics of how insecurity works, we are on our way to a more emotionally stable, less stressful and happier life, no matter what the external manifestations of our problems up to that point in time. It is not important whether we could not hold jobs, whether we are compulsive gamblers, whether we do not get along with our children or whether we fight constantly with our spouses, these types of self-destructive behaviors will start to drop away.

We begin to realize as well the actual self-destructive nature of these behaviors because we will see the choice between how we feel and experience things when we are in those states of insecurity versus how we feel and what we experience when we go to higher levels of consciousness, by dropping the thoughts of insecurity that make up our images of self-importance.

We could say that humility and the willingness to be ordinary break through the ego and lead people to nicer feelings and to mental health, which in turn leads to wisdom and rich enjoyments of life that few people have found in their rush to prove themselves. When therapists live in these feelings, they are truly qualified to help others. We also know that there is no technique that can give anyone these feelings. The most we can do is become happy and give our clients as clear a choice as we can for themselves, through sharing the principles of separate realities and the common-sense nature of mental health.

THE GHOST OF A PSYCHOLOGY PAST

To date, no psychological approach has ever been effective in truly helping us to find our own mental health. The reason for this is that the old psychology has attempted to teach people to incorporate someone else's psychological theories concerning why we behave the way we do.

The only true benefit, however, will come when we as people begin to realize that we ourselves are living psychological systems which function on the basis of our own thoughts. We will begin to experience and to learn our own psychology;

how our thoughts create content, emotions and experience; and how our levels of consciousness are related to our tendencies to search for the causes of our own separate realities.

Presently, psychology will begin to step outside the boundaries of its own theoretical limitations and accept the deeper sense of understanding we are calling common sense or wisdom. At this point, psychology will begin to become the most potent source of help this culture has ever known.

For a short period of time, specialization and diversification can provide a field with a temporary postponement of having to acknowledge that no answers have been found for the problems we ourselves have conceived. We honestly feel that this point has now been reached by the field of psychology, which will now begin to undergo a full change of direction and perspective — a direction away from searching in our pasts to find the answers to our own mental health, and a perspective from which to understand that our pasts are really non-existent but are present in our experiences only in the forms of thought-retrieved memory; and that as memories these experiences have no factual reality, power or effect other than that which we think into them.

SECTION VI

THESE BREAKTHROUGHS IN PRACTICE: THE RESULTS IN MAJOR HEALTH CARE SETTINGS

CHAPTER 22

Applications of This Breakthrough to the Functioning of Health Care Organizations

In Section III of this book we discussed the implications of what we are learning for the field of psychology. In Section IV we spelled out these implications in terms of their applications to therapy and counseling. In these next few chapters we would like to relate our experiences to date in working in health care organizations, with patients, professional staffs, administrators and management on issues of patient management, employee relations and stress. Areas of consultation included staff conflict, job performance, motivation, patient care, communication, supervision and decision-making. These issues are all important to anyone's management role and to organizational efficiency and productivity, as well as to the areas of burnout and professional stress.

Training and consulting in health care settings today is filled with a variety of psychological techniques, methods and approaches to managing people. Models abound for decision-making, problem-solving, communication skills, group dynamics, and motivation. Simulations of interaction processes, conceptual models of communication and stress management are becoming more and more popular. While on the surface these seem to be helpful, and in some ways are helpful, the field of management training in this respect is much like the field of psychology in terms of "technique" oriented therapies. All organizations, particularly health care settings such as hospitals and mental health centers, are made up of a mix of professionals, skilled labor, technicians and clerical and unskilled personnel. Each of these people bring to their work who they think they are; that is, their prejudices and biases, their perceptions of what is important to them at work in terms of how they are treated and how others see them, their self-images and their present levels of insecurity.

ORGANIZATIONAL COMMUNICATION

Within most organizations there is interpersonal conflict and misunderstanding since people react to others who they do not like or whose behavior they don't understand. If one were to talk to two employees, for example, both of whom had told their supervisor that they could not work together, each would tell a consistent and believable story about what was wrong with the other. Each would probably have about the same degree of truth and of insecurity. The most difficult part of such a supervisor's job is to get each side to see past personal positions to see any legitimacy at all in the demands of or constraints on the persons on the other side of the table. The same situation often exists between patients and staff, between wards, and between professional groups in hospitals. These frictions, to the degree they exist, add stress and frustration to people's jobs. These stresses are the result of everyone using a different way of looking at things to assess the same situation in terms of how important it is, its meaning, and what should be done. Nurses blame doctors and vice versa when in reality often neither is at fault in the way that each group describes the other. For example, it is often the situation that nurses may have preferred styles or ways of working with patients which conflict with the attending physician's training. In these situations people will often react to one another from their habits and the insecurities around their perceived role differences. In other words, the bulk of these problems involve ego and insecurity more than any particular technical skills.

PROFESSIONAL STYLES AND HABITS

In a similar way throughout the organization, people

develop habitual ingrained ways of approaching problems, situations and others. When they feel more insecure than usual — that is, when they are in lower moods or states of consciousness — these conditioned or preferred ways of doing things become even more important to them. They then attempt more strenuously to impose their feelings and ideas on the people around them. Since insecurity leads people to hang on to or to remember incidents in which there were conflicts, bad feelings and disagreements, people develop resentments and attitudes toward each other that affect their willingness to work together, to cooperate or to provide their assistance or expertise when needed. Many of these conflicts develop into an ingrained *we-they* or opposition mentality between professional groups and between employees and management. This mentality, in turn, leads to poor work performance; performance levels that become ingrained as minimally acceptable performance standards as the most prevalent condition in many health care organizations.

The overall motivational climate of any organization is affected by the day-to-day conflicts, misunderstandings, personality differences and coordination problems between people and between departments within an organization. When managers actually begin to see with more common sense the source of these conflicts and misunderstandings, they also begin to see common sense or more obvious ways to affect the motivational climate, the work performance of individuals and the efficiency of how things actually get done.

A danger with all pre-set techniques and theories of management is that no technique or model can fit itself to the unique set and combination of forces and factors that actually exist in any one situation. A second danger is that these techniques are used instead of understanding and, therefore, actually get in the way of or obscure a truer understanding or common sense about what is actually going on in any given situation and what the most effective action would be at that time with those people.

Another danger stemming from the second is that techniques

are often used by management on workers in much the same manner as psychotherapeutic techniques are used on patients or clients. This aspect of the problem is critical. We have found consistently in our experiences over the last five years with various organizations that the farther away people are from a job, the less practical idea they have of what it actually takes to get that job done and the demands involved. As management relies more on someone's theoretical model, its understanding of the actual situations and crucial contingencies on the line becomes less concrete.

MOTIVATION AND PRODUCTIVITY

This trap is a greater danger in the area of employee productivity. Rather than finding out directly what changes in people's jobs would make them more productive and motivated to perform better, management usually applies someone's theory on motivation to institute workshops to analyze and figure out other people, redesign jobs, introduce certain incentives into the work place in order to achieve a particular form of participatory management. These programs may even show a short-term effect. The early Hawthorne Studies revealed that any change that makes employees feel responded to or their needs considered will temporarily increase motivation and productivity.

We have seen lasting changes in these areas come when administrators, managers and supervisors begin to honestly see for themselves and to change things that are frustrating to employees (those things that inhibit their abilities to do their jobs better). This deeper understanding is, in actuality, not difficult to achieve. In fact, once we begin to see how people perceive themselves in relation to their jobs, our understanding of our employees' behaviors and attitudes becomes more common sense and obvious. Yet many managers do not feel that they have a clear enough perspective about people to enable them to easily see ways to get people into their jobs, to involve and excite them about their work, to give them a good feeling about their jobs that leads to active steps to contribute more to the organization.

In the next two chapters we will describe how we have observed the principles we have introduced in psychiatric and medical/surgical hospital settings, and in personnel who have begun to realize what common sense is and have gone beyond thinking and acting on the basis of their own insecurities. Over the past several years, we have witnessed changes in people which have resulted in increased senses of well-being and reliability in their jobs and home lives. These observations have contributed to our understanding of how people's insecurities interact to create what is today being labeled *job-related stress* and *burnout,* and its effect on patient care.

These stress-related phenomena not only become the bases for administrative, managerial, and employee working relationships, but also go on to contribute to the overall negative context within which the treatment of patients is experienced. All this adds up to create an atmosphere which actually contributes to the insecure reactive behaviors of both staff and patients, resulting in the gross compromise of the organization's mission, not to mention the impact this has on this society.

This situation has been, to some degree, recognized by every large health care agency, especially the Veterans Administration Hospitals, which several years ago initiated agency-wide programs to help the situation. Although in one sense they were a step in the right direction as far as reflecting a willingness to help, these programs consisted mainly of traditional psychological theories, models, techniques and rituals to explain cooperation, communication, interpersonal skills, problem-solving and so on. One of the authors participated and later conducted these workshops. The results, however, were always similar: employee morale improved for a short period of time with people subsequently falling back into old patterns. (Such short-term effects are seen following the implementation of any intervention program.) Since then, we have seen that lengthy and costly workshops are not necessary. In fact, we have found that engaging people in analyzing their interactions, teaching strategic psychological methods and techniques is counterproductive. The ritualization actually gets in the way of insights rather than facilitating them.

COSMETIC SOLUTIONS

We now know that what all such workshops accomplish is that they provide tangible approaches to alleviate these types of problems, while at the same time keeping intact the prevailing frameworks of functioning which created the problem in the first place; thus, providing disguises with which to avoid or by-pass dealing with the true sources of these problems. For example, we were recently told by a group of supervisory-level nurses about a consultant who had been hired by the nursing service in their hospital to help pinpoint the causes of low morale being experienced by the particular service. It did not take long for the consultant to begin seeing that most of the problems this nursing service was experiencing were coming from upper-level nursing personnel, especially the chief nurse. These people were insecure themselves so their methods of running the service were based on distrust, disrespect, hostility and aggressiveness toward their employees. Yet, because of insecurity and a lack of understanding on the part of the consultant as to how to operationalize what had been seen, a new consultant was hired. The new consultant quickly implemented a workshop which included traditional exercises and rituals dealing with communication, interpersonal skills and so on to supposedly help the morale of the staff. This approach fit much more comfortably with the prevailing level of functioning of this service. It provided an acceptable route to deal with a recognized problem, but in a manner that disguised everyone's insecurity. Through this program the service would not have to be truthful about what it knew to be the sources of much negativity, and the chief nurse and her associates would not have to face the fact that they like everyone else in that service were creating and holding on to their own problems.

In looking at examples such as these, we have seen that in

one sense it is the overall prevailing levels of insecurity on the part of people which allow such conditions to develop and persist. In the meantime, hospitals such as the one from which our example is drawn do not even have a vague idea that insecurity is the true source of their problems. Thus, millions of dollars are annually allotted to bring consultants in to do the very same workshops dealing with leadership, communication, management and stress that they did six months prior all the while that these problems are getting worse.

More important than anything, however, is that we have found that when an organization is honestly willing to change, these costly, self-defeating and negative realities stemming from people's lack of common sense can be eliminated and do not have to be worked around, coped with or swept under the rug. They can, in fact, be eliminated merely in the course of doing our jobs every day.

IN DISGUISE AS ISSUES

If there is one thing we have learned working with professionals in the health care settings, it is that the specific details of what the problems are, what profession is involved, or what specialty is represented are irrelevant to bringing some efficient relief to any problem situation. These are merely the explanatory disguises for insecurity and negativity which interfere with people's lives. We have seen insecurity and the feelings and behaviors it generates take on every disguised form conceivable in hospital settings. Suffice it to say that when insecurity is present, any issue can be used to manifest negativity and boost someone's ego. The real, true, long-lasting relief only comes when the people themselves actually begin to look past the disguises to see what is really going on in life, whether at home or in a hospital, whether in a staff member or a patient. It is only at this point that positive, creative solutions for situations emerge and are utilized.

To date we have been asked to work with almost every kind of group existing in a hospital setting including administration/management, medical, and auxiliary support staffs. We have been able to literally see that behind the details all groups are suffering from the same basic problem. Many of these groups had within the last year devoted personnel, time and money to fund some form of stress, communication and human relations workshops for their workers. The effects of all such workshops have been everything but what was hoped would be gained.

THE LACK OF COMMON SENSE IS THE PROBLEM

The results and the changes we have observed are merely the tip of the iceberg. We have merely scratched the surface of what is possible. What is really and truly needed in the area of health care today is not necessarily more psychologists or other mental health professionals. What will help is more people who know how insecurity works and use their common sense to see what is happening. They can therefore guide others to find this same understanding for themselves, rather than searching in the details of negative illusions.

The changes we have observed in many people and the subsequent effects these have had on their work and working environments have resulted from these people beginning to see what is evident and obvious — no theories, models, techniques, machines, rituals or psychologists can tell them what to do at every turn. Many of these people, by virtue of their senses of well-being, security, stability and genuine desire to help others, are contributing far more than the vast army of mental health professionals who are still searching, debating and arguing theories.

We have been asked to work with some of the top people nationally in the field of organizational development. We have never, in over a decade of work in this area with people in all kinds of organizations, seen any technique, method, or style of management taught get any lasting results. Many reasons are given for this outcome in the literature, usually involving extraneous or unanticipated variables. Yet we have more recently watched people in organizations pick up common sense and start doing common sense things that dramatically and immediately improve the motivational climate and the productivity of the unit while issues of burnout and stress become literally nonexistent in those people's jobs. Again the results are striking, yet the direction and the focus of change are very different from traditional management development or organizational development programs.

CHAPTER 23

Applications of This Breakthrough to the Effectiveness and Quality of Work Life of Health Care Professionals

Our hospital consulting experiences in the public and government sector have provided us with a wealth of insights regarding the principles we have presented. Our work with the upper levels of supervisory medical personnel have provided us a clearer view of the actual working interrelations, misinterpretations and insecurities that exist to produce barriers to successful organizational functioning in health care settings. We have not approached this from the point of view of unraveling the details of any specific problems, but rather to help people see from a deeper common-sense perspective how misunderstandings are generated. Regardless of the profession, educational level, organizational unit or nature of the problem, we have concluded that the vast majority of problems seen were often self-generated as a result of people's insecurities leading to negative feelings, resentments, prejudices, biases and defensiveness. We have often been able to help these people see how it is their personalized experiences of insecurity which are translated and implemented into their work settings in the forms of counterproductive behaviors.

THE MENTAL HEALTH OF THE HEALTH CARE PROFESSIONAL

An example of what we are talking about can be seen in our

work with nursing supervisors and staff. Our initial goal was aimed at attempting to help head nurses and supervisors relieve or solve problems which they considered to be occurring on their wards or units. These problems were seen and felt to be a source of continuing annoyance, negativity and reactivity by these supervisors. In turn, many of these supervisors had over years of experience developed rigid and counterproductive methods to achieve what they thought to be better control over their employees in order to keep them in line. Added to this was the pressure they felt coming from their superiors (using similar methods) to control the situation. It was clear to us from the beginning that this frame of reference itself was a major barrier to solving any problem without the added negativity getting in the way.

Likewise, the situation on the units and the wards that these supervisors oversaw were identical in nature although differing in details. Here the situation was seen as constant negativity and stress as a result of non-compliance and reactivity of patients, the pressure coming from supervisors, and the negative prejudices, jealousies, and general discontent existent among ward staff members themselves. The behaviors of other medical personnel (the physicians) and hospital management were also seen as causes of their situation, which in general, was experienced as one of conflict and hassle. The result was a *we-they* environment.

As a result of this *we-they* atmosphere many endeavors, regardless of how simple, were often seen as problems. Supervisors, for example, often found it difficult and irritating to find volunteer replacements for extra evening or night work when needed. In many instances, they would have to "insist." Nurses would automatically defend other nurses in conflicts involving other professionals or patients no matter what the issue. Supervisors would be called to act as advocates in problems simply because those were their roles. Much of the administrative and/or professional work often revolved around tactical and strategic moves relative to other services or departments which were perceived as issues which caused problems. This *we-they* framework was so ingrained as a given that, without anyone being aware, it surfaced to create negativity within the department supervisory heads themselves.

We have observed these very same illusory forces operating in all units, departments and/or specialties (including psychology) in health care settings. The details of the particular issues, of course, vary according to the nature of the profession or specialty (surgery, psychology, administrative), but the results are always the same — misunderstanding, negativity, and problems.

TRADITIONAL PSYCHOLOGY IN HEALTH CARE

The traditional role of psychology in the health care setting ties in with the prevailing illusion that psychologists have the power, via rituals and techniques, to change other people's levels of understanding, motivation, mood, reality, compliance and so forth. Thus, for example, most psychologists function as consultants who see patients in different departments and units who have been designated as being in need of change — whatever that may mean. The psychologists in turn review the details of the problems, tests and/or assesses the underlying dynamics or behavioral causes, and suggest some form of psychotherapy to eliminate the specific problems. Changes in the behaviors of the patients are in theory assumed to eliminate the problems perceived by the referring staff, however this is rare.

Along the same lines, psychologists' interactions with individuals in other disciplines for the purpose of consultation and staff education usually take the form of theoretical explanations of patients' behaviors — diagnostic labels and plans of therapy. Methods and techniques may be suggested to staff to better control certain patients. Because in many instances these explanations and techniques are utilized by people who, without knowing it, are caught up in their own negative judgments and biases, the results usually add to more confusion.

Ironically, there are many instances where people in other

disciplines actually become angry and hostile at a psychologist, if the patient was not perceived to have changed in the desired manner. Staff personnel quite often expect a mental health professional to be able to change the behavior of patients. The target behavior to be changed can include anything ranging from lack of motivation for therapy to not acting courteously. It is somehow considered justifiable in many situations as these for staff (but not patients) to become angry and frustrated because someone cannot change someone else's mind. Thus, a common pattern is for physicians to blame nurses for not controlling a patient's behavior; nurses to blame psychologists for being a patient advocate; occupational and physical therapists to blame nurses for not bringing a patient to therapy; and on and on. Incidentally, such working environments as these contribute to what today is being labeled *professional burnout*. Situations such as these are deterrents to honest staff development, especially if psychologists are also functioning from insecurity. With insecurity present on all sides it is something that is not recognized for what it is, and discussions focus on theory.

GAINING THE ABILITY TO SEE CHANGE

Early in the career of one of the authors, wards or units would request treatment of patients for acting out, non-compliance of some type, or some other complaint. In many instances, patients would change their behaviors, but the staff would continue to treat them as they had previously (for example, a trouble maker who is presently not making trouble). At the time the significance of what was happening went unnoticed. It was impossible in these instances to figure out how people could slip back so easily into these old patterns after changing. Although the importance of staff-staff and staff-patient interrelationships were often referred to at conferences, meetings and conventions, it was taboo to really specifically point out when staff were off base, especially when it involved professional staff.

It was indeed quite frustrating to find that such problems never ended. They would appear in a variety of forms, details, issues, events and situations involving different combinations of personnel and patients. There was always some patient or staff member (new or old) causing trouble and problems. Six years later we could look at these experiences and realize all that was happening in these situations. It became obvious that staff really could not see when change occurred, when they were caught up in their own insecure thought patterns, negative feelings and judgments from the past about these patients or other staff members. It was at this point that we fully realized that mere information about psychological care or change — no matter how voluminous, detailed, or precise — was of no use without the presence of what we are calling common sense, wisdom and understanding.

These insights about how insecurity is disguised led to working with staff and sharing not the unbelievable volume of memorized theoretical information picked up over the years, but the knowledge of what all of these data were pointing to; the implications of what was occurring and the fact that we are the ones who create any overall working experience.

GOING BEYOND THE DETAILS OF PROBLEMS

It was only in instances where a few staff personnel themselves began to see that they were living in their own worlds of insecure thoughts and feelings that some began to realize they possessed any ability to solve problems. Initially and understandably, there was resistance, skepticism and even negative reactivity to what we were pointing to. It was normal for everyone to be defending what was thought to be the cause of their predicament in life. Admittedly, it was sometimes quite difficult at first to speak up and talk directly to what we saw occurring because of our own insecurity about the reaction we would get. However, it soon became clear to us that the only difference between the fears and the insecurities of staff and patients was in the form through which they were exhibited. Our work became much easier when we realized that although we had to be truthful we also had to be as gentle and compassionate toward staff as we were toward patients.

Once staff personnel became more aware of how their own bundles of insecurities, fears, and biases operated via their thoughts, changes occurred in their abilities to do their jobs. Avoiding gossip, reactivity, arguments and paranoid witch hunts became easier. Many noticed they were more deeply enjoying their chosen livelihood. With stronger and more stable senses of well-being the reactivity and/or non-compliance on the part of patients or staff became less important and was seen in a more understanding manner. The nurses found they could more effectively offer their skills and services and not get so totally caught up in judging and reacting to these events as personal. Many became aware that they had been taking their jobs home, which had contributed to family, marital, and health problems. In essence, they learned to mind their own business! As a result, some of the supervisors of these people became interested in what was going on. They were provided with a *break in the action* and a chance to take a look at their own roles and contributions to problems. As these supervisors and workers became more secure and dropped the tendencies to become lost in the details of problems, the general overall positive feelings for each other as people emerged to replace the antagonistic *we-they* relationship that existed previously. They began to realize how simple it was to solve, avoid or eliminate many problems that once resulted in negativity toward themselves and others. They all subsequently became more interested in enjoying their lives including work, home, family and recreation rather than defending, prosecuting, or looking for trouble.

For example, a head nurse recently consulted with us concerning some interpersonal problems being experienced among several professional staff members in a particular unit. This particular supervisor's expanded ability to see beyond details effectively put her in the desired position of being able to be objective, truthful, and yet at the same time not lose perspective on the goals of the unit. When the problems were presented by the people involved, it became obvious that those details were irrelevant because all staff were angry, reactive, and blind to the fact that they were causing the problems.

In the past when such problems arose, decisions were made on the basis of analyzing the details. This was a long, drawn out process involving compiling, verification, and substantiation of details as evidence supporting one side or the other. In contrast, this nurse could be honest in sharing with these people the truth about what they were collectively doing to themselves without beating about the bush. She could do so with humor and security about what she was saying. The result to the surprise of everyone involved was everyone's acknowledgment of personal responsibility in creating the negativity feeding the problem. In the six years of working in medical health settings and coming into contact with hundreds of nurses, we had honestly never seen that quality and ease with which such a problem was eliminated.

In another instance, year-long problems which once plagued a head nurse involving other nurses and staff literally vanished when she began realizing some common sense, became more secure, and stopped worrying about analyzing and intervening in what she saw as everyone's problems. Later she could see that many of her own staff's problems with other personnel and patients represented nothing more than a mutual display of insecurity put in the form of some hospital issue. It became more evident to her why every time she attempted to intervene in many of these problems involving professional staff and patients she would end up with another problem, this time involving herself. She is now better able to distinguish what situations do require some change and which represent nothing but mere insecurity and negativity in staff and patients. At present, many people who once considered this head nurse as a definite liability to be gotten rid of now see her as an asset to have on the ward.

Subsequently, many supervisors are learning to more appropriately get out of the way and let those under them fully utilize their skills, whether administratively or professionally, more creatively and common sensically, rather than crushing such efforts for fear of loss of control. All this has occurred without a single theory, method, technique or need to analyze, dissect or figure out the details and causes for problems.

The benefits of such changes as these are immeasurable since they affect not only patient care, but also help those staff members not yet aware of what is going on by not adding to the fire.

STRESS IS IN THE EYE OF THE BEHOLDER

Another prime example of how the illusion of problems can be created exists in the belief prevalent today that certain settings, events, or conditions *per se* are problematic, stressful or negative. Many of these illusions, supported by theories, models, and explanations, have actually been counterproductive and harmful to those who have believed them. There are hundreds of newspaper articles quoting a mental health professional who states that such and such a job can lead to stress, burnout, and even death. We have, unfortunately, seen many workers who by virtue of their suggestibility have self-fulfilled that prophecy.

INTENSIVE CARE UNITS

The three-year experience of one of the author's continual work with surgical intensive care unit nursing personnel illustrates the point in a dramatic way. Such intensive care units are today considered by psychologists to be among the most stressful job environments found. These units are indeed relatively fast-paced (compared to other wards), involve critically ill patients and involve more frequent life or death crises. This being the case, units such as these require much more precise teamwork and cooperation. The physical environments are often geographically small, compact and packed with personnel from a variety of disciplines. In some cases such units have been so involved in hostility between factions that their very functioning was being impaired when we were consulted.

Because of lack of understanding of what insecurity is, negativity is created and manifested in many disguised forms in nearly all work situations in this society. A hospital is no exception. Every unit or ward contains individuals (like everywhere else) who think and see all their feelings, including the negative ones, as real and see their moment-to-moment experiences of life as created for, in spite of, or somehow against them. Thus, they become defensive, reactive, angry and hostile toward those around them.

Although this happens everywhere, when it occurs in a setting such as an intensive care unit which involves mostly critically ill patients, it creates the illusion that the unit, or the situations occurring in it, are in and of themselves stressful. The obvious fact, however, is that this illusion represents merely a greater concentrated number of negatively behaving individuals who would not be as high-profile somewhere else, even though they would behave in a similar manner in some other settings.

The intensive care unit at one hospital was a prime example of this type of situation in action, until one of the authors began working as a consultant with this group. He was able to show the professional staff how to see past their insecurities about themselves and their jobs. As a result, they began to get to know the other staff better, to relax and start looking in positive manners for ways that they could actually help one another to make their jobs easier and more enjoyable. Their habitual reacting, judging and proving started to disappear. As these dynamics changed, stress and other work-related problems started to disappear as well. This particular intensive care unit is now one of the most enjoyable, supportive and efficient work environments we have ever observed.

Just recently, a group of nurses from this particular intensive care unit (ICU) attended a conference on critical care nursing. One of these nurses attended a workshop on burnout in ICU's. The presentation consisted of presenting data to ICU nursing personnel proving surgical ICU's to be the most stressful of places, along with techniques with which to offset the stress. In the course of his discussion, the presenting psychologist shared with the workshop participants that he was himself very stressed on a daily basis in his job as a psychologist. It is doubtful that anyone, with the exception of this particular nurse, realized the full implications of what this stressed man was saying about his knowledge and understanding concerning stress and how to eliminate it. He, in fact, was promoting a set of theories and beliefs which for many people in attendance will result in more stress. To a large extent, many of the nurses we know have manifested a far greater working common-sense knowledge of human behavior than some experts.

We now have many examples of intensive care unit nurses who have experienced changes in their perceptions of their jobs as a result of taking deeper looks at what stress really is and where it originates. They now, more than ever, enjoy and thrive on helping people in a setting that attracted them to begin with. The overall environment of one of these units in particular is so positive and attractive that it is literally one of the least stressful places to be found in the hospital. Everyone from the assistant chief of nursing to the unit supervisor, head nurse and staff nurses, has begun to appreciate how lucky they really are to have such jobs and such friends to work with. The mutual respect has resulted in more spontaneity, openness, and creativity on the part of the staff. More important than anything is the psychological benefit to patients. Patients have, without anyone knowing, received the best psychological care that money can buy simply by being cared for by people who possess common sense. Many problems that beforehand were thought to require psychological intervention no longer come up even as issues.

MEDICAL/SURGICAL WARDS

To varying degrees, similar situations and results have been observed on the many other wards in this hospital. Those people (including many head nurses) who have even gotten mere glimmers or insights of what we are learning have found it easier to understand the behaviors of their employees, patients and other professionals and avoid creating the negative feelings of stress that can be taken home and experienced as job dissatisfaction and stress.

One of the authors of this book had a student in one of his industrial psychology courses who was working his way through school as a waiter. In the course of his job, he encountered customers who were upset, impatient, were never satisfied, demanded special service, or who otherwise took out their frustrations on him as a convenient target. He would often walk back into the kitchen boiling and fuming, getting upset at the cook or other waiters. One day he realized that he was accepting and taking on their realities. He saw that they would do that to anyone who happened to be in front of them, that it really had nothing to do with him personally, but was merely the personalities and the insecurities of the customers. He said later that he felt a tremendous sense of relief and began to enjoy his job more all of the time. He could then ignore the negativity of some customers and still take pride in his work.

The vast majority of nurses and other health care professionals with whom we have worked have picked up a similar understanding of people, particularly with regard to patient management. They can treat patients with positiveness, consideration and efficiency without reacting to the patients' states of mind. This clarity and absence of reactiveness in these professionals has a positive effect on the patients as well. They become in turn more relaxed, less anxious about their conditions and go through less unnecessary suffering and concern about their conditions.

RESULTS ON REHABILITATION UNITS

Among the most rewarding results we have observed occurred on the spinal cord injury unit where one of the authors was working. Units such as these treat individuals in all adult-age ranges who have sustained injuries to the spinal cord resulting in some degree of paralysis, quadriplegia or paraplegia. Psychological treatment for these injuries is designed to help individuals adjust to what is considered by the field of mental health to be a condition to which it is difficult to adjust (like intensive care units)! Spinal cord injury typically is accompanied by psychological distress. Initially, many patients are in states of disbelief, depression, or anxiety. Sooner or later, in the vast majority of cases they begin to function psychologically in a manner that is considered normal.

Psychologists have taken note of how people in general adjust to such physical changes. In an attempt to help, theories, models, and concepts have been thought up and promoted to intervene in adjustment. Thus, *stage* theories (similar to those pertaining to dying) guide the therapy to aid in readjustment. Many of the mental health experts in the field consider the stages of denial, bargaining, depression and acceptance to be gospel. Thus, the psychological management of spinal cord injured patients on this particular unit was so based. Patients would be asked to think about their injuries, rather than deny them, and relate them to their lives. Many times patients were actually told that depressions, anger or some other negative emotion would help in their readjustments. Thus, they were encouraged to verbalize their thinkings and to manifest their real emotions. This was to aid in the transition through the stages. Psychological tests were administered for classification of their distress or lack of it, and a variety of psychotherapeutic rituals prescribed. Many of the prescriptions instead of helping these patients use their own common sense merely added to their insecurities by raising more doubts in their minds. Once the patients' doubts were raised with regard to their social skills and sexual functionings, for instance, they were subjected to all sorts of *how to* films, programs and books which kept the ball rolling.

ADDING TO THE PROBLEMS

Added to this psychosocial treatment environment, this unit was also characterized by the before-mentioned negativity existing within and between disciplines. As with other wards the general atmosphere here was also one of defensiveness, scapegoating of problems and general bad feeling.

The validity of the principles we are introducing was most evident when one of the authors and a social worker attended a two-day national level conference focusing on job stress, dissatisfaction and burnout and other barriers facing psychosocial teams (psychologist and social worker) on a number of government spinal cord injury units throughout the United States. Many of those who attended were frustrated, angry, stressed and themselves admittedly burned out. The conclusions regarding the source of this negativity pointed to the system, to other professional staff and personnel (that is, nurses, physicians), and to patients and the monetary compensation they receive for their injuries. Many of these mental health professionals were insulted and reacted with hostility when we suggested that the described situation might well exist but the negativity was self-generated. It was at this conference that one member of a psychosocial team expressed pride that she was able to get a veteran to cry nine years after injury by having him relive his injury. In this way she helped him work through the depression she considered him to have skipped.

A NEW REHABILITATION ENVIRONMENT

Major changes began to occur in this particular spinal cord injury unit, however, when a significant number of staff personnel including the social worker, physicians, and some nurses, began to acknowledge and utilize their common sense. Many began to accept the possibility that they could enjoy doing their jobs without getting caught up themselves in other people's negative illusions. These people became much more understanding regarding the lack of common sense among staff and patients and to a great degree stopped feeding the fire.

When patients were caught up in their fears and reactions, staff found they could be compassionate for the actual suffering the person was experiencing without commiseration. They were able to do this because they could themselves see how commiserating would keep the patient in that version of reality longer. The staff spent much less time responding to patients' upsets and the patients were benefiting tremendously merely from the more relaxed, positive and assured manner of the staff.

The perspective on the psychosocial care of patients changed and the management was turned in the direction of common sense. The psychosocial team began to share with patients what we know about feelings of insecurity, depression, anxiety and so forth; how they relate to our thoughts; and how they interfere with any and all positive results. In short, they stopped commiserating with negativity and ceased to stir up, relate to and analyze the muck. In some cases over the past two years many of the new injuries (many of them young men in their early twenties) have adjusted beautifully and without going through any such theoretical stages as described. As a matter of fact, we have seen that about 90 to 95 percent of all such patients adjust on their own with minimal or no psychological intervention. When we do intervene, it is simply to share some common sense and not rituals. In turn, these patients become more confident to do whatever is necessary at the time to help themselves. We have seen patients with many years of problems (criminal, social, psychological) drop their thoughts of insecurity and begin to enjoy life. They have begun to look to their own common sense, beyond their thoughts of insecurity, to realize that any negative thoughts or self-pity they retain are merely their holding judgments and evaluations of the significance of their conditions in their own minds.

From our recent observations of these people, we have found that they are becoming one of the more mentally healthy groups in the hospital! They have begun to realize that happiness and getting the most out of the moment-to-moment experience of life has absolutely nothing to do with what is happening on the outside, with accomplishments, with abilities or successes judged by the external norms of society. In fact, these patients are becoming wiser and freer than most people in society today. We are realizing that many of these patients are happier and more sane than most people we know.

We in the field of psychology must begin to realize that we cannot continue to take the credit for an individual's adjustment and hand it over to a theory or a ritual. Rather, we must begin to direct people to the fact that they themselves are changing and getting healthier. Contrary to the fears of many professionals, this will not lead to the elimination of our jobs; quite the opposite. It will bring us the results we seek, for there will always be people around who, for whatever reason, have forgotten how simple life is.

THE PSYCHIATRIC SETTING

Our experiences in psychiatric settings have provided us with yet more proof concerning the common applicability of the principles we have been discussing. Many people today hear the words *mental illness* and associate them with mental conditions which are incurable or are at best only controllable. We have begun to see, however, that this is not the case. Although many of these mental illnesses can be intensely dramatic in their manifestations, they nonetheless represent the negative realities created by severe degrees of insecurity. As such, they are curable or incurable only relative to our thinking and that of those who think they are incurably mentally ill.

One question which always comes up is why would anyone in the field of mental health ever tell a patient seeking help that he or she has a mental condition that is *"incurable"* or *"unchangeable?"* The answer is that this type of thinking is traditional. Psychiatric hospitals have grown up around a framework of traditions, psychiatric/psychological legacies and established ways of thinking. As a result, change on the part of patients and/or staff is not the order of the day. When viewed from within, both patients and staff have very well-defined roles to act out with regard to each other. Very little variance is tolerated.

This attempt to systematize behavior has resulted in the institutionalization of fixed views concerning psychological change in people. This has manifested itself over the years in the tendency for psychiatric hospitals (especially the large ones) to become stagnant. Instead of changing people they become warehouses of institutionalized patients where, because of their own views, even the therapists themselves no longer believe that their patients will ever change and become mentally healthy.

Thus, it is no wonder that many psychiatric illnesses are considered to be life-long processes which are incurable. Accordingly, for the purposes of research these illnesses are increasingly being conceptualized by the field as resulting from causes which are supposedly beyond our controls and, thus, incurable. Yet these same professionals reverse their logic to describe psychosomatic illnesses where our thinking causes our physiology to change to a disease form.

One of the present authors three years ago carried out a two-year longitudinal study for the Experimental and Special Projects branch of the National Institute of Mental Health. In this research program we trained therapists from over forty mental health agencies in a variety of approaches to change. The one area that had the most significant impact was the realization that the way the therapists personally saw life was a frame of reference — that is, a bundle of thoughts, beliefs, biases, reactive patterns and theories they had picked up over the years. As was the case in strictly medical/surgical settings, once psychotherapists working with so-called psychiatric populations realized that the way they saw life themselves was primarily an illusion, a subjective frame of reference made up of a bundle of memories and distorted biases and judgments, they began to drop this bundle of thoughts and became free of their own pasts. They started to see the futility of going back into the past to see where client's problems came from in an attempt to work through their negative feelings.

As they picked up this understanding, they saw their clients caught up in their own subjective and illusionary realities. Once they saw this fact with that degree of clarity and objectivity, they stopped commiserating with their clients and trying to work with their problems. With empathy and lightness, they merely began to show them how to drop that bundle of negative and insecure thought patterns, to let their natural sense of self-esteem and common sense about life come through.

The results these therapists report are hard for current practitioners to swallow. We receive letters continually from therapists telling us that they now see clients only two or three times rather than what in the past would have involved years of therapy. By going directly to the source of difficulty — a person's insecurity attached to his or her thought system — they often break their clients completely out of their problem worlds to the point where the clients themselves have the wisdom to not create problems in their lives.

We have colleagues in large psychiatric hospitals who have begun to see past the specific theoretical details and labels which have contributed to the institutionalized mentality seen in many thousands of chronic psychiatric patients. They, in turn, have begun to share these insights with the staffs and the patients they work with. Their jobs have become increasingly more rewarding learning experiences rather than uphill efforts to maintain psychiatric patient warehouses.

Perhaps for the first time in our careers we have begun to see chronic institutionalized people who have begun to realize some responsibility in their lives by virtue of what some mental health professional with some common sense pointed out to them. Many of these people would have spent the rest of their lives in the realities of mental institutions. Instead they have begun to free themselves from the prisons of their own thinking. We honestly hope that some day soon the entire field of mental health will realize that it is our own institutionalized ways of thinking about people's mental health that have resulted in institutionalizing people.

RESULTS WITH PHYSICIANS

Over the past several years we have also had the opportunity to work with physicians who have taken more commonsensical looks at their work instead of seeing it as a stressor. Most physicians today work in a perceived atmosphere of societal confusion about their roles as healers. On the one hand, they possess skills that help those people who are injured or diseased. On the other, they are often blamed when their skills fail or lead to compromised recovery. The atmosphere is one of legal responsibilities and litigations with patients and their relatives. Furthermore, the field of medicine involves intense inter- and intra-professional competitiveness and territoriality. Thus, many physicians feel they are serving a society which does not care or lacks gratitude for what they are receiving within a context of societal, institutional and professional barriers.

In addition to their own feelings about health care today and intraprofessional competitiveness among specialties, physicians also experience the confusion of working with multi-disciplinary staff who are themselves involved in the confusion previously described. The results are unfortunately well known to any hospital worker.

In talking with many physicians who have begun to drop much of their self-generated stress, we have greatly profited from the insights they have shared. For example, we have worked closely with a general surgeon working in a large medical school associated with a large county hospital. Like many other people in his position he frequently experienced stress, frustration and anger over such things as lack of nursing coverage and cooperation, facilities, secretaries, students, interns, residents, administrative red tape, uncooperative patients, inter- and intra-department intrigues and the like. When he began to realize that the negative feelings he was experiencing and blaming on others were his own thought system doing what everyone else's thought system was doing, his entire perception of his job began to change. He found it easier to stay out of the inter- and intra-department intrigues, arguments, and confrontations, which were now seen for what they are: insecurity. He began to better understand how these same patterns manifested themselves in students, interns, residents, and senior staff members, which in turn excluded any meaningful learning. It was more obvious why truly worthwhile case reviews of possibly mismanaged cases were difficult or impossible; insecurity dictated total defense or total attack, depending on which side of the review one was on. The goal of learning something new was lost in the smoke.

Simple insights such as these have directed many physicians to realize the role of common sense and mental well-being in the medical profession. They have been able to utilize this knowledge more effectively in their teaching and allow their students' own common sense and creativity to emerge. It has paved the way to more effective management of their patients, many of whom are caught up in the details and negativity of their illnesses, so as to not reinforce these patterns. It has simplified their interactions with other disciplines which in the past were many times seen as intrusions. Many of these people began to find it easier to leave their work and their medical practice at the hospital. They began to take better care of themselves and enjoy their homes and their families to deeper degrees. One aspect of these changes that has surprised many doctors is that problems that they never even attempted to solve (marital and family) began to disappear and drop away. Many of these people did not even realize how much thought they devoted to their work during non-working hours. They would be talking medicine or thinking it on Sunday afternoons at the park, waiting in line to go to the movies, at restaurants, in the shower, and so on. All of the doctors we have talked to who have found even a glimmer of these principles have experienced significant changes not only in their jobs but in their overall well-being.

As in other cases we have mentioned, many of these physicians have appreciated and welcomed the perspective we are sharing, not being invested in the defense of any theory of human behavior and being more interested in concrete results. It is always of interest to us when many of these people tell us that what we are pointing to not only makes sense, but also that they have always known this to some degree but somehow never made the connection to their professional activities.

SECTION VII

IMPLICATIONS OF THESE DISCOVERIES FOR THE FUTURE EVOLUTION OF THE FIELDS OF PSYCHOLOGICAL RESEARCH AND MENTAL HEALTH PRACTICE

CHAPTER 24

The Future Evolution of Psychological Research: Building on the Clues Already Recognized

When Freud came out with his theories about the sources of emotional and behavioral patterns in the past, his thoughts were then considered a major breakthrough. He created a context for the field of psychology as it is known today. Although many of the more modern schools act as if Freud were antiquated, the frame of reference he was speaking from is still the basis for the direction of most psychological research and for most therapeutic rituals, including the newer schools of transactional analysis, gestalt, encounter and others.

Yet, quite innocently, Freud actually did a disservice to mankind by pointing toward the past and by asserting the existence, the reality and the difficulty of changing psychic tendencies, ingrained habits and the resultant personality traits. Psychology is still largely wedded to a framework of seeing these traits, personality styles and characteristics as fixed or given, of tracking them back where they came from, and in a descriptive way attempting to predict how they affect a person's mental health and success in dealing with other people. What psychology keeps telling people over and over again in many different ways is how much they are products of their pasts, prisoners of their present habits and styles, and how difficult it is to change any of these.

RELATIONSHIP TO PRESENT DAY PSYCHOLOGY

We cannot say that Freud or anyone else was wrong in whatever manner they experienced life as working. We are talking rather about the evolution of our understanding of how the mind does work in relation to people's experiences of life. At one point in history, those of us who were healers thought that people were possessed by demons and that a cause of physical illness was bad blood. As a result, people were exorcized, burned or drowned as witches; and bloodletting was a common medical treatment. Both psychology and medicine have relatively evolved a long way since that time in our understanding of how the body and mind function.

Freud suggested, and many others who followed him agreed, that much of our present responses to the world originate in early traumas and conflicts with parents and later through other experiences. However, to say that these experiences are still around and that they can only be expunged through years of analysis or through altered patterns of reinforcement or through getting out repressed feelings or whatever technique is picked to work on the problems is still searching one step removed from an understanding of the phenomena we are studying. For example, the most common result that occurs from getting in touch with negative feelings and somehow expressing them to get them out of our systems is that we learn to more easily generate and express negative feelings. This process does not allow us to realize that these feelings are not really there (repressed and waiting to come out), but are created the moment we create the thought.

Whatever theory a therapist has about the source or cause of our problems creates a set of interpretations and significance in our minds because that therapist, by virtue of education alone, is seen as the expert. Recently, some therapists like Milton Erickson have focused on and used this very principle (labeled hypnosis), claiming success with that method. What the hypnotic state seems to represent is a receptive condition in which our computers, our brains, are disengaged from the normal hypnotic programming of our acquired habits, and then new thoughts or associations are introduced which the therapist hopes will get plugged into the computers. In the same manner, if a therapist's theory plugs the thoughts into our computers that all our problems come from our mothers or our cultural upbringings or our lack of socialization in school, these interpretations can then be used to generate anger at our mothers or at society or literally anything.

The field of psychology cannot go any further until it realizes that it is looking one step removed from the center or source of emotional patterns. Thus, it is unwittingly contributing to the ongoing ignorance of the clients of the mental health system, creating the illusion of change through altering the form or formats through which people express insecure or negative feelings.

The proliferation of theories and techniques is a sign of the frustration of the field in breaking through to an answer within the context of the framework of basic assumptions now accepted about change. This year it may be encounter groups; next year perhaps gestalt; then on to assertiveness training and bioenergetics through the wide array of techniques now available; and later back to encounter groups to get angry at parents, once again. While we are going through all these experiences, the phenomena pointed to by these deeper principles are occurring all the time, at every moment in each of these experiences. We are not noticing the obvious going on because we are not looking in that direction deeply enough from a common-sense understanding of these principles.

THE CLUES LEFT AROUND IN PRESENT-DAY PSYCHOLOGY

What we are saying about the present *status quo* of psychology has nothing to do with the rightness or wrongness of any specific therapeutic ritual or process. All processes are results of the frames of reference at given levels of understanding, what we call the underpinnings, the underlying assumptions and beliefs held in common by the field today as a whole: the contexts from which present theories emerge.

When astronomers, for example, had as an underlying assumption that the earth was the center of the universe, all studies of the stars and planets were carried out within this frame of reference. The equations and formulas used to describe the movements of these bodies were totally different from what we use today because the earth was seen as the center around which everything else revolved in some patterned manner. Studies were carried out to discover more about this pattern. The equations became more and more complicated and disparate with large margins of error or unaccounted for variances. The field in an attempt to explain its lack of results became diverse and spawned a variety of different theories and models. All of the theories were too complicated to visualize or to grasp. Some of these were more strongly connected to an ideology rather than to the evident logic of the mathematical descriptions.

Then someone came up with the notion that the earth was not the center and that the planets, including earth, revolved around the sun. Initially this discovery was seen as heresy. Yet there was a compelling logic that was there in the patterns of what had already been discovered. The change in the frame of reference of astronomy suddenly made all the equations simple and consistent in describing the movements of the planets relative to earth, to the stars and to the sun.

In fact, there had been an increasing number of clues popping up in the research and observations up to that time which had been ignored or distorted to fit the existent frame of reference. What constitutes a breakthrough are that the clues add up in a different way than had been recognized previously, and form a pattern that brings more integration, simplicity and clarity. It seems that it is time for this kind of breakthrough to occur for the field of psychology as a next step in the evolution of our understanding of the mind. The field as a whole is now spawning more and more divergent theories and techniques, many of which are contradictory; yet all conform within the context of certain basic assumptions about the effects of our pasts and the limitations of our abilities to change our minds.

At the same time, the clues are starting to build up and to be noticed. When we first discovered a little bit about the power of separate realities and their existences, we saw it as something to incorporate into the context of what we were already doing; in helping people, in teaching, or in therapy. Yet as our exploration in this direction proceeded, we realized that everything else we were doing was a manifestation or a demonstration of the principles of separate realities, insecurities and levels of consciousness; and that the outcome was a demonstration of the power of thought.

Once this shift in our direction toward a more accurate, deeper pattern occurred, other results and unexplained variances made a much simpler and logically more consistent sense, a common sense. This shift was the key to tying together the wide variety of manifestations of emotional and mental illness, of how people behave in groups, in marriage, in compulsive or addictive behavior patterns, at work, and as cultures.

The documented psychological phenomena which exist within psychology presently hold all the implications a profession needs that could trigger this shift. Up until now, however, the field has been generating theoretical conclusions concerning these phenomena. The theoretical conclusions are centered around explaining the observed results to extract methods or techniques for replicating them. The focus in psychology, therefore, has involved and has been misdirected by a preoccupation with methodology, based on the assumption that some method will eventually be found that achieves better results.

THE CLUE OF IMPLICATIONS

Before Einstein laid out the principles of general relativity, the clues were building up within the research of the field of physics. Phenomena had been observed and measured that did not fit easily without creating forced and complicated explanations into the frame of reference of underlying assumptions of Newtonian physics. This same phenomenon is now beginning to happen within the field of psychology. The object now is to begin to look at these clues not through the filters of what we think we already know, but with no preconceptions, with no set ideas about any relationship or pattern that we bring with us. We must approach merely with an openness that allows us to see the logic or principle that emerges from their implications.

The direction of our evolution as people and as a profession is our common sense emerging as a willingness to accept something new and evidently implied; that the world is not as flat as we think, that the earth is not necessarily the center of the solar system, that energy, space and matter are all related in principle, and that perhaps by shifting our focus away from manifested problems to the power of thought in psychology we will see the connection of separate frames of reference, insecurity, human behavior and mental health.

One set of clues comes from the studies in the areas of hypnosis and biofeedback which have demonstrated the power of a person's state of mind and thought on bodily functioning. For example, it has long been documented and accepted that in some instances scores of people have undergone surgical operations without any pain sensations and without anesthesia — solely as a function of so-called suggestion or hypnosis. There are thousands of cases involving the use of hypnosis to alter bodily functions and sensations.

In the case of biofeedback, it has been demonstrated that ordinary people can alter their patterns of brain waves, blood pressure, blood flow, temperature and the conductance of their skins — all previously thought impossible by most of the field fifteen years ago. The basis for the skepticism was that textbooks taught us these were involuntary functions controlled by the autonomic (autonomous and thus not subject to our control) nervous system. This belief persisted through two hundred years of documentation of people who before biofeedback could control such functions in some way.

Yet another set of implicit clues is the measurement of stress in relation to meditative states, in relation to brain wave frequencies as well as in relation to changes in important dimensions of people's lives, lifestyles or jobs. The clues are in fact around us every day, all the time, in our own lives, in our friends, on television and in the movies. When we become open to seeing a new pattern from all of these clues, the bigger picture begins to fall into place to become more obvious and simple.

Psychology has always been interested in the principles of learning and conditioning. Experts in the field tell us how the world is conditioned to the pattern of a learned reality in which people then exist and react. Knowing this, psychology will soon go further to the realization of the implications of what it is saying, that the explanatory details of any given reality are conditional.

BEYOND THE SHADOWS OF OUR DOUBTS

Today's psychology, as a collection of theories, concepts, constructs, methods and techniques, has naturally attempted to explain the phenomenon of change (insight, growth and so forth). The explanations of such phenomena have been in terms of theories of methods and techniques and not in terms of the evident power of mind and thought. This has led to the misperception that the explanation is the route to any given result. Results, however, already exist. It is the many explanations which are the shadows of our doubts.

Instead of accepting and sharing the implications of these results, we have been studying the varied rituals we think responsible (therapy, hypnosis, biofeedback). There is nothing to be found in studying and in explaining the attributes of placebo sugar pills or water injections since it is a person's power of thought that brings results.

CHAPTER 25

The Direction Provided by an Understanding of These Principles: The Emergence of a New Understanding of the Mind

To experience our own development — the natural changes which need no intellectual participation — is to truly understand the direction called evolution. The insight leading to the next evolutionary level for psychology will emerge from the direction of principles which are already implied, rather than from specific detailed data. The data point in the direction leading to the fragmented misunderstanding of detail; the direction of principle, toward the more unified understanding of what the details are.

After a significant shift in the focus of any field we can look back and see that the implications had been there all along to give direction. The barrier which always stands in the way is that the implications pointing to a new framework are always one step removed from the details in the existing frame of reference. We must remember, however, that even when someone gets a glimpse of the implied there is an attempt to validate that implication using the details with which we are familiar. It is, however, impossible to prove the new using the old frame of reference.

THE EVOLUTION FROM THE STATUS QUO

Psychology as an inquiry will begin to move in the direction of what is implied and will start to see the dangers in formulations of conceptual conclusions. We will begin to realize that we learn more about human behavior and develop a deeper understanding of the mind by being open and continuing to move to higher levels of wisdom and happiness ourselves, rather than by accepting any fixed explanations in the forms of theories or models.

Once psychology as a field begins to look beyond the seductiveness of theoretical conclusions, it will begin to appreciate the implications of what it already has in order to find the knowledge it seeks. Implications cannot have a conclusory end. Rather they are aimed at the realization of principle. A conclusion is the illusory end of an implication. It blocks principle by its conceptualization. Conceptualization by its very nature must relate back to the old details. Since the details of every human being's life differ and could change, concepts trap us in a stagnant reality and are actually blocks to our evolution.

For example, at one point in history the phenomenon associated with what is today known as hypnotism or suggestion was thought to be due to *animal magnetism,* which was an available concept of the times. Later, these results were attributed to the specific ritual of hypnotic induction. Within the last two decades it was then noted that many induction procedures worked equally well. That is, the phenomenon associated with hypnosis could be achieved with a variety of methods. Most recently it is thought that the essential ingredient involved in hypnotic phenomenon is the set of specific details of a person's belief systems and resulting expectations; that is, that the nature of the content is what is important. There are present-day authorities in the field of hypnosis who are beginning to realize that the hypnotic induction ritual is only conditionally necessary to induce the receptiveness of an individual through developing or shaping his or her expectations, and its effectiveness is limited to that placebo effect.

It was when our direction became one of relative simplicity that we benefited from taking another look at the set of clues in the hypnotic phenomenon. As we look at these results from a higher perspective, it becomes more evident that we have viewed results backwards and missed what was implied. For example, the results associated with hypnosis were traditionally associated with the method or ritual of *trance induction* which was supposedly responsible for allowing the powers of the mind to be manifested. In reviewing the many varied hypnotic induction techniques several years ago we noticed that all held the same principle in common. Firstly, they required a compliant subject who would be willing to cease a production of thoughts and listen exclusively to the hypnotherapist. Secondly, the subject would be asked to entertain the hypnotherapist's thoughts and just allow themselves to image them, without question; without getting in the way.

These conditions met, the resultant state of a thought system is one of neutrality toward the usually acquired thought patterns. This condition, in turn, avails all the usual resources of the mind, normally devoted to an inconceivable number of details making up the habit patterns in life, available to one simple image, accepted without question (thought). It is no wonder that, in these states of receptiveness people accomplish changes which they normally do not accomplish in their usual ways of thinking and living.

Concommitantly, we also realized that such conditions of receptiveness and quietness of mind already existed normally in people and were most evident in those who we realized were happy, content and successful. We began noticing that some people, who were stable and successful, were also flexible and ever-changing. They were simply becoming more successful and proficient in all aspects of their lives (studies, jobs, families, and so forth), yet these people were at the same time ordinary. We began to recognize the quality of novelty which accompanied the openness to accept positive changes in themselves. The vast majority of these people had never even heard of psychology. We began to see that these people were, to degrees, living closer and closer to creative and responsible realities every day. We began to understand why it was becoming easier and easier for these people to be truly content. Yet, even as psychologists, we had not even begun to realize the power of thought.

As our willingness to listen and learn something new increased, we ourselves could see that it is natural to be able to change, drop and become free of our negative habitual thought patterns. It was no small insight for us to begin to realize that the states of mind that we mostly had been functioning in during our lives and professions were more hypnotic than that of many ordinary, successful and happy people we were observing. What we were seeing — extraordinarily healthy and flexible people — was certainly not hypnosis. Hypnosis was more what we were doing in our realities, where our habitual thought patterns of theories, concepts, analyses, beliefs, *do's* and *don'ts, shoulds* and *shouldn'ts, oughts* and *ought nots,* were keeping us busy trying to figure out how to explain, prove or change ourselves by changing the details of what we thought and perceived to be our environment.

As psychology takes the next step, we will acknowledge that the power behind phenomena such as change lies not in the specific details of a person's beliefs, but in the power to think these details. The change will no longer be seen within the limits and patterns of a specific thought in order to conform to the specific belief. This type of change is placebo. Whether a person attributes the cause to *animal magnetism,* the ritual, the hypnotist, or the content details of individual thoughts and lives, the results are the same. What will begin to be realized within the psychological profession is that the power which gives life to all illusions related to the principle of change, including such illusions as the placebo effect, is available directly to people without need for a middle man.

FUTURE DIRECTIONS

Psychology as a field will begin moving in the direction of the implications of the emerging evidence and common sense of separate realities and wisdom. Shifts will begin to occur as we realize more clearly the principles of how our minds shape our realities, irrespective of what the details of any reality includes. For example, the criteria for evaluating the efficacy of therapy will shift away from evaluating people based on the details of other people's theories or models. We will become more sensitive to the conditions of our own lives as helpers, and the quality of the good feelings and common sense we pass along to our clients.

Present research and existing data will be reviewed again from a new perspective. The field will begin to shift more in the direction of true integration and to recognize commonalities rather than looking for differences. The relationship of meditative states (not the theories or techniques of meditation), insights and insecurities will be experimentally related to stress and mental health, to manifestations of mental illness, to alcoholism and other addictive behaviors, and on to issues including weight loss and psychosomatic illnesses.

The present definitions of what we call now a *therapeutic milieu* will change as we observe more clearly that the objects or activities, behaviors and specific rewards we place around people are not as important as the field of feelings and level of understanding in the people with whom they interact, with whom they associate, or to whom they look for direction.

Psychology will then begin to look in an opposite direction from where it is searching now, straight to a deeper understanding of the core processes of how the mind as an individual's thought system operates moment to moment to create an experience of whatever is going on at the time. Rather than looking for more detailed descriptions of types or categories of problems and sources of discomfort or bad habits, psychology will begin to explore deeper into the underlying thought that keeps it caught in neurotic or distorted thought patterns, the thought of insecurity.

We will become less concerned with the specific mechanisms used to create change, but rather will begin to recognize and look for the correlation of the recognition of the principles of separate realities and levels of consciousness; then on to dropping irrational fears and self-destructive behaviors and having successful marital and family relationships; finding the relationship to our self-confidence, performance and results in our professional lives; and finally looking in relation to our physical health and habits.

The field will begin to see the common grounds in the principles pointed to by the various forms of consciousness of awareness disciplines or schools; to relate to and identify with these principles in a more direct and common sense manner; to realize their practical implications and psychological common sense; to discard the trappings of the association with a particular culture, lifestyle, dogma and the accompanying rituals of each conceptualization. Rather, we will begin to explore and observe how these principles are related to the way that each of us functions psychologically all the time to produce the content of our thoughts.

Many therapeutic rituals already considered inhumane, yet which continue to attempt the manipulation and forcing of behavior without the understanding of the client, will be used less and less once the deeper nature of the irresponsibility of these methods is seen more clearly. The field as a whole will move away from a reliance on therapeutic placebos and the need for their continued, repetitive, periodic application. Rather, the implications of these associations will be made more directly accessible to people in general.

If we continue to study placebos, we will remain one step removed from a deeper understanding of our emotions and of mental health. The studies, explanations and investigations become the placebos we will count on for results. The field of psychology will take a new and exciting direction, when we begin to look directly toward the mental power we as human beings possess. Once this new wisdom is shared with people, the benefits will spill over to society to help many people who are now looking for relief from emotional distress, from their own fears and anxiety, from mental illness and a recurrent life of self-destructive behaviors that seem always just out of individual control.

We will start to see the therapeutic danger in focusing on

the past and in categorizing people's problems. Therapy will be turned more in the direction of the potential of people and the discovery of their own common sense, moving away from a problem-oriented search for solutions, and a destructive labeling of patients as diseased in some way. In return, the results that psychology now seeks will become evident as we, our clients, families and friends begin to manifest an overall greater degree of mental health, happiness and creativity than before.

The most exciting research will not be focused on mental distress at all; but will explore, through our own deepening common sense, the higher levels of consciousness available to us as human beings. This direction is also the one that will help the most people in the long run.

The next evident level in our evolution of understanding of human behavior has already broken ground. It is clearly implied in principle and direction. The next step is up to us and our willingness to honestly and humbly look for something new. Our understanding of the mind, the psychological principles of states of consciousness, and the relationship of these principles to how we now experience life is still in its infancy. We feel that we are beginners who have stumbled onto a clue, a link that is the key to the relationship of what we are right now and our potential to gain the wisdom of separate realities and live beyond our previous experiences of ordinary ups and downs in life; in essence the cure to mental illness.

We sincerely hope that this book can point some people, even a few, in the direction of common sense. Once a few people catch on, their wisdom and levels of clarity will help many, many more. We feel that it is a privilege to have had the opportunity to share the little we have learned ourselves.

INDEX

Addictions, 51
Advice (psychological), 237, 245
Alcoholism and insecurity, 102
Astronomy,
  scientific development of, 69, 288
Attitudes: see Thought Systems
Behavioral Therapies, 173-174
Beliefs: see Thought Systems
Brain, 45, 77;
  and thought systems, 38-39
Brainwashing, 136;
  see also Conversion Process
Biofeedback, 62, 290-291
Breakthroughs
  in psychology, 31-33, 159;
  nature of, 117
Burnout, 44
  in Health-Care Settings, 266
  in Intensive Care Units, 270-273
  in Psychotherapy, 238-240
  prevention of, 238-240
Cause & Effect
  in psychological theories, 157-162, 185-186
  in psychotherapy, 157-162, 185, 186
Catharsis, 51, 192
Change, 116, 242
  psychological interpretation of, 291, 296-298
  psychological resistance to, 111
Cognititive Therapies, 175
Commiseration, in therapy, 215, 239
Common Denominators in Psychology, 30, 45, 217
Common Sense, 37, 52-53, 73, 81, 133, 243, 276, 281
  and insecurity, 126
Communication, 85
Concepts, in Psychology, 161;
  See also Framework of Contemporary Psychology
Conditioning
  and beliefs, 77, 136
  and brain, 77
  and illusions, 77-78
  and mental health, 205
  and rituals, 129-130

Conditioning (cont.)
  and thought systems, 77
Consciousness
  and beliefs, 42
  and feelings, 205
  and problems, 206
  and psychology, 42
  thought systems, 42
  consultant (role of), 258-260, 263
Conversion Process, 136, 150
Decision Making & Insecurity, 269
Diagnostic Categories and Labels, 162
Ego, 111-114
  and image of self importance, 48
  and insecurity, 111, 113
  and level of consciousness, 112, 114-116
  and mental health, 126
  and psychology, 158
  and self-image, 93, 111
  and thoughts, 111
Einstein, Albert, 28, 33, 35, 41, 43, 49, 72, 159, 160, 184, 289
Emotions and Feelings
  and insecurity, 124-125
  and levels of consciousness, 53
  and mental health, 54, 123-124, 205, 210, 218-222
  and psychotherapy, 123, 207, 217-222
  and thought, 217
Erickson, Milton, 286
Evaluation
  of psychology, 58, 72, 290, 293
  and therapy, 217-219
  and mental health, 219-222
Field Theory
  analogy in psychology, 33-35, 49-50
  in physics, 35, 49-50
Frame of Reference, 84, 108
  and conditioning, 109
  and ego, 111
  and reality, 110
  and thought, 84
  and relativity, 43
  first and second order, 136-137
  of contemporary psychology, 157-201
Freud, Sigmund, 45, 59, 76, 173, 179, 285-286

Happiness and Mental Health, 149, 181
Health Care-Settings
and communication, 254-255
and health care professionals, 268-269
and insecurity, 271
and intensive care units, 270-272
and medical/surgical wards, 272
and motivation, 256
and organizational behavior, 260-264
and productivity, 256
and psychology consultation, 265
rehabilitation wards, 273-276
and staff development, 253, 257-261
and stress, 263
Hospitals, see Health Care
Hypnosis, 175, 286, 294
and change, 175, 286, 295
and placebo effect, 175
and problems, 286
and psychotherapy, 286
and rituals, 294-295
and thought, 295
Individual Differences, 36
and principle of separate realities, 39
Information:
and insight, 53
and psychology, 70
Insecurity, 47, 89-96
and ego, 93, 126
and learning, 89-91
and mental illness, 92, 141, 188
and thought, 50
and common sense, 126
and relationships, 137, 144
Insight:
and change, 123, 135, 151
and conditioning, 81, 136
and information, 267
and mental health, 81, 92, 108, 135
Intellectual Understanding, 82, 183, 232-233
Intelligence Testing, 169-170, 198
Intensive Care Units, 270-273
and stress, 171
Kantor, Rosabeth, 136
and learning, see Conditioning
Internal Consistency of Systems, 48

Levels of Consciousness, 97
and ego, 114-116
and feelings, 99, 145
and insecurity, 100, 145
and insight, 100-101
and thought, 98-103
and therapy, 206-208, 239, 242-243
and therapist, 210, 242-243
Listening, 213-214, 233-234, 236, 296
Love, 142-143
and ego, 142
and insecurity, 146
and level of consciousness, 142
and relationships, 143
Memory and Separate Realities, 39
Mental Health:
direction of, 121-122
nature of, 48, 67
practice of, 60-64
Mental Illness, 88, 123, 140
and levels of consciousness, 192, 197
Methods in Psychology, 199-202
Mid-Life Crisis, 185
Mind, 82
Newton, Isaac, 185
Organizational Behavior, 93-96;
in health-care settings, 253-261
Parenting, 147, 189
Pavlov, Ivan, 39, 77-78, 173, 191
Penfield, Wilder, 39
Perceptual Filters, 33
Personal Growth, 200
Personality Theories:
nature of, 76
Positivity, 124-125
Physics, 23
and psychology, 27
evolution of, 35, 49
Placebo Effect, 79, 131, 183, 191
and contemporary psychology, 296-298
and psychotherapy, 223-226, 298
and rituals, 131
Principles:
and direction in therapy, 125, 226-228, 290-291, 292
and learning, 235-237
and psychological theories, 45, 107
Post Traumatic Stress Disorders, 185-188

Psychology:
  contemporary theories, 180, 287-288
  future evolution, 160, 293-299
  status as a science, 24-27, 160-163, 289-291
  and results, 24-25, 68-70, 73, 165, 175, 179, 185, 279, 280, 289
Psychological Theories:
  and diversity, 157
  and logic, 160
  and testing, 164, 167-172
  as thought systems, 51, 76, 159, 210
Psychotherapist, 148
Psychiatric Settings, 270-279
Psychotherapy:
  and therapist, 169, 210
  and symptoms, 215-216
Physicians and Mental Health, 280-282
Reality (nature of), 86
Relationships
  and insecurity, 141-148
  and love, 142-143
Relativity:
  and measurement, 33, 162
  and thought, 43
  in psychology, 33, 43, 68
Research:
  in contemporary psychology, 163-166
  in future, 299
Resistance to Change, 116, 209
Responsibility, 175, 228, 241-242, 244
Rituals:
  and change, 291, 298
  and conditioning, 129
  and insecurity, 131
  and placebo effect, 131, 291
  and therapeutic techniques, 138, 201
Schizophrenia, 194
Science:
  nature of, 23, 27
Scientific Breakthroughs (nature of), 159
Scientific Method in Psychology, 163
Scientific Principles, 29

Searching, 127
  and frames of reference, 128-129
Second Order Frame of Reference, 137
Self-Destructive Behavior, 102, 248
Self-Fullfilling Prophecy, 191,
  and concepts in psychology, 157, 161-163
Self Image, 89
Separate Realities, 30, 85
  and communication, 85
  and ego, 91
  and frame of reference, 81, 83
  and insecurity, 89
  and learning, 86, 91
  and psychotherapy, 242-243
  and thought, 110
Skinner, B. F., 39, 173
Specialization:
  in physical sciences, 25, 41
  in psychology, 41, 246-247
Stress:
  and cancer, 62
  and health care and mental health, 237-238
  Professionals, 44, 238-240, 257, 270
Stress Scales, 170-172
Suggestion, 79
Suggestibility:
  and insecurity, 76
  and mental health, 176, 223-226, 298
Symptoms (and Mental Health), 215
Systems Perspective, 32, 34
  and analogy to ecology, 37
  and succession, 40
Techniques in Psychology, 123, 176, 181, 189, 191-192, 213-214, 225, 255
Therapist, 148-149, 151, 167, 184, 231-232, 245
Theories:
  and information, 68, 87, 157
  and level of consciousness, 286-287
  and mental health, 67-68, 76, 78, 174, 278
  and testing, 167-172
  in psychology, 68, 157, 274, 286
Therapeutic Milleau, 297

Therapy:
   and thought systems, 46-47, 157, 201
   and insecurity, 149
   future direction, 206, 210-212

Thought Systems, 30, 32, 37-39, 46-49
   and beliefs, 217-219
   and feelings, 217-219
   and relativity, 43, 75, 84-85, 103, 139, 159.

Variation in Psychology, 45, 60

Wisdom, 118, 119, 148
   see also, Common Sense,
   and beliefs, 119
   and mental health, 119, 205
   and psychotherapy, 232
   and therapist, 232